ROUTLEDGE LIBRARY EDITIONS: EDUCATION

RACE RELATIONS AND CULTURAL DIFFERENCES

RACE RELATIONS AND CULTURAL DIFFERENCES

Educational and Interpersonal Perspectives

Edited by
GAJENDRA K. VERMA AND
CHRISTOPHER BAGLEY

Volume 126

LONDON AND NEW YORK

First published in 1984

This edition first published in 2012
by Routledge
2 Park Square, Milton Park, Abingdon, Oxfordshire OX14 4RN

Simultaneously published in the USA and Canada
by Routledge
711 Third Avenue, New York, NY 10017

First issued in paperback 2014

Routledge is an imprint of the Taylor and Francis Group, an informa company

© 1984 Gajendra K. Verma and Christopher Bagley

All rights reserved. No part of this book may be reprinted or reproduced or utilised in any form or by any electronic, mechanical, or other means, now known or hereafter invented, including photocopying and recording, or in any information storage or retrieval system, without permission in writing from the publishers.

Trademark notice: Product or corporate names may be trademarks or registered trademarks, and are used only for identification and explanation without intent to infringe.

British Library Cataloguing in Publication Data
A catalogue record for this book is available from the British Library

ISBN 13: 978-0-415-69456-8 (Volume 126)
ISBN 13: 978-0-415-75107-0 (pbk)

Publisher's Note
The publisher has gone to great lengths to ensure the quality of this reprint but points out that some imperfections in the original copies may be apparent.

Disclaimer
The publisher has made every effort to trace copyright holders and would welcome correspondence from those they have been unable to trace.

Race Relations and Cultural Differences

EDUCATIONAL AND INTERPERSONAL PERSPECTIVES

Edited by
GAJENDRA K. VERMA and CHRISTOPHER BAGLEY

CROOM HELM London & Canberra
in association with
The International Centre for Intercultural
Studies, University of Bradford

ST. MARTIN'S PRESS New York

© 1984 Gajendra K. Verma and Christopher Bagley
Croom Helm Ltd, Provident House, Burrell Row,
Beckenham, Kent BR3 1AT
Croom Helm Australia, PO Box 391, Manuka,
ACT 2603, Australia

British Library Cataloguing in Publication Data

Race Relations and cultural differences.
   1. Childrenof minorities--Education
   I. Verma, Gajendra K.   II. Bagley, Christopher
   371.91   LC3701

ISBN 0-7099-2606-5

All rights reserved. For information, write:
St. Martin's Press, Inc., 175 Fifth Avenue, New York, NY 10010
First published in the United States of America in 1984

Library of Congress Cataloging in Publication Data
Main entry under title:

Race relations and cultural differences.

   1. Race relations--Addresses, essays, lectures.
2. Intercultural communication--Addresses, essays,
lectures. 3. Intercultural education--Addresses, essays,
lectures. 4. Minorities--Addresses, essays, lectures.
I. Verma, Gajendra K.
HT1521.R2356 1984   305.8   83-43000
ISBN 0-312-66140-1

Printed in Great Britain by Biddles Ltd, Guildford, Surrey

CONTENTS

Other Books by G.K. Verma and
    C. Bagley
Editors and Contributors

INTRODUCTION

 Multicultural Education: Problems
 and Issues
  G.K. Verma and C. Bagley 1

Part I: RACE RELATIONS, CULTURAL DIFFERENCES
   AND ETHNOCENTRISM

1. Race Relations and Cultural Differences:
 Some Ideas on a Racial Frame of
 Reference
  Peter M.E. Figueroa 15

2. Toward An Explanation of Ethnocentrism
 Versus Ethnorelativism Based Upon
 Reference Group Orientation
  James C. Mayer 29

3. Toward a Typology of Stranger-Host
 Relationships
  William B. Gudykunst 40

Part II: LANGUAGE, EDUCATION AND
    MINORITY GROUPS

4. Multiculturalism and Education:
 Prelude to Practice
  Gajendra K. Verma 57

5. Education, Language and Ethnic Groups
 in Britain
  Olav A. Rees 78

CONTENTS

6. Language, Disadvantage and Minority Education
    John Edwards 87

7. The Education of Children of Immigrant Groups: A Comparative Perspective of Britain, France, The Netherlands, The Federal Republic of Germany and Sweden
    Arpi Hamalian & Joti Bhatnagar 99

8. Using a Multicultural Context as a Basis for a Core Curriclum: Cultural Difference as Educational Capital
    James Lynch 143

9. Children's Books and Ethnic Minorities
    Gajendra K. Verma & Kanka Mallick . . 163

10. Second Languages in the Primary School: The Australian Experience
    Barbara McLean 184

Part III: MINORITY GROUP CHILDREN IN MULTICULTURAL CONTEXTS

11. Cultural Diversity, Migration and Cognitive Styles: A Study of British, Japanese, Jamaican and Indian Children
    Christopher Bagley 217

12. The Welfare, Adaptation and Identity of Children from Intercultural Marriage
    Christopher Bagley & Loretta Young . . 247

13. Native Indian and Metis Children in Canada: Victims of the Child Welfare System.
    Bradford Morse 259

14. A Matched-Guise Methodology for Measuring Attitudes Toward Sign-Language Speakers
    R. Bruce Anderson & Robert Benford . . 278

Author Index 290

Subject Index 293

EDITORS AND CONTRIBUTORS

EDITORS

GAJENDRA K. VERMA is Reader in the Postgraduate School of Studies in Research in Education, and Director of the International Centre for Inter-Cultural Studies, University of Bradford, Bradford, West Yorkshire, England

CHRISTOPHER BAGLEY holds the Senator Patrick Burns Chair of Child Welfare at the University of Calgary, Calgary, Alberta, Canada

CONTRIBUTORS

PETER M.E. FIGUEROA, University of Southampton, Southampton, England

JAMES C. MAYER, Portland State University, Portland, U.S.A.

WILLIAM GUDYKUNST, Rutgers University, New Brunswick, U.S.A.

OLAV A. REES, University of Bradford, Bradford, England

JOHN EDWARDS, Francis Xavier University, Prince Edward Island, Canada

ARPI HAMALIAN, Concordia University, Montreal, Canada

EDITORS AND CONTRIBUTORS

JOTI BHATNAGAR, Concordia University, Montreal, Canada

KANKA MALLICK, West London Institute of Higher Education, London, England

BARBARA MACLEAN, MacQuarry University, Sydney, Australia

LORETTA YOUNG, University of Calgary, Canada

BRADFORD MORSE, University of Ottawa, Canada

R. BRUCE ANDERSON, University of Texas at Arlington, U.S.A.

ROBERT BENFORD, University of Texas at Arlington, U.S.A.

JAMES LYNCH, Sunderland Polytechnic, Sunderland, U.K.

OTHER BOOKS BY GAJENDRA K. VERMA AND
CHRIS BAGLEY, JOINTLY AND INDIVIDUALLY

Social Structure and Prejudice in Five English Boroughs

The Social Psychology of the Child with Epilepsy

The Dutch Plural Society: A Comparative Study of Race Relations

Race and Education Across Cultures (Editors)

Race, Education and Identity (Editors)

Racial Prejudice, The Individual and Society

Illusion and Reality in Indian Secondary Education (with K. Mallick)

Personality, Self-Esteem and Prejudice (with K. Mallick and L. Young)

What is Educational Research? Perspectives on Techniques of Research (with R.M. Beard)

Multicultural Childhood: Education, Ethnicity and Cognitive Styles

Child Welfare and Adoption: International Perspectives

Problems and Effects of Teaching About Race Relations (with L. Stenhouse and R. Wild)

The Impact of Innovation

Introduction

MULTICULTURAL EDUCATION: PROBLEMS AND ISSUES

Gajendra K. Verma
and Christopher Bagley

Multiculturalism began to emerge as an idea and as an area of study in Europe and the United States in the late 1960s. Since that time a terminology has developed which has featured increasingly widely in research reports and in the media and thence into the everyday language of those interested in the educational process. Much confusion exists over the terminology - 'multi-cultural education', 'multi-racial', 'multi-ethnic', 'education in a plural society', all having developed from 'multiculturalism'. This confusion stems from at least two sources. Firstly, within the field of research the terms have a variety of often conflicting applications because of the particular perspective employed by different researchers, seeking to give shape to some ideology or aspect of a complex subject. Secondly, the terms have been widely used beyond the field of research and have become a form of shorthand for defining or tackling problems faced in the classroom in a rhetorical or non-systematic way.
This problem of confusion over terminology is not peculiar to Britain. Considering the approaches used in the United States to examine the field of multicultural education, Gibson (1976) observed:

> The literature on multi-cultural education lacks clarity with regard to key concepts and abounds with untested and sometimes unsupportable assumptions regarding goals, strategies and outcomes.

These comments might equally be applied to programmes developed recently in Britain, Canada, Australia and Sweden.

The observations that follow attempt to highlight some of the problems and issues that relate to multicultural education. The selection of areas is undoubtedly arbitrary but should, taken in toto, serve to illustrate the complexities of the subject.

THEORETICAL PROBLEMS

The first of these concerns the nature of 'culture'. What is 'culture?' How does one describe it? The task of defining 'culture' may seem relatively easy; let us say provisionally that it represents a series or collection of relatively interconnected attitudes, values and beliefs shared by a particular group of people because of common experience based on a common tradition and a common present. Even assuming that this definition can be applied with confidence to the task of identifying a particular culture (and that is a big assumption), such a definition does not allow for two important factors. Firstly a 'culture' (whatever it is) is not a static entity, a 'culture' is dynamic; it changes over time. Secondly, a 'culture' is not 'objective'; any attempted description of it must allow for the way in which it is perceived by the individuals living in that particular culture. Personal experience may well dictate a different attitude to or perception of some particular aspect of a shared culture. Taken singly, differences about some aspect of that shared culture may not amount to much but collectively these differences may well be of considerable importance to individuals or sub-groups within those having what seems superficially to be a 'shared' culture. One has only to consider the important differences that exist among those whose culture could be generally characterised as 'Christian'.

Another theoretical problem concerns the non-coincidence of cultures with national boundaries. This non-coincidence is at the base of any definition of "multiculturalism" as opposed to "interculturalism". Different cultures living within the same nation state have differing and sometimes competing claims to political, social and economic resources, power, and representation; these competing claims can be met by responses ranging from racism and class domination to "consociational" democracy which strives to establish equality between cultures (Bagley, 1972; Lijphart, 1977). The recent overuse of the plural society concept, originally developed in order to describe colonial societies in Burma and Indonesia and later used in a description of Dutch society (Bagley, 1972; Lijphart, 1975) reflects a rhetorical and indeed a crude political attempt to rationalise cultural domination. The South African case is the most flagrant example of this, where the preservation of cultural difference is used as an excuse for the preservation of economic and political domination of one race by another.

Another theoretical problem concerns the definition of "ethnicity" around which culture groups are frequently mobilized (Rex, 1970). In theory, though not often in practice, cultural groups which have a particular relationship to the means of production can, if they are relatively endogamous over a long period of time, form both ethnic and cultural groups. However, modern industrial societies usually maintain social concensus across most cultural and ethnic groups by a variety of social control and inducement strategies, which may lead to a type of "false consciousness" (Bagley et al., 1979, Chapter 8). This raises the additional problem of the personal consciousness of a particular cultural identity. The idea of multiculturalism in Western societies may in fact be a response to the development of a particular consciousness by ethnic, cultural, religious and language groups, and may be a strategy for conceding only a minimum of economic and political power. This thesis is argued by Moodley (1981) for Canada, and by Mullard (1981) for the United Kingdom.

PRACTICAL PROBLEMS IN MULTICULTURAL EDUCATION

Multicultural education is a logical and practical reflection of the idea of a multicultural or plural society. Education, presumably must be appropriate to the needs and aspirations of different cultural groups. What is not clear however is whether the trends of education are (like the differing trends of education for different ability classes posed by the Hadow Report of 1927 - Simon, 1974) a proposal for relative or net equality, based on the implicitly assumed inferiority of non Anglo-Saxon cultures. The alternative, a 'strong' model of multicultural education based on the equal power of cultural and ethnic groups within a particular nation, is intrinsically more attractive, and pleasingly revolutionary in its implications for the reform of British society.

Since the 1950s and throughout the 1960s and 1970s the increased migration to Britain of a variety of racial or ethnic groups, mostly from former British Colonies (e.g. the Caribbean, the Indian sub-continent, and West and East Africa) has generated discussion about the nature of British society. As a result of that process individuals of different and potentially conflicting cultures now inhabit the same country, town or classroom, in the same way that social classes have done in these same areas for many centuries. This new diversity is attributable to an admixture of religious, linguistic and ethnic characteristics of the newly migrant populations. Thus the need has arisen for the process of education to adapt itself to the resultant new forces from this changed society (Mallick and Verma, 1982). Added to this has come the increasing importance of educational qualifications as regards employment opportunities. The advent of the CSE and later examination systems has heightened the focus on measurement of educational performances further across the ability range than ever before.

With regard to educational provision for the 'New Commonwealth' immigrants, there have been a series of changes reflecting the perceived needs of the time. At first provision was very much 'ad hoc' and the early emphasis was on compensatory programmes - in the case of many on their needs to acquire English. As the scale of the perceived problem grew, other measures were felt desirable; one example, the 'bussing' type of policy, where children from immigrant neighbourhoods were distributed to various schools in the authority rather than allowing their concentration in particular schools, usually innercity ones, reflected the policy of seeking to 'assimilate' or absorb different ethnic/cultural groups into a relatively homogeneous British society. Such thinking and resultant policy decisions are considered as being part of the 'dominant culture' model.

In the early 1970s, there began a shift in thinking and policy, away from the assimilationist strategy, towards one of 'integration'. The focus in educational provision moved towards the design of programmes intended to promote unity while allowing for diversity; such programmes were designed to meet the 'special needs' of ethnic minority children in Britain. Research conducted during this period shows that the education of ethnic minorities was perceived as 'problem oriented' (Verma and Bagley:

1975, 1979). Perhaps a parallel could be traced in the evolving philosophy of comprehensive education, away from the naive 'grammar school education for all' to the recognition that education should seek less to fit children to meet a particular mould and rather to recognise the differences among children and to seek to meet the needs of the individual. The integrationist approach has not been without its critics, who have accused it of being a subtle form of racism directed at cultures and life styles which provided a challenge to traditional British practices and beliefs (Mullard, 1981; Stone, 1981).

Currently in fashion is the model of cultural pluralism, which is often confused with multiculturalism. This perspective regards each ethnic group as having a need to develop and retain its distinct culture and traditions within a political framework which involves a dynamic relationship with the other ethnic groups within a larger nation.

Thus it can be seen that, from the point of view of both researcher and educational practitioner, apart from the theoretical problems which underly multiculturalism, the practical problems are ones of understanding change within a framework of movement towards political equity.

One further problem appears when looking at the educational process from an international or comparative framework. Multicultural education is still too localised; it could be seen, even with its present imperfections, to be a response merely to local needs, whether to those of the community as a whole or to those of particular groups within the community; as a result, those schools, those areas where presently the number of ethnic minority children is negligible or even nil often assume that the issues involved in multiculturalism are irrelevant. There is still no national value consensus on even the problem of multiculturalism. The only unfortunate consensus on the part of the majority of whites in Britain is on the rejection of the aspirations of ethnic minorities (Bagley and Verma, 1979). This response is, in essence, racist.

RESEARCH PROBLEMS

Quite apart from the 'theoretical' and 'practical' problems which have already been referred to, there are a number of research problems relating to multiculturalism.

A key problem is that of making comparisons. When seeking to establish whether educational needs are identical among different cultural groups, it would be neat to think of the parallel needs of the Asian 12 year old, the West Indian 12 year old and the English 12 year old (all of them, of course, British). What would emerge would be a series of gross generalisations, because although the South Asian child may look as different from the West Indian, as both do from the English, the comparison is only skin-deep and does not allow for the distinct differences that exist within that group which may well be attributable in part to different religion, linguistic and sub-cultural traditions. It is important also to avoid generalising from 'average' profiles of particular ethnic groups to all of its members. Such generalisations can have a stereotypical effect

Even assuming that distinct cultural groups have been identified for the purposes of making that comparison, there are further problems when it comes to measuring differences; these centre on the issues of reliability and validity. Tests that have met those criteria with a particular group may well not be appropriate to another group, because of what is called 'cultural bias'. This may well be true of other devices intended to 'measure' some aspect of behaviour/performance/attitude in two or more different cultural groups.

On the basis of what has gone before, one might feel tempted to question the point of attempting to investigate multiculturalism. It is a question to which there is no easy answer. The pessimist or the sceptic will argue that there is no point at all. The optimist will counter that investigation should improve over time. Perhaps the most realistic answer lies somewhere between the two viewpoints. The field is ripe for investigation that must, if nothing else, promote discussion and debate and in the process provide insight that will lead to increased understanding of intercultural issues.

The essays in this book explore varying aspects of the problems of interculturalism: multiculturalism, education and interpersonal relations. The papers demonstrate the fascinating complexity of the field, and different or complementary approaches in Britain, America, Canada and Australia. It is perhaps inevitable, and indeed desirable, that the complexities of race and culture co-existing in the same national boundaries call forth such a complexity of approaches and types of interpersonal relationships.

A uniting theme may be perceived in the paper in this volume on mixed marriages, in which we suggest that mixed marriages (mixed by race, language, ethnicity or religion) can have a variety of interpersonal styles and balances of the interests of the two parties, and the needs of children. Similarly, the relationship between two cultural, religious, racial or ethnic groups in society is a matter of balance, compromise and integration which can frequently serve the needs and aspirations of both parties involved. Marriage, like intercultural relations between groups, is a dynamic, dialectical process in which imbalances of power and resource access have to be negotiated and sometimes fought for!

It may surprise some readers to find a paper on attitudes to deaf people in a volume on "race relations". However, with the emerging philosophy of normalisation, and the understanding that handicapped people have, or should have, rights of equal access to power, fulfillment and resources, it has no longer become insulting to compare one minority group (such as an ethnic group) to another minority group (such as a physically handicapped group). Recent writing on deaf people for example, has drawn on literature of race relations in suggesting that the interests of deaf people are best served by seeing themselves as a minority cultural group with special types of language and communication (Bagley and Bowhay, 1983). The interaction of different statuses in defining social roles and degrees of stigma and powerlessness (for example, in ethnic minority women, or in ethnic minority handicapped people) is an important area for research.

A CHANGING PERSPECTIVE

In the past eight years we have written and edited a number of volumes on the themes of race relations, education, prejudice and multiculturalism. (Verma and Bagley, 1975, 1979 and 1982; Bagley and Verma, 1979 and 1983; Bagley, Verma, Mallick and Young, 1979). Our declared aim in these papers has been to integrate "radical and scholarly" approaches from the integrating discipline of social psychology, in the study of multiculturalism and education. Verma's paper in this volume on conceptual problems in multicultural education reflects a change and development in our thinking. We have, in the past decade, been involved in an intimate way with the development of a variety of models, including those of multicultural and pluralism, and have advocated the development of a plural model in British race relations (Bagley, 1973). However, we have been alarmed and dissatisfied with two recent trends in Britain and to some extent elsewhere: the first is a retreat into the rhetoric of unreason by different groups on right and left, with a rejection of systematic, intellectual studies of phenomena such as academic or linguistic difficulties in some groups. The bearers of bad or difficult news are too easily condemned: attacking the messenger leaves fundamental problems untackled(1).

Another unwelcome trend is the trivialisation of concepts and problems in the field to the extent that the term "multicultural education" has become a synonym for minor curriculum accommodations to the needs of some ethnic groups, without beginning to address the problems of racism, and the need to educate all ethnic groups (including whites) for intercultural living in a non-exploitive world. Although we offer no clear academic or educational model for addressing these issues at the present time, we are anxious that a rational debate and dialogue on these issues should continue, without premature specialisation at a trivial level, and without a degeneraiton of the debate into political rhetoric or dogma. In this continued debate, to which the International Centre for Inter-Cultural Studies at the University of Bradford will hopefully make an important contribution, we commend the important work of the Greek-American social psychologist, Harry Triandis (Triandis, 1976).

Finally, we must draw attention to perhaps the most profound but infrequently recognised problem of race relations: the gross intercultural misunderstanding, oppression and exploitation of aboriginal peoples in North America and Australia by white settlers. Bradford Morse's paper in this volume on the fate of Native children in Canada is a salutory reminder of the gross dimensions of this racism in a country which in other areas of race and ethnic relations is relatively enlightened. Relations between the Natives and Whites in Canada have been marked by the most astonishing misunderstanding. Recent work by anthropologists, such as Hugh Brody's <u>Maps and Dreams</u> (1982), have shown the parameters of this misunderstanding and some ways in which the reflective, intuitive and harmonising lifestyles of

Native people can become balanced in some harmonious way with the aggressive, thrusting, exploitive, planful lifestyles of the White invader-settlers. It is the task of cross-cultural social psychology to provide the intellectual basis for an intercultural education which can approach such profound problems of intergroup relationship.

Most of the chapters in this volume are revised and updated versions of papers that have been presented at international conferences in Europe and North America in the past two years: in particular, we have drawn on a number of papers given at the Third International Conference on Intercultural Relations of the Society for Intercultural Education and Training at the University of Bradford in July, 1981.

NOTES

1. One of the issues is that of achievement of minority groups. We have argued that there is no good evidence for a genetic loading for "intelligence" in any ethnic group (Bagley, 1975); but we do point to the significant underachievement in Britain of West Indian groups, particularly those of Jamaican parents, a conclusion based on research in both Jamaica and Britain; this underachievement is based on both historical and social circumstances (Bagley, 1979 and 1982). Denying the reality of that underachievement denies the possibility of addressing this problem in a constructive way. We are currently undertaking comparative research on the achievement of Jamaican children in Canada, Britain, and Jamaica: the initial results point to signficantly higher achievement of Jamaican children in Canada suggesting, as did Thomas-Hope (1982), that structural factors including a generally non-racist environment are important factors in the achievement of black children in Canada. A similar claim can be made with regard to the adjustment of South Asian children in Canada and Britain (Bagley, 1983).

REFERENCES

Bagley, C., 'Pluralism, Development and Social Conflict in Africa', Plural Societies, Summer, 1972, 347-354.

Bagley, C., *The Dutch Plural Society: A Comparative Study of Race Relations*, Oxford University Press, London, 1973.

Bagley, C., 'On the Intellectual Equality of Races', in Verma, G.K. and Bagley, C. (eds.), *Race and Education Across Cultures*, MacMillan, London, 1975.

Bagley, C., 'The Education of Black Children in Britain: a Cross-cultural Perspective', *Comparative Education*, vol 15, 1979, 63-81.

Bagley, C., 'Achievement, Behaviour Disorder and Social Circumstances in West Indian and Other Ethnic Groups', in Verma, G.K. and Bagley, C. (eds.), *Self-Concept, Achievement and Multicultural Education*, MacMillan, London, 1982.

Bagley, C., 'A Comparative Perspective on the Adaptation of Children of South Asian Migrants in Canada and Britain', Paper given to State of the Art Conference, Graduate Centre for South Asian Studies, University of Toronto, February, 1983.

Bagley, C. and Verma, G. *Racial Prejudice, the Individual and Society*, Saxon House, Farnborough, 1979.

Bagley, C. and Verma, G.K. (eds.), *Multicultural Childhood: Education, Ethnicity and Cognitive Styles*, Gower Press, Aldershot, 1983.

Bagley, C. and Bowhay, C., *Social and Psychological Factors in the Adjustments of Deaf and Hearing Impaired Children*, Faculty of Social Welfare Monograph, University of Calgary, 1983.

Bagley, C., Verma, G., Mallick, K. and Young, L., *Personality, Self-Esteem and Prejudice*, Saxon House, Farnborough, 1979.

Brody, H., *Maps and Dreams: Indians and the British Columbia Frontier*, Pelican Books, London, 1981.

Gibson, M., 'Approaches to Multicultural Education in the United States: Some Concepts and Assumptions', *Anthropology and Education Quarterly*, vol 7, 1977, 7-18.

Lijphart, A., 'Consociational Democracy', in McCrae, K. (ed.), Consociational Democracy: Political Accommodation in Segmented Societies, McLelland and Stewart, Toronto, 1975.

Lijphart, A., Democracy in Plural Societies: A Comparative Exploration, Yale University Press, New Haven, 1977.

Mallick, K. and Verma, G.K., 'Teaching in the Multi-Ethnic, Multicultural School', in Verma, G.K. and Bagley, C. (eds.), Self-Concept, Achievement and Multicultural Education, MacMillan, London, 1982.

Moodley, K., 'Canadian Ethnicity in Comparative Perspective', in Dahlie, J. and Fernando, T. (eds.), Ethnicity, Power and Politics in Canada, Methuen, Toronto, 1981.

Mullard, C., 'Black Kids in White Schools: Multiracial Education in Britain', Plural Societies, vol 12, 1981, 1.

Rex, J., Race Relations in Sociological Theory, Weidenfeld and Nicolson, 1970.

Simon, B., The Politics of Educational Reform 1920 - 1940, Lawrence and Wishart, London, 1974.

Stone, M., The Education of the Black Child in Britain: The Myth of Multiracial Education, Fontana, London, 1981.

Thomas-Hope, E., 'Identity and Adaptation of Migrants from the English-Speaking Caribbean in Britain and North America', in Verma, G.K. and Bagley, C. (eds.) Self-Concept, Achievement and Multiracial Education, MacMillan, London, 1982.

Triandis, H., 'The Future of Pluralism', Journal of Social Issues, vol 32, 1976, 179-208.

Verma, G.K. and Bagley, C. (eds.), Race and Education Across Cultures, Heinemann, London, 1975.

Verma, G.K. and Bagley, C. (eds.), Race, Education and Identity, MacMillan, London, 1979.

Verma, G.K. and Bagley, C. (eds.), Self-Concept, Achievement and Multicultural Education, MacMillan, London, 1982.

PART I

RACE RELATIONS, CULTURAL DIFFERENCES AND
ETHNOCENTRISM

Chapter One

RACE RELATIONS AND CULTURAL DIFFERENCES:
SOME IDEAS ON A RACIAL FRAME OF REFERENCE

Peter M.E. Figueroa

INTRODUCTION

It is typical of social reality, as distinct from the natural world, that people construct over time and in interaction with each other - and within the constraints of the given (cultural, social and natural) - their own reality. The model of efficient causality, which may usefully be applied to the natural world, is thus of very limited service in considering the social world. To say this, however, is not to espouse an atomistic model in regard to the social world, which is characterised by what may be termed an 'internal causality'. People determine to act in various motivated ways. They invest the world with meaning. They have intentions. They interpret reality, their own situations, and the actions of others, and they act and react accordingly, in view of their intensions - and given the actual possibilities. (And as a result, their interpretations and intentions may be re-inforced, or modified, and will further inform action.)

The phenomenon which we significantly continue to refer to as "race relations" is, in my view, a typical social phenomenon which cannot be adequately comprehended within the bounds of an efficient causal model. Instead, an adequate understanding of 'race relations' needs to include the notion of 'race' as a social construction or reality. Central to this social construction, according to the present view, are certain largely taken-for-granted understandings, which are shared by the majority in Britain, are closely associated with British identity, and provide as it were a basic 'backdrop' to perception, knowledge, judgement and action. This is what I refer to as the 'racial frames of reference', and it is this in particular on which this paper focusses.

RACISM

Whether or not actors differ in genetic, cultural, or social characteristics, they have certain views and tend to make certain assumptions about themselves, other members, the in-group as such, non-members and outgroups. The racial frame of reference is of this order and it permits a conceptualisation of racism which goes beyond the traditional parameters of prejudice and tolerance. It is possible for a person to be tolerant and free of prejudice and yet still to be racist in his or her thinking or behaviour. Such a person may, for instance, be paternalistic in behaviour or stereotype in thinking. Thus, for example, a teacher who stereotypes all 'West Indians' (including youngsters born in Britain) as 'by nature' good at games, art and music (but inherently bad at mathematics, language and academic subjects generally) is racist in his or her thinking however well-disposed such a teacher may be towards these 'West Indians'.

The popular debate about racism subsequent on the publication of the Interim Report of the Committee of Inquiry into the Education of Children from Ethnic Minority Groups (1981) illustrates well the importance of developing a concept like racial frames of reference. The Rampton Committee (page 12) itself defines racism as "a set of attitudes and behaviour towards people of another race which is based on the belief that races are distinct and can be graded as 'superior' or 'inferior'". The first point here is that this quote suggests with the words 'towards people of another race' that the Committee itself believes that there are distinct 'races'. The main point in the Rampton Committee's definition is that the racist considers his or her own 'race' as 'superior'. This, however, is too narrow a definition. What matters is in effect taking 'race' as a general determining factor at all.

In a paper in the Times Educational Supplement of 26th June 1981 critical of the Rampton Committee's supposed exclusive stress on racism as a determining factor, research by Peter Green of Durham University was reported which seems to show that the self-concept of 'West Indian' children varies little between those taught by 'tolerant' and those taught by 'intolerant' teachers. This, however, does not necessarily tell us anything about the importance of racism as a way of seeing people and (in effect) of accounting for social phenomena in terms of 'races'. The definition of racism has been too narrow, the 'tolerant - intolerant' dimension being far from the only important one in racism and 'race relations'.

A similar example can be found in the now classic survey of 'race relations' in Britain (Rose, 1969). It was concluded that "contrary to the general view, the majority of the population are tolerantly inclined". This would seem to imply that 'racial prejudice' was not an important factor in 'race relations' in Britain. In fact, however, much of the data set out in the same report (1969, e.g. pages 567, 569, 570 and 587 - see Figueroa, 1974, pages 412-414) suggests on the contrary that racism as a negative or narrow way of seeing (without any hostility necessarily implied) was a widespread phenomenon. A careful reanalysis of the survey data indicated in fact, that prejudice was widespread (Bagley, 1970).

What I am suggesting is that even if prejudice in some narrow individualistic sense (rigid and hostile rejection, intolerance or even feelings of superiority) is apparently of little widespread importance, nevertheless racism as a shared racial frame of reference, involving 'race' (and, inseparably, 'race relations') as a social construction, may be of basic significance.

CONSTRUCTION OF REALITY

There are two central aspects to the notion of the construction of reality. The first is that people act on the basis of how they see the situation, in other words on the basis of their 'definition of the situation'. What matters is not just what objectively is the case, but what people believe to be the case. Banton (1979) cites what has now become a sociological axiom, "if men define social situations as real, they are real in their consequences". This axiom does not in my view entail that material forces are of no consequence for human behaviour and for social reality. Nor does it mean that the consequences which follow from people's definitions will necessarily be in <u>accord</u> with those definitions. Even in ambiguous social reality it is metaphorically possible to walk into a brick wall. One's definition of the situation may be in conflict with that of other parties to the situation and one may soon realise in such a case that the outcome of one's actions was not what one would have expected from one's definition of the situation - especially where the other parties to the situation hold more power than one does. Nevertheless, and this is basically what is being stated in the first point, each actor's definition of the situation will affect his or her action (and may thereby influence the action of others - in terms of their own 'definition'). The actor is not simply acted on by the situation (nor, however, are his powers of definition of the situation absolute - or exercised other than through interaction with some others).

The second point is that the actor is always in a situation which is not just of his or her making, but is the net result of interaction with and among others (as also of forces of the natural world). Social reality is constructed in and through interaction within the parameters of the given in view of shared and contested perceptions, beliefs, interpretations, values, norms, intentions and affects. It is the very net-working that is the social reality and that constructs the social reality.

RACIAL FRAMES OF REFERENCE

In the definition of the situation actors bring to bear on that situation any previous knowledge of experience (including feelings, judgement or action) which may seem relevant to it. It is 'maps' of such 'knowledge' or 'experience', which serve to orientate the actor, that I refer to as frames of reference. They are part of our interpretational system. Like a language they are themselves produced in and through interaction, yet are always given, being learned through a process of reproduction, so that they are actively taken up and may be modified in use. These frames of reference are not to be taken in an individualistic or subjectivist sense. They are inherent to social interaction in and through which they are constructed. They are shared with other members of the in-group, are socially learned, and fulfill important social functions.

'Race', like education (Young, 1971), sex (Ardener, 1978) and childhood (Holland, 1980), is a social construction. This is not to try and deny the existence of different looking populations, any more than one denies that the physics syllabus in schools tells us something about natural phenomena, or that there are anatomical differences associated with reproduction, or that age and maturity differences exist. However, cultures differ, for instance, in the roles, status and image they assign to women and children. People, through interaction and the mutually interpretive process this involves, categorise, highlight and make sense of the given in particular ways and establish order through particular patterns of relations. What matters is not just actual differences (in appearance for instance), but the way these are related to, invested with meaning and importance through interaction. What is significant are the patterns of relations that are established, the lines along which they are drawn, and the myths and assumptions that go along with, and inform this. 'Race' refers both to the network of largely unspoken, taken-for-granted assumptions and the actual constellation of relationships and the patterned distribution of power which gives rise to and express it and which it informs and justifies.

The myths and assumptions that serve in the modern world and in particular in Britain in defining and structuring particular situations in terms of 'race' are the racial frames of reference. They provide an important definition and boundaries along which power is distributed, and in terms of which relations and social interactions are patterned in terms of an inherent and basically <u>inexplicit</u> 'interpretive process'. Such a racial frame of reference, broadly speaking, is a socially constructed, socially reproduced and the learned way of orienting with and towards others and the world involving ultimately tacit assumptions such as: there do actually exist objectively different 'races'; these share 'by nature' or genetically or inherently certain common characteristics, including or closely linked with certain social characteristics; the different 'races' are mutually exclusive if not hierarchically ordered; each person belongs to one and only one such 'race', thereby possessing certain physical and cultural characteristics and occupying a certain social location.

However, a racial frame of reference does not refer just to a set of beliefs. The assumptions and myths are not to be understood just cognitively. Apart from the given conceptual framework, the symbols and beliefs, are the existing evaluations and patterns of affective orientation, and the already given patterns of actions and interactions, the exciting social relations - and all these go to 'define' or provide the 'lived' frame in terms of which any new action, perception, judgement, thought, knowledge, feeling or experience is situated, given meaning and value, and realised. This 'definition', however, usually takes place implicitly, rather than being a reflexive operation. The racial frame of reference is rooted essentially at the level of the subsidiary awareness or the taken-for-granted, at the level of hidden structures or even of the social 'deep structures'.

FUNCTIONS OF RACIAL FRAMES OF REFERENCE

First, in a broad sense, is the interpretive function. It permits the categorisation, managing and ordering of the experienced world, and provides a simple, stable explanation of various social phenomena. Closely related to this, it contributes significantly to the 'definition' of group identity and self-identity (see Husband's 1979, very aposite analyses). It is thus of central importance for it concerns "a crucial aspect of the determination and co-ordination of social action and interaction, namely the very way in which groups, their membership and their relative social location are defined, symbolised, judged and treated" (Figueroa, 1974). The racial frame of reference provides the underpinning to what Blumer (1961) has called a 'sense of group position', which for him 'is a general kind of orientation...a sense of where the two racial groups belong...a norm and imperative' - not just 'a set of feelings'. Thus the racial frame of reference provides those who share it with a rallying point for group loyalty and cohesion. The racial frame of reference helps to bridge the worlds of a socially divided nation and to maintain its national unity against 'outsiders'.

It also provides a simple basis for action, incorporating as it does a view of the world, that is both a way of accounting and a value position. Finally, and again closely related to the above, the racial frame of reference provides a rationale for the existing order of institutionalised racism and a simple justification for 'racially' exploitative social practices and arrangements. It also papers over the schisms in what Ruth Glass (1964) has called the 'parent' society by 'constructing' a scapegoat. It thus performs a systems maintenance function, and so serves the interests of the privileged classes, of those who hold the balance of power.

SOCIO-HISTORICAL SOURCES OF RACIAL FRAMES OF REFERENCE IN BRITAIN

However, the order of institutionalised racism - in which 'blacks' are typically in a low social location - itself leads to and supports a racial frame of reference. There tends to be in brief a circular and mutually reinforcing relationship betwen a (de facto) racist power structure and the racial frame of reference. The racial frame of reference springs from, expresses, is embodied in, and supports or underpins certain forms of social relations, that is the power structure of institutionalised racism. So, although the term 'race' has little objective validity as a socio-biological reality, 'races' as actually 'constructed' through social interaction constitute important structural features of a stratified (or divisive) social system, and are characterised by differential access to power.

There is quite a lot of evidence suggestive of such a racial frame of reference in this country. In a study (Figueroa 1974 and 1976) of West Indian, British and Cypriot school-leavers, the researcher found that: The British respondents had negative stereotypes especially of West Indians; the West Indians had on the whole a positive group self-image, though not one as completely favourable as the group self-image held by the British; rather than patterns of friendly interaction between these groups, the data pointed "to negative or rejecting patterns of action on the part of the British vis-a-vis the West Indians"; there were some limited data "implying negative or rejecting affects or feelings on the part of the British regarding 'immigrants'"; several statements by respondents indicated racial thinking and a linked negative evaluation, but did not suggest that virulent hostility was a particularly salient phenomena.

Brittan (1976) in some contrast, has reported feelings suggesting widespread and negative or narrow stereotyping of West Indian pupils by school teachers, and Bagley and Verma (1975) have reported results showing marked 'racism' and stereotypes among pupils. Husband's research (1979) is particularly suggestive of how blacks have been symbolised as 'immigrants' (rather than, e.g. as settlers) and have been seen as a 'threat', the implicit assumption being that they and their ways are undesirable. Margaret Thatcher's much published statement that "this country might be rather swamped by people with a different culture" takes on its full meaning and impact only if the unspoken assumption is made - not just that those people's culture is different - but that it is not really desirable or valid as one's own. Similarly, if 'blacks' as such are particularly seen as a threat in housing, jobs, etc. this is because they are not accepted as having equal rights. Along, moreover, with these assumptions, judgements, evaluations and stereotypes is the commonly known, and exaggerated fact (see E.J.B. Rose, 1969) that on almost any index (employment, accommodation, education) the 'blacks' have tended to be over-represented at the lower end of the scale.

Even before 1555, which seems to be the first recorded date of 'blacks' in Britain, there already existed in Britain, partly on the basis of adventurers' accounts (Walvin, 1973), a negative or subordinating orientation towards 'blacks' similar to the one existing today. Little (1948), in putting forward his 'colour-class hypothesis', was one of the first scholars to stress the importance of beliefs associating 'colour' with low status, and to suggest that in Britain 'coloured' people are considered inferior and not very desirable socially as a result of the British colonial past and especially of the slave trade.

Walvin (1973) quotes a 16th century writer, Eden, who refers to Africans as "Moores, Moorens, or Negroes, a people of beastly lyvynge, without a god, law, religion or commonwealth" - all of which was, of course, false. Walvin (1973) also quotes from a 1788 number of the Gentleman's Magazine, "perhaps the most popular and influential periodical of the day":

> The Negro is possessed by passions not only strong but ungovernable; ...a temper extremely irascible; a disposition insolent...As to (most of the) fine feelings of the soul, the Negro,... is nearly deprived of them.

The Encyclopaedia Britannica of 1810, also quoted by Walvin (1973) characterised the Negro as "this unhappy race...strangers to every sentiment of compassion,...an awful example of the corruption of man left to himself". Carlyle (1853) in his polemics also depicts a stereotype of the Negro as crude, lazy and depraved.

But, not only was there this generally negative orientation towards blacks, they did actually on the whole fill the lowest strata in the social system, both within Britain and in the Empire. Besides, the structural relationship of Britain, the metropolis or the 'mother country', to the rest of the Empire was essentially similar to that which existed, and exists, between whites and blacks within Britain. As Rex and Tomlinson (1979) have argued, present-day British society, and especially 'race relations' in Britain today, cannot be understood without an understanding of Empire. Great Britain and the colonies formed one complex economic, political, and social system, with the metropolis as the 'overlord', with the 'whites' in the dominant positions, and the slaves, the 'coolies' and the other 'natives' as the exploited groups. The frames of reference which developed were an expression of this relationship, helping to produce, justify and perpetuate it, and have themselves developed as part of the British cultural tradition. They are embedded in the particular social structure and are part and parcel of the society's culture.

RACIAL FRAMES OF REFERENCE, SOCIO-CULTURAL CONSEQUENCES AND CHANGE

Some of the theories put forward in Britain in recent years to account for the oppressed position of 'blacks', especially of West Indians, in the educational system and in society in general, can actually be understood within this tradition. It seems significant, for instance, that the greatest aspiration Rex and Tomlinson (1979) seem able to hold out for the 'blacks' in Britain is that they should be integrated into the working-class (1).

The notions of linguistic or cultural deficiency on the part of 'blacks' fit into the traditional British racial frame of reference. For instance, the British Department of Education and Science (DES, 1971) seems to assume that 'non-English speaking immigrant children' suffer from 'the restricted code' of the 'culturally deprived' and are thus hindered from developing 'certain kinds of thinking'. In other words the dubious assumptions are made that: there is a correlation between linguistic code and cognitive ability; and standard English permits higher levels of thought than the 'immigrant' languages. Difference tends to be equated with deficiency.

Cultural difference, such as linguistic differences, differences in patterns of child-rearing, differences in habits of dress and food, differences in family and religious patterns, and differences in values can lead to misunderstandings and conflicts, and can help to account for 'race relations'. But such differences need not lead to conflicts and difficulties. Sharp and Green (1975) have argued that parents can work the school system even when their values differ from those of the teachers. Besides, cultural differences could also be turned to positive advantage in 'race relations' - for instance, in the multi-cultural classroom. Culture contact can be a source of positive social change. What seems to be more important than cultural difference is the orientation towards such difference: the extent to which they are exaggerated - or even 'fabricated'. What is also important is a mismatch between the way each group sees itself, is seen, and sees each other, each having a different perspective and different interests. It is difficult for these groups, given their different locations, different perspectives and the way they interrelate, to identify such mismatch, which only helps to feed racial frames of reference, making it more difficult for these to be modified or discarded.

The racial frames of reference are part and parcel of the institutionalised separateness of the 'white's' and 'black's' social worlds, closely linked as they are to group identity, cohesion and distinctiveness, and to the interaction between the groups. Each group tries to develop its own strategies for control - given its situation and its definition of that situation - so as to sustain its construction of reality and accomplish what it sees as its interests. The strategies of the different groups will be rather different: on the one hand, the dominant racial frame of reference, discrimination, legal exclusion from the society or its citizenship, 'law and order' enforcement, and the distribution of knowledge; and, on the other hand, protest, disruptive behaviour, non-conformity, acceptance of a racial frame of reference and a group identity exalting blackness and cultural distinctiveness, rejection of the educational system, an attempt to set up one's own, or even an attempt 'to play' the existing system. This institutionalised separateness and these opposing strategies for control make the welding of common experience and structures rather difficult.

However such a situation of race relations, being dynamic, may also be quite unstable. There is an in-built tension between the dominant and subordinated groups because of their differing structural positions. This tends to result in their having different and probably conflicting constructions of reality. Even oppressed groups actively interpret their situation, give it meaning, and build as far as possible a positive group identity. (Maureen Stone, 1981, is one of the most recent black social scientists to effectively assert this). However, the exploited, oppressed or subordinated group may be likely to take over the general racial frame of reference orientation of the dominant group while rejecting essential particularities of the dominant frame of reference - and thus rejecting its own subordination. For instance, 'black is beautiful' (but oppressed and unfairly treated) involves a racial frame of reference, but one different from (and tending to be a mirror image of) the dominant group's. A group constructing its reality in anti-dominant terms such as these, and not having many avenues of power, is likely to seek to assert itself in various non-conformist, non-cooperative, protest or even violent forms - such as in Britain in the early 1980s. Although this can result in reinforcing the dominant group's racial frame of reference - and so increase conflict and confrontation - it can also lead to change. It can, for instance, lead people to become more clearly aware of the social realities of their situation, to discuss the issues, and to question and modify their assumptions, strategies and tactics.

CONCLUSION

The idea which I have tried to develop is that of 'race' as a social construction in terms of a taken-for-granted racial frame of reference, which is shared by the members of the 'in-group', but not, or only imperfectly, with the members of the 'out-group'. This idea clearly has implications for the study of 'race relations' and for policy and action. Some of the important implications are:

1. Since the 'objective' socio-economic factors cannot be separated from the shared, interactive and interpretive dimensions, research, policies or action which focus exclusively on the former will at best only be partially successful.

2. Since one is not concerned merely with individual psychological or pathological phenomena, a primary focus on say, depth interviews or psychological information campaigns aimed primarily at individuals would not of themselves be appropriate.(2)

3. Since however, the social construction of 'race' and the racial frame of reference are the expression and result of interaction, and both help to 'define' and to be 'defined' by relative social positions, research and action aimed at the structural and political reality are appropriate.

4. Teachers and others who want to change the existing order need to join together so as to have a chance of intersubjectively realising new frames of reference, and of being able to contribute towards establishing new power relations.

5. Since 'race relations' is a group or intersubjective phenomenon involving, along with a largely camouflaged structure of relations, a largely taken-for-granted orientation and cultural reality, institutions like schools can help to facilitate social change by raising social consciousness through various forms of group projects.

6. Within this context positive steps can be taken to show, treat and explore cultural differences as cultural riches. This implies also taking care to try and avoid any one culture seeming a threat to any other.

7. The process of the reproduction of racial frames of reference among young people - e.g. in schools - needs to be studied. It is also important to try and study the relationship between the racial frames of reference of teachers and pupils (especially of 'white' teachers and 'white' pupils) and between 'black' and 'white' pupils, and to explore any link with academic performance.

NOTES

1. This view is of course compatible with the orthodox Marxist view that unity of black and white working class will lead to a general unmasking of the alienating forces of racism, and ultimate social change that is profound in nature.

2. See Bagley et al. (1979) and Bagley and Verma (1979) for attempts to link the 'culture of racism' to individual dispositions to prejudice and discrimination.

REFERENCES

Ardener, S. (ed.), *Defining Females: The Nature of Women in Society*, Croom Helm, London, 1978.

Bagley, C., *Social Structure and Prejudice in Five English Boroughs*, Institute of Race Relations, London, 1970.

Bagley, C. and Verma, G., 'Inter-ethnic attitudes and behaviour in British multi-racial schools', in Verma, G.K. and Bagley, C. (eds.), *Race and Education Across Cultures*, Heinemann, London, 1975, pp. 236-262.

Bagley, C., Verma, G., Mallick, K. and Young, L., *Personality, Self-Esteem and Prejudice*, Saxon House, Farnborough, U.K., 1979.

Bagley, C. and Verma, G., *Racial Prejudice, the Individual and Society*, Saxon House, Farnborough, U.K., 1979.

Banton, M., *Race Relations*, Tavistock Publications, London, 1967.

Banton, M., 'The idea of race and the concept of race', in Verma, G.K. and Bagley, C. (eds.), *Race, Education and Identity*, Macmillan, London, 1979, pp. 15-30.

Blumer, H., 'Race prejudice as a sense of group position', in Masuoka, Jitsuichi and Valien, Preston (eds.), *Race Relations: Problems and Theory*, University of North Carolina Press, Chapel Hill, N.C., 1961.

Brittan, E., 'Teacher opinion on aspects of school life: pupils and teachers', *Educational Research*, vol. 18, no. 3, June, 1976.

Carlyle, T., *Occasional discourse on the Nigger Question*, Thomas Bosworth, London, 1953.

Committee of Inquiry Into the Education of Children From Ethnic Minority Groups, *West Indian Children in Our Schools*, (Chairman: Anthony Rampton, OBE), H.M.S.O., London, 1981.

Department of Education and Science, *The Education of Immigrants*, (Education Survey 13), H.M.S.O., London, 1971.

Figueroa, P., *West Indian School-Leavers in London: A Sociological Study in Ten Schools in a London Borough, 1966-1967*, unpublished PhD thesis, School of Economics, University of London, 1974.

Figueroa, P., 'The Employment Prospects of West Indian School-Leavers in London, England', Social and Economic Studies, vol. 25, no. 3, September, 1976, pp. 216-233.

Glass, R., 'Insiders and outsiders: the position of minorities', Transactions of the Fifth World Congress of Sociology, Washington, September 1962, vol. 3, ISW, Louvain, 1964.

Holland, D., The Ideology of Childhood - A Marxist Reappraisal of Theories of the Cultural and Historical Specificity of Modern Childhood, unpublished Masters dissertation, Department of Education, University of Southampton, 1980.

Husband, C., 'Social identity and the language of race relations', in Giles, H. and Saint-Jacques, B. (eds.), Language and Ethnic Relations, Pergamon Press, Oxford, 1979, pp. 179-195.

Little, K., Negroes in Britain: A Study of Racial Relations in English Society, Kegan Paul, London, 1948.

Rex, J. and Tomlinson, S. (with the assistance of David Hearnden and Peter Ratcliffe), Colonial Immigrants in a British City: A Class Analysis, Routledge and Kegan Paul, London, 1979.

Rose, E. and Deaken, N., Colour and Citizenship: A Report on British Race Relations, Oxford University Press, London, 1969.

Sharp, R. and Green, A., Education and Social Control, Routledge and Kegan Paul, London, 1975.

Stone, M., The Education of the Black Child in Britain: The Myth of Multi-Racial Education, Fontana, Glasgow, 1981.

Walvin, J., Black and White: The Negro in English Society, 1555-1945, Allen Lane, London, 1973.

Young, M., Knowledge and Control: New Directions for the Sociology of Education, Collier Macmillan, London. 1971.

Chapter Two

TOWARD AN EXPLANATION OF ETHNOCENTRISM VERSUS ETHNORELATIVISM BASED UPON REFERENCE GROUP ORIENTATION

James C. Mayer

INTRODUCTION

Ethnocentrism is a broadly defined term. Although generally viewed as an attitude or ideology, and usually imbued with negative feelings, ethnocentrism may alternatively be approached as a perceptual process from which, for example, negative attitudes or an authoritarian ideology may result. As a perceptual process, ethnocentrism has been defined in this way: an ethnocentric person uses a "frame of reference that denies the existence of any other frame of reference" (Porter, 1976, p. 10). This definition illuminates the basic nature of ethnocentrism. It also allows us to state a converse notion, ethnorelativism, in terms that are just as specific as those used for the definition of ethnocentrism: an ethnorelative person uses a frame of reference that allows him to accept the viability of other frames of reference.

Furthermore, this definition does not confuse the notion of ethnocentrism with closely related concepts. Usually, these concepts describe the effects or results of an ethnocentric perspective. In fact, most tests and scales that have been used to measure ethnocentrism in the past thirty years are concerned with identifying attitudes that are directed toward specific issues such as prejudice, social distance, intolerance, nationalism and anti-worldmindedness. It is suggested in this paper that a clearer understanding of ethnocentrism will result if we distinguish ethnocentrism, both theoretically and empirically, from closely associated, though not equivalent, concepts.

One way to gain a clearer understanding might be to apply the reference group concept to an analysis of ethnocentrism. Any application of the reference group concept must utilise an interactionist perspective on the social process. That is, the responsibility for maintaining the social process is shared, however unequally, by an individual and individual and society. By holding an ethnocentric position, a person limits the quantity and quality of his or her interpretations of the social process. Possibly, an ethnorelative position can be attained through gaining an awareness of one's reference group orientations. The more that one is aware of his or her own reference group orientation, the more he or she could appreciate that others have established their own equally viable reference group orientations.

ATTITUDES DIRECTED TOWARD SPECIFIC GROUPS

Most notions of ethnocentrism are based upon the distinction between ingroups and outgroups, terms which were first coined by Sumner (1906). The widely acknowledged definition of ethnocentrism comes from Sumner also:

> ...a view of things in which one's own group is the center of everything, and all others are scaled and rated with reference to it. Each group nourishes its own pride and vanity, boasts itself superior, exalts its own divinities, and looks with contempt on outsiders. Each group think its own folkways only right ones, and if it observes that other groups have other folkways, these excite its scorn (p. 13).

The impact of his analysis has been felt for most of this century. From his definition, four main aspects of ethnocentrism can be isolated: 1) that one's own group or customs are used as a standard, 2) that the rating of other groups is hierarchical, i.e. in terms of greater or lesser similarity, 3) that one evaluates differences, i.e. he points out things that are peculiar and that differentiate him from others, and judges these differences, and 4) that one expresses ingroup acceptance, positiveness, loyalty, amity, superiority and outgroup rejection, negativeness, hostility, inferiority. This aspect will henceforth be simplified to 'ingroup acceptance/outgroup rejection'.

These aspects have been primarily relied upon by subsequent writers who have contributed to the ethnocentrism literature - especially those writers who have attempted to measure ethnocentrism. I will, therefore, consider them as the traditional aspects of ethnocentrism.

Quite often, when ethnocentrism is conceived as an attitude directed toward other groups, it is not sufficiently distinguished from ethnic prejudice. A study significant investigation of ethnocentrism, The Authoritarian Personality (Adorno et al., 1950), actually defined ethnocentrism as "prejudice, broadly conceived". In all four versions of the California E scales, the notion of ethnocentric ideology is based upon the traditional aspects of ethnocentrism, especially the ingroup acceptance/ outgroup rejection distinction. For individuals responding in an ethnocentric direction on the E tests, the ingroup is typically a) Anglo-Saxon, b) politically conservative, c) white, d) male, e) American. Outgroups include blacks, Jews, foreigners, hippies, the insane, radicals, incapable people, even women. Thus, subjects are actually expressing their readiness to accept or oppose prejudice toward these outgroups.

Williams (1964) makes a helpful separation between ethnocentrism and prejudice. He claims an ethnocentric person indulges in feelings of social distance and stereotyping behavior before his behavior moves onto what could be called prejudice. Moreover, ethnocentrism does not always lead to prejudice, according to Williams, because ethnocentrism is not always characterised by negative feelings toward other groups. That is, positive feelings toward one's own group may include merely neutral feelings, such as ignorance, or lack of interest in, other groups.

Other investigations of ethnocentrism also fail to distinguish ethnocentrism from ethnic prejudice. The Social Distance Scale (Bogardus, 1933) purports to measure personal-group distance, i.e. the distance that someone perceives to exist between herself and members of other ethnic groups. Because this conception of social distance involves all of the aspects traditionally attributed to ethnocentrism, especially the aspect of scaling and rating other groups in a hierarchical fashion, the Social Distance Scale has often been used to measure ethnocentrism. The Internationalism-Nationalism Scale (Levinson, 1957) has been used to measure ethnocentric thinking in the realm of international relations. Nationalism is considered here as "a facet of a broader ethnocentric orientation".

Levinson bases nationalism on the traditional aspects of ethnocentrism, especially the ingroup acceptance/outgroup rejection distinction. The Worldmindedness Scale (Sampson and Smith, 1957) distinguished conceptually between pro-worldmindedness/antiworldmindedness and internationalism/nationalism. That is, the authors wanted to show that it is possible to be, for example, worldminded without necessarily having interest or knowledge in international affairs. Whereas the Internationalism-Nationalism Scale measures one possible facet of ethnocentrism, in turn, ethnocentrism is one part of what the Worldmindedness Scale attempts to measure. The Intolerant-Tolerant Scale (Prentice, 1956) also widely used as an ethnocentrism scale, has statements concerning only blacks and Jews. Half of its items state tolerant attitudes and the other half state intolerant attitudes. However, the standard used in making the statements is not necessarily a Jewish or black person's standard. The Black Ethnocentrism Scale (Chang and Ritter, 1976) also considers a partial or biased conception of ethnocentrism. Although a few items on the scale are directed against groups which could include non-whites, most outgroup rejection statements on the test express anti-white sentiments. Thus, the text actually considers an extremely narrow conception of ethnocentrism.

THE NEED FOR A TEST THAT MEASURES AN ETHNOCENTRIC PERSPECTIVE

The tests reviewed above are representative of the scales used in the past thirty years to measure ethnocentrism. The designers of these tests have been influenced by the four traditional aspects of ethnocentrism. As a result, feelings of favour toward ingroups and disfavour toward outgroups are associated with ethnocentrism. These feelings are most commonly portrayed on the tests as prejudicial attitude statements. Occasionally, the prejudicial attitude and a prejudicial belief are combined in one statement.

However, ethnocentrism is not best understood as being attitudinal in nature. Certain attitudes and beliefs may be results of an ethnocentric, or ethnorelative, perspective. Agreement with negative attitudes may show that someone is nationalistic, intolerant or prejudiced, but not necessarily that he is ethnocentric.

Also, there is no necessary correlation between the extent of a person's ethnocentrism and his score on one of these tests. For example, on the California E Scale, a white respondent who is actually quite ethnocentric, yet doesn't happen to agree with the anti-black statements on the test, could receive an inaccurately low score. However, the evidence adduced by Wilson (1973) for the 'general factor' theory of conservatism does suggest that for most individuals, ethnocentrism is a good predictor of prejudiced attitudes.

Generally, these tests have not been able to accommodate the difference between a subject's indication of negative or positive feelings for himself with respect to a behavior reflects in an attitude statement, and his acceptance of the viability of that behavior for others. For example, one's initial negative reaction to a statement concerning interethnic marriage may have only an indirect connection with tolerance of that behaviour in others. The problem of inferring specific attitudes and specific behaviors in relation to a more general attitude such as ethnocentrism has to be carefully considered (Bagley and Verma, 1979).

A major criticism of many of these tests is that they do not attempt to capture the nature of an ethnocentric perspective in their attempt to encapsulate multiple perspectives. Thus, the first priority in designing a test of ethnocentrism is to consider ethnocentrism <u>before</u> it becomes an attitude toward other groups or <u>their</u> assumed behaviour, or a statement of behavioural intent in relation to particular groups.

ETHNOCENTRISM AND THE NEED FOR THE REFERENCE GROUP CONCEPT

The notion of reference group orientation owes much to our propensity for what Mead called, "taking the attitude of others" (Mead, 1934, p. 154). The taking of others' attitudes begins in early childhood. By adulthood it has become so well-practised that one has eventually lumped all of these attitudes into one common impression, which Mead called, 'the generalised other'. The generalised other assures that a person can operate socially whether she is in face to face involvement with other people, or thinking about interacting with someone, even someone that she has never met before.

Most explanations for the development of the reference group concept point to its usefulness in accounting for all those people with whom one is psychically involved, and not simply physically involved. The explanations point out that non-membership groups have as much influence on an individual as do his membership groups (Merton and Rossi, 1968; Sherif, 1968; Kuhn, 1972). A widely accepted division of the reference group concept is the distinction between normative and comparative groups (Kelley, 1968). In the comparative reference group, a person views himself with respect to that group. In the normative reference group, a group evaluates a person according to the standards, or norms, of that group. Either aspect, comparative or normative, describes only half of the social process.

The utility of the reference group concept is that it should help us to focus on the interaction of society and the individual (Urry, 1973). This interaction must involve a synthesis rather than a separation of the normative and comparative reference groups. One way of explaining this synthesis is by viewing reference group orientation as a perceptual process.

The synthesis of the comparative and normative aspects is analogous to the dynamic relationship between Mead's 'I' and 'me', in which the 'I' sets up responses from our 'generalised other', and the 'me' imagines what those responses would be. Just as one's 'I' sets up a response, an individual, by referring to a reference group, sets up, or expects, a potential response from it. When this comparative aspect has barely begun, the normative aspect, similar to the 'me', has taken over. That is, as soon as the set-up occurs, one imagines how it would be to see himself through that reference group's eyes, i.e. he develops their outlook, and this immediately affects how he perceives the world.

The most important resultant of the simultaneous actions of setting up and imagining a response from a reference group is the formation of a frame of reference. This frame of reference, which has been induced through adoption of a reference group's perspective, is a perceptual filter that is replaceable depending upon the reference group as a perceptual filter is that it allows us to account for fictional or imaginary reference groups as easily as real ones, or for reference groups which exist in the present as well as those which existed in the past or will exist in the future.

Fundamental to this view of reference group orientation is the notion that each individual constructs her own reality. That is, the reference groups that each of us uses depend upon our construction of reality. In these constructions, we use 'typificatory schemes' (Berger and Luckman, 1967), which may be as concrete as 'my friend Harry', or as anonymous as 'my immigrant great grandparents'. The ability to use 'typificatory schemes' is the basis for orienting ourselves to reference groups.

Both ethnocentrism and reference group orientation are perceptual processes. They can be placed in a similar framework in which, first, reference group orientation is defined as a person's use of a frame of reference that is formed through adoption of a reference group's perspective. Second, ethnocentrism is defined as a person's use of a frame of reference that keeps him from accepting any other frames of reference. The reason for bringing them together into the same theoretical framework is to discover whether or not there are some aspects in the nature of an individual's adoption of a reference group's perspective which will indicate why that individual would deny or accept the viability of other frames of reference.

ENCULTURATION AND THE FORMATION OF CULTURAL IDENTITY

Each individual is imprinted with his culture. The degree of the imprintation of culture is realised by the process of enculturation. Enculturation has both a direct and an indirect effect. Its direct effect concerns the choices of behavior that a particular culture offers to its members. Its indirect effect concerns the fact that those choices were the result of our being presented with only a single set of alternatives.

The indirect impact of the enculturative experience is the more powerful one, because of the effect it has on our perceptions of people who have grown up in other cultural settings. Typically, we fail to acknowledge that people undergoing other enculturation experiences have had available to them sets of alternative choices of behavior, attitudes, perceptions, learning styles, etc. In fact, the most enculturated individuals are the people who are least able to recognise that other people have been enculturated differently. Also, as Segall et al.

(1966) point out, "The most enculturated person is the least aware of his culture's role in molding him".

The formation of a cultural identity begins in childhood. A child's early enculturative experience helps determine whether this formation will transpire in a more or less flexible way. The claim has been made in the literature that ethnocentrism is rooted in the early years of enculturation (Adorno et al., 1950; Caditz, 1976; Thomas, 1975). Specifically, some authoritarian childrearing practices during early enculturation have been identified as contributing to ethnocentrism (Thomas, 1975). I suggest that the dimension of authoritarian/non-authoritarian child-rearing by parents is directly related to the dimension of rigid/flexible development of self images by children in the formation of their cultural identities. Since a person's use of self-mage is the basis for his reference group orientations, the rigid/ flexible development of self-images can also be stated in terms of the 1) multiplicity and 2) structural variation of reference group orientations. Multiplicity of reference group orientation refers to the number of reference groups that a person is aware of using. Structural variation of reference group orientation refers to the amount of variation in the structure, or make-up, of reference groups that a person is aware of using.

PILOT STUDY

The subjects for the two tests comprising this pilot study of some of the ideas developed above were 21 undergraduate students at Portland State University. Twelve women and nine men took part. Fifteen of the respondents were Americans and six were International students.

The 'Who are you?' test, adapted from the 'Who am I?' test (Kuhn and McPartland, 1954), consisted of a sheet of paper covered with blank lines. The test was made up of two parts, although the first part appeared to the subjects to be the entire test. During this part, the subjects gave as many answers as they could think of in seven minutes to the question, 'Who are you?'. At the end of the seven minutes, directions for the second part were given orally: to go back and put a check mark after a response if the subject felt that other people think of him that way also. The rationale for including the second set of directions was to assure that the reference group selection is a bi-directional process.

For each subject taking this test, two raw scores were derived. The 'multiplicity of reference group orientation' score cosisted of all the responses having check marks beside them. The dichotomous categorisation technique used by Kuhn and McPartland to divide responses into 'consensual' and 'subconsensual' references was also used here. Discrepancy in agreement between three judges in categorising the responses was slight, occuring on the average less than five percent of the time. The structurally varied reference group was accounted for by a 'subconsensual' response, i.e. that which refers to "groups, classes, attributes, traits or any other matters which would require interpretation by the respondent to be precise or to place him relative to others" (ibid., p. 115). 'Consensual' responses are those which would require no interpretation by the respondent. The 'structural variation of reference group orientation' score consisted of all the responses having check marks beside them that were also 'subconsensual'.

The 'Acceptance/rejection of other cultural frames of reference' test consisted of five questions that each utilised a seven-point semantic differential technique in responding to them. The five questions, taken together, were representative of the notions of ethnocentrism and ethnorelativism. Three of the five questions concerned significant aspects of ethnocentrism and ethnorelativism: the assumption of cultural similarity and the assumption of cultural difference; the acceptance of denial of the viability of other cultural frames of reference; and the utilisation or non-utilisation of a frame of reference which denies the viability of other cultural frames of reference. The first question concerned a philosophical basis for having an ethnocentric or ethnorelative perspective: the construction of a single reality or multiple realities. One question concerned the ability or nonability for empathy. The 'acceptance of other cultural frames of reference' score was found by totalling the numbers 'X'-ed for each question and dividing by five.

The pilot study was carried out to test the following hypothesis:

> There will be a direct correlation between both (1) high/low 'multiplicity of reference group

orientation' scores and (2) high/low 'structural variation of reference group orientation' scores on the 'Who are you?' test and high/low scores on the 'Acceptance/rejection of other cultural frames of reference' test.

Results of correlating the raw scores using the Pearson 'r' coefficient were all statistically significant, and suggest that 1) a moderately positive correlation (.47) exists between multiplicity of reference group orientation and the acceptance of other cultural frames of reference; and 2) only a slightly less positive correlation (.41) exists between structural variation of reference group orientation the acceptance of other cultural frames of reference. Based upon these results, it may be concluded that further explorations should be undertaken which test the validity of multiplicity and structural variation of reference group orientation as aspects of ethnocentrism and ethnorelativism. The present results do suggest a measure of reference group orientation, based on Mead's theory can explain at least some of the variance in the dimension of ethnocentrism versus ethnorelativism.

REFERENCES

Adorno, T.W., et al., The Authoritarian Personality, Harper and Brothers, New York, 1950.
Bagley, C. and Verma, G.K., Racial Prejudice, the Individual and Society, Saxon House, Farnborough, U.K., 1979.
Berger, P. and Luckman, T., The Construction of Social Reality: A Treatise in the Sociology of Knowledge, Anchor Books, Garden City, 1967.
Bogardus, E.S., 'A Social Distance Scale', Sociology and Social Research, vol. 17, Sept. 1932-Aug. 1933, pp. 265-271.
Caditz, J., 'Ethnic Identification, Interethnic Contact, and Belief in Integration', Social Forces, vol. 53, 1976, pp. 632-645.
Chang, E.C. and Ritter, E.H., 'Ethnocentrism in Black College Students', The Journal of Social Psychology, vol. 100, 1976, pp. 89-97.
Kelley, H.H., 'Two Functions of Reference Groups', Readings in Reference Group Theory and Research, Hyman, H.H. and Singer, E. (eds.), The Free Press, New York, 1968.

Kuhn, M.H. and McPartland, T.S., 'An Empirical Investigation of Self-Attitudes', American Sociological Review, vol. 19, 1954, pp. 68-76.
Kuhn, M.H., 'The Reference Group Reconsidered', Symbolic Interactionism: A Reader in Social Psychology, 2nd ed., Manis, J.G. and Meltzer, B.N., (eds.), Allyn and Bacon, Boston, 1972.
Levinson, D., 'Authoritarian Personality and Foreign Policy', Journal of Conflict Resolution, vol. 1, 1957, pp. 37-47.
Mead, G.H., Mind, Self and Society, The University of Chicago Press, Chicago, 1934.
Merton, R.K. and Rossi, A.K., 'Contributions to the Theory of Reference Group Behavior', Readings in Reference Group Theory and Research, Hyman, H.H. and Singer, E., (eds), The Free Press, New York, 1968.
Porter, R.E. and Samovar, L.A., 'Communicating Interculturally', Intercultural Communication: A Reader, 2nd ed., Samovar, L.A. and Porter, R.E., (eds), Wadsworth Publishing Co., Inc., Belmont, 1976.
Prentice, N.M., 'Critique and Notes: The Comparability of Positive and Negative Items in Scales of Ethnic Prejudice', The Journal of Abnormal and Social Psychology, vol. 52, 1956, pp. 420-421.
Sampson, D.L. and Smith, H.P., 'A Scale to Measure Worldminded Attitudes', The Journal of Social Psychology, vol. 45, 1957, pp. 99-106.
Segall, M.H., et al., The Influence of Culture on Visual Perception, Bobbs-Merrill Co., Indianapolis, 1966.
Sherif, M., 'The Concept of Reference Groups in Human Relations', Readings in Reference Group Theory and Research, Hyman, H.H. and Singer, E., (eds), The Free Press, New York, 1968.
Sumner, W.C., Folkways, Ginn and Co., New York, 1906.
Thomas, D.R., 'Authoritarianism, Child-Rearing Practices and Ethnocentrism in Seven Pacific Islands Groups', International Journal of Psychology, vol. 10, 1975, pp. 235-246.
Urry, J., Reference Groups and the Theory of Revolution, Routledge and Kegan Paul, London, 1973.
Williams, R., Strangers Next Door: Ethnic Relations in American Communities, Prentice-Hall, Englewood Cliffs, 1964.
Wilson, G. (ed), The Psychology of Conservatism, The Academic Press, London, 1973.

Chapter Three

TOWARD A TYPOLOGY OF STRANGER-HOST RELATIONSHIPS

William B. Gudykunst

Since Simmel's (1908) original introduction of the concept of the stranger (der Fremden) and the first translation of his seminal essay by Park and Burgess (1921, pp. 322-7) (1); there has been an abundance of research and theorising based upon the concept (e.g., Hamilton-Guerson, 1921; Wood, 1934; Schuetz, 1944; Siu, 1952; Zajonic, 1952; Nash & Wolf, 1957; Herman & Schild, 1961; Schild, 1962; Nash, 1963; Skinner, 1963; Williams, 1964; Nash & Heiss, 1967; Tiryakian, 1973; Fortes, 1975; Shack & Skinner, 1979). The overwhelming amount of work related to the concept has led such writers as Alex Inkeles to conclude that "there is a special and well-developed sociology of the stranger" (1964, p. 12). However, as two recent critiques (McLemore, 1970; Levine, 1977) have pointed out, the literature on strangers is confused by several different conceptualisations of the term.

According to Simmel's (1950) conceptualisation of the concept, there is a paradox for the stranger in terms of space:

> If wandering is the liberation from every given point in space, and thus the conceptual opposite to fixation at such a point, the sociological form of the 'stranger' presents the unity, as it were, of these two characteristics. This phenomenon too, however, reveals that spatial relations are only the condition on the one hand, and the symbol, on the other, of human relations. The stranger is thus being discussed here, not in the sense often touched upon in the past, as the wanderer who comes today and goes tomorrow, but rather as the person who comes today and stays tomorrow. He is, so to speak, the <u>potential</u> wanderer:

> although he has not moved on, he has not quite overcome the freedom of coming and going. (p. 402).

Thus, Simmel's paradox is one of "complete liberation and absolute fixation" (McLemore, 1970, p. 86).

Not all writers on strangers concur with Simmel's conceptualisation. One writer who differs is Wood (1934) who describes the stranger:

> As one who has come into face-to-face contact with the group for the first time. This concept is broader than that of Simmel....For us the stranger may be, as with Simmel, a potential wanderer, but he may also be a wanderer who comes today and goes tomorrow, or he may come today and remain with us permanently. The condition of being a stranger is not, for the present study, dependent upon the future duration of the contact, but it is determined by the fact that it is the first face-to-face meeting of individuals who have not known one another before (pp. 43-44).

Similarly, Schuetz (1944) diverges from Simmel's conceptualisation. For Schuetz the term stranger means:

> ...an adult individual of our times and civilization who tries to be permanently accepted or at least tolerated by the group which he approaches. The outstanding example for the social situation under scrutiny is that of the immigrant....But by no means is their validity restricted to this special case. The applicant for membership in a closed club, the prospective bridegroom who wants to be admitted to the girl's family, the farmer's son who enters college, the city-dweller who settles in a rural environment, the 'selectee' who joins the Army, the family of the war worker who moves into a boom town--all are strangers according to the definition just given (1944, p. 499).

Levine points out that Wood's "work might well have laid the groundwork for an extensive sociology of the stranger, in which Simmel's formulations would properly have been understood as referring to a special type; but...subsequent sociologists of the stranger tended to cite Simmel as the primary point of reference for the topic and, even when citing Wood, tended to miss the distinction between Wood's newly arrived outsider and Simmel's stranger" (1977, p. 25).

Prior to continuing it is necessary to point out that there is one essential feature of Simmel, Wood, and Schuetz's conceptualisation of the stranger-host relationship which differs from the more common usage of the term stranger. That is that the stranger-host relationship is "a figure-ground phenomenon, in which the stranger status is always defined <u>in relation to a host</u>" (Levine, 1977). This differs from broader uses of the term where strangerhood is viewed as a function of the degree of unfamiliarity between any two people. For example, Lofland (1973) views people as strangers if they lack biographical and/or personal information about the other person.

McLemore, (1970) argues that there are at least two research traditions which are classified under rubric of the sociology of the stranger. These traditions include research based upon Simmel's original conceptualisation of the term, as well as the study of the 'newcomer' which "has been subordinated to and largely undifferentiated from the study of the 'stranger'" (McLemore, 1970, p. 93). Further, McLemore suggests that the issue is confounded by the attention the stranger concept receives in the study of marginality. Levine (1977) indicates that the conceptual confusion is furthered by the lack of differentiation between work on the stranger and research on social distance. More specifically, he concludes by saying: "one finds in the literature which draws on the excursus, both in that on social distance and that on the stranger proper, a sprawling and confused assortment of statements" (Levine, 1977). In other words, there is not a welldeveloped area of the sociology of the stranger as Inkeles would have us believe (2).

One of the major attempts to clarify the conceptual confusion with regard to the sociology of the stranger is Levine's (1977) specification of a typology of stranger relationships. Levine contends that the critical variable is not the length of time a stranger spends in the host community. Rather he argues that the focus should be upon the type of relationship that the stranger aspires to establish with the host (e.g. to visit, for residence, for membership in the host group). Whatever the stranger's aspiration, there is a response by the host community to the stranger. According to Levine this reaction will involve feelings of anxiety or latent antagonism. He goes on to describe the host's response as "compulsive, reflecting the reality of a persisting ambivalence underlying all stranger relationships and the related fact that these relationships are invested with a particularly high degree of affect. It will be compulsively friendly if positive feelings predominate, compulsively antagonistic if negative ones are dominant" (1977). By cross-classifying these two variables Levine ends up with a typology which contains six categories: guests, sojourner, newcomer, intruder, inner enemy, and marginal man (3).

Given that Simmel's conceptualisation of the stranger focuses upon both the nearness and farness - or in other words, ambivalence - of the stranger-host relationship, Levine's typology may oversimplify the potential relationships between strangers and hosts (4). The objective of the remainder of this paper is to expand and modify upon Levine's typology to develop a typology which will allow us to subsume the writing of Simmel, as well as that of Wood and Schuetz and other writers on the subject.

Figure 1 presents a modified typology of stranger-host relationships. The typology was constructed using the strangers interest in the host community and the host's reaction to the stranger as the two critical variables following Levine (1977). The strangers interest in the host community is trichtomised into visit, residence, and membership. Similarly, the host's reaction is broken down into a trichtomy: friendly, ambivalent, and antagonistic. It is here where the current typology differs from Levine's. As noted above, Levine uses the dichtomy 'compulsive friendliness' and 'compulsive antagonism'. The argument being made is that if Simmel's stranger-host relationship is basically ambivalent, such a category must be included otherwise Simmel's stranger does not fit into the typology. Further, if the underlying stranger-host relationship is basically ambivalent, if the host's reaction does in fact lean toward positive or negative, it will, in all likelihood not be 'compulsive'. The present typology yields nine types of stranger-host relationships: (1) guest, (2) newly arrived (for a discussion of why 'newly arrived' rather than sojourner, is being used to describe this cell, see note 3), (3) newcomer, (4) sojourner (for a discussion of why 'sojourner' is used for this cell, see note 3), (5) Simmel's stranger, (6) immigrants, (7) intruder, (8) middle-man minority, and (9) marginal men. (5)

Prior to discussing each of these types separately it is necessary to briefly examine the factors which affect the particular status a stranger assumes vis-a-vis the host community. Following Levine (1977), the factors affecting the aspirations of the stranger and the factors affecting the response of the host will be discussed separately. However, it should be noted that the stranger-host relationship is a transactional one and each set of factors will inevitably influence the other.

Levine specifies two factors which influenced the stranger's aspirations: (1) "Reasons for leaving home (alienation, boredom, calling, disaster, economic hardship, political oppression, etc.)" and (2) "Condition of entrance into the host group (amount of prestige, movable resources, special skills, etc.)" (1977). In addition to these two factors there are several additional factors which will influence the strangers aspirations regarding the host community. These will include, but are not limited to: (1) the attitudes of the stranger toward the host (Gudykunst, 1977), (2) the general intercultural attitudes of the stranger (e.g., is the stranger a person whom, Adler, 1976, would refer to as a 'multicultural' person or one whom Walsh, 1973, would label 'cosmopolitan'?), (3) prior contact between the stranger and the host community (Gudykunst and Halsall, 1980), (4) contact with other strangers (Gudykunst and Halsall, 1980) (6).

In his paradigm of a sociology of the stranger Levine (1977) specifies four factors which will affect the hosts response toward the stranger: (1) "Extent of strangerhost similarity (ethnicity, language, race, religion, value orientations, etc.)", (2) "Existence of special cultural categories and rituals for dealing with strangers", (3) "Criteria for group and societal membership (classificatory kinship, religion, citizenship, professional certification, etc.)", and (4) "Conditions of local community (age, size, homogeneity, degree of isolation, etc.)".

Given the above discussion of the factors which can influence the particular status a stranger assumes vis-avis the host community, the specific types of strangerhost relationships can now be examined. The nine types of stranger-host relationships presented in Figure 1 cover a wide variety of different research areas. For example, the typology covers the traditional writings on the stranger, marginal-men, immigrants, and sojourners. If looked at from the perspective of the strangers aspirations toward the host community, the typology includes work on sociology of tourism (to visit), intercultural adjustment (residence), and assimilation/acculturation (membership). Space does not allow for an elaborate discussion of each of the specific types nor an integration of the types; therefore, what follows should be considered only an overview.

GUEST

Given the typology, a guest's interest in the host community is to visit, while the host's reaction toward the guest is leaning to positive or friendly. This type includes some, but not all, tourists. Using Doxey's (1976) four-stage model of the host's attitude toward the tourist, this category would involve the stage he labels 'euphoria,' or a positive attitude toward the host (7).

NEWLY ARRIVED (8)

The newly arrived outsider's interest in the host community is one of residence, but not membership, while the host's reaction toward the stranger is friendly and/or positive. Like the guest, the newly arrived is a desirable person in the host community. Included in this category would be a large portion of diplomatic personnel residing in foreign nations, business persons invited to set up operations in a foreign culture, change agents (e.g., Peace Corp) invited into a host community, and other outsiders living in a foreign culture where there is a need and/or desire for the services offered.

NEWCOMER

The newcomer's interest in the host community is one of establishing membership, and the corresponding host reaction to the newcomer is positive or friendly. In general newcomers constitute desired migrants, including migrants whose skills the host community needs and political migrants whose orientations the host community views as positive. The differentiating characteristic of the newcomer, like the guest and newly arrived, is the positive attitude of the host toward the sojourner.

SOJOURNER (9)

A sojourner's interest in the host community, like the guest's, is to visit, and then leave. However, the host community response to the sojourner is not inherently positive as in the case of the guest. Rather, the host's reaction toward the sojourner can best be classified as ambivalent and/or indifferent. This category entails much of the study of sociology of tourism. In discussing indifferent attitudes of the host toward the tourist, MacCannell indicates that "The local people...have long discounted the presence of tourists and go about their business as usual...treating tourists as part of the regional scenery" (1976, p. 106).

SIMMELL'S STRANGER

When the stranger's interest in the host community is one of residence and the host's reaction is one of ambivalence, the relationship is identical to the one Simmel discussed in his essay "der fremden". Therefore, this type has been labeled Simmel's Stranger. In that Simmel's position has been summarised above, it is unnecessary to elaborate further here.

IMMIGRANTS

The immigrant's interest in the host community is one of membership, while the host community's response can best be described as one of ambivalence or indifference. This type would include the vast majority of research/writing on people aspiring to assimilate and/or acculturate in a new culture. So much has been written on this category that it is impossible to begin to summarise the writing here (for an overview of research on immigrants, see Kim, 1979; Kitano, 1980; Padilla, 1980).

INTRUDER

Similar to the guest and the sojourner, the intruder's interest in the host community is only to visit, however, the host community's reaction toward intruders is leaning toward negative or antagonistic. This type includes visitors who are unwelcome in the community they are visiting. Included in this category would be visitors like the late Shah of Iran during his visit to the United States during the time when the U.S. embassy personnel were being held hostage in Iran. Following Doxey's (1976) four stage model for the development of host's attitude toward tourists, this type includes those he labels 'antagonism'.

MIDDLE-MAN MINORITY (10)

This category of stranger strives toward residence in the host community, but must overcome the same antagonistic or negative host reaction as the intruder. Traditionally, the middle-man minority involves a group that is higher in status than other minorities, but at the same time is lower in status than the dominant group (Blalock, 1967; Bonacich, 1973). These minorities "often serve as buffers between dominant and subordinated groups and can become the targets and scapegoats for the stress of that system (for example, Jews in Germany during the Nazi era)" (Kitano, 1980, pp. 216-17). In that these minorities act as a buffer between dominant and subordinate groups, there is often antagonistic feelings associated toward their members.

MARGINAL MAN

The final type of stranger-host relationship is the marginal man. This type of relationship involves a stranger who strives for membership in the host community. This category encompasses the research and writing, often categorised under work on the stranger, which stems from Park's (1928) work on "Human Migration and the Marginal Man". Park conceived of the marginal man as a person who was 'more or less of a stranger' in two cultures, while aspiring to membership in the host community. A conceptualisation significantly different from Simmel's, yet similar enough that future writers often failed to recognise the distinction (11).

The present typology, like Levine's (1977) typology, allows for research the marginal man to be differentiated from other types of writing on strangers. Levine (1977) suggests that other writings can be subsumed under this type, including Schuetz's (1945) work on the 'homecomer' and Tiryakian's (1973) discussion of the 'estranged native'.

CONCLUSION

The typology outlined above, is only a beginning attempt to explicate the various types of stranger statuses vis-a-vis the host community. Space does not permit a more complete discussion here. However, a more complete elaboration is necessary. When fully articulated the typology will integrate previous research on each of the individual stranger statuses, specify individual characteristics which impact upon strangers, elaborate on the factors which influence the type of status a stranger assumes and the factors influencing changes in stranger status, and, finally, specify how the typology can be integrated with the study of other forms of social relations.

NOTES

1. Although Park and Burgess were the first to translate Simmel's original essay, the most frequently cited is Wolff's which appears in Simmel (1950). In writing this paper I have drawn heavily upon Levine (1977). Although I disagree with him at several points, this paper would never had been written if I hadn't read this paper and disagreed with Levine in several areas.

2. Space does not allow a thorough, complete review of the writings on the sociology of the stranger. For two excellent reviews see McLemore (1970) and Levine (1977). However, exposure to these reviews is not a substitute for the original writings on the concept (Simmel, Wood and Schuetz).

3. I disagree with Levine's choice of terms both in his typology and in the text of his article. My disagreement centers around the use of the terms 'sojourner' and 'newly arrived'. For me a sojourner is a traveler, a visitor, not a person who has come to the host community to reside. On the other hand, a newly arrived implies a person who has come to stay. I would contend that these are more common uses of the terms in the literature and Levine's uncommon use of the terms can lead to conceptual confusion on the readers part if he/she is not careful.

4. Although Levine's typology oversimplifies the potential relationships, he does present a 'paradigm' for the sociology of the stranger which is extremely useful.

5. Following Levine's argument each of these types can be applied to either individual strangers or a collectivity of strangers.

6. This list is not all inconclusive. For a further discussion of attitudes of strangers toward the host see Brein and David (1971) and Gudykunst (1977).

7. Cohen (1979) points out that linear models such as Doxey's (1976) can not do justice to the differential dynamics under varying tourist conditions. For example, Doxey's model does not take into account how tourism was introduced into the host community or the attitudes of host prior to the introduction of tourism.

8. As indicated in note 3, Levine (1977) uses the term sojourner to label this type. I have chosen newly arrived, because sojourner is a term usually used to apply to visits (one writer Siu, 1952, has used sojourner to talk about a group which clings to the culture of its ethnic group--again a non-traditional use of the term).

9. I am not sure that sojourner is the ideal label to use for this type. It is better used here than to describe the newly arrived type. Possibly a better term would be 'traveler', but this term has additional connotations which are not desirable (Fussell, 1980).

10. Levine uses the term 'inner enemy' to label this type and argues that middle man minorities fit into his sojourner (our newly arrived) category. I have modified the terms for several reasons. First, in reviewing the literature I found very little reference to inner enemy. Second, it did not seem appropriate to classify middle man minorities into a category involving positive attitudes on the part of the host. Even though the writings on middle man minorities do not always emphasise negative feelings on the part of the host, but they are often scapegoats and subject to antagonistic feelings. Therefore, this term has been chosen to label this type even though it is not ideal.

11. Stonequist (1937) made the necessary distinction, but a decade later it was lost in the writings of Hughes (1949).

REFERENCES

Adler, P., 'Beyond Cultural Identity', in Samovar, L. and Porter, R. (Eds.), Intercultural Communication: A Leader 2nd ed., Belmont, CA: Wadsworth, 1976.

Antonovsky, A., 'Toward a Refinement of the "Marginal Man" Concept,' Social Forces, Oct. 1956, pp. 57-62.

Blalock, H.M., Toward a Theory of Minority-Group Relations, New York: Capricorn Books, 1967.

Bonacich, E., 'Toward a Theory of Middle Man Minorities,' American Sociological Review, vol. 38, 1973, pp. 583-594.

Brein, M. and David, K.H., 'Intercultural Communication and the Adjustment of the Sojourner,' Psychological Bulletin, vol. 76, 1971, pp. 215-230.

Cohen, E., 'Towards a Sociology of International Tourism,' Social Research, vol. 39, 1972, pp. 164-182.

Cohen, E., 'Expatriate Communities,' Current Sociology, vol. 24, 1977, pp. 5-133.

Cohen, E., 'A Phenomenology of Tourist Experiences,' Sociology, vol. 13, 1979, pp. 179-201.

Cohen, E., 'Rethinking the Sociology of Tourism,' Annals of Tourism Research, vol. 6, 1979, pp. 18-35.

Doxey, G.V., 'A Causation Theory of Visitor-Resident Irritants,' in Impact of Tourism, Salt Lake City: The Travel Research Association, 1976.

Fortes, M., 'Strangers,' in Fortes, M. and Paterson, S. (Eds.), Studies in African Social Anthropology, London: Academy Press, 1975.

Fussell, P., Abroad, London: Oxford, 1980.

Gudykunst, W.G., 'Intercultural Contact and Attitude Change,' in Jain, N.C. (Ed.), International and Intercultural Communication Annual, vol. IV, Falls Church, VA: Speech Communication Association, 1977.

Gudykunst, W.B. and Halsall, S., 'The Application of a Theory of Contraculture to Intercultural Communication,' in Nimmo, D. (Ed.), Communication Yearbook, 4, New Brunswick, N.J.: Transaction, 1980.

Hamilton-Grierson, P.J., 'Strangers,' in Hastings, J. (Ed.), Encyclopedia of Religion and Ethics, Edinburgh: T & T Clark, 1921.

Herman, S.N. and Schild, E.O., 'The Stranger-Group in a Cross-Cultural Situation,' Sociometry, 1961, pp. 165-176.

Hughes, E., 'Social Change and Status Protest: An Essay on the Marginal Man,' *Phylon*, vol. 10, 1949, pp. 58-65.

Inkeles, A., *What is Sociology?*, Englewood Cliffs, N.J.: Prentice-Hall, 1964.

Kim, Y.Y., 'Toward an Interactive Theory of Communication Acculturation,' in Nimmo, D. (Ed.), *Communication Yearbook, 3*, New Brunswick, N.J.: Transaction, 1979.

Kitano, H.L., *Race Relations*, 2nd ed., Englewood Cliffs, N.J.: Prentice-Hall, 1980.

Levine, D.N., 'Simmel at a Distance: On the History and Systematics of the Sociology of the Stranger,' *Sociological Focus*, vol. 10, 1977.

Lofland, L., *A World of Strangers*, New York: Basic Books, 1973.

MacCannell, D., *The Tourist*, New York: Schocken Books, 1976.

McLemore, S.D., 'Simmel's Stranger: A Critique of the Concept,' *Pacific Sociological Review*, vol. 13, 1970, pp. 86-94.

Nash, D., 'The Ethnologist as Stranger,' *Southwestern Journal of Anthropology*, vol. 19, 1963, pp. 149-167.

Nash, D. and Wolf, A.W., 'The Stranger in Laboratory Culture,' *American Sociological Review*, vol. 22, 1957, pp. 400-405.

Nash, D. and Heiss, J., 'Sources of Anxiety in Laboratory Strangers,' *Sociological Quarterly*, vol. 8, 1967, pp. 215-221.

Padilla, A.M. (Ed.), *Acculturation: Theory, Models and Some New Findings*, Boulder, CO: Westview Press, 1980.

Park, R.E., 'Human Migration and the Marginal Man,' *American Journal of Sociology*, May, 1928, pp. 881-893.

Park, R.E. and Burgess, E.W., *Introduction to the Science of Sociology*, Chicago: University of Chicago Press, 1921.

Schild, E.O., 'The Foreign Student, as a Stranger,' *Journal of Social Issues*, vol. 18, 1962, pp. 41-54.

Schuetz, A., 'The Stranger: An Essay in Social Psychology,' *American Journal of Sociology*, vol. 49, 1944, pp. 499-507.

Schuetz, A., 'The Homecomer,' *American Journal of Sociology*, vol. 50, 1945, pp. 369-376.

Shack, W.A. and Skinner, E.P., *Strangers in African Societies*, Berkeley, CA: University of California Press, 1979.

Simmel, G., 'Exburs iiber den fremden,' *Sociologie*, Leipzig: Dunker and Humblot, 1908.

Simmel, G., 'The Stranger," in Wolff, K.H. (Trans. & Ed.), *The Sociology of George Simmel*, New York: Free Press, 1950.

Siu, P.C.P., 'The Sojourner,' *American Journal of Sociology*, vol. 58, 1952, pp. 34-44.

Skinner, E.P., 'Strangers in West African Society,' *Africa*, vol. 33, 1963, pp. 307-320.

Stonequist, E., *The Marginal Man*, New York: Scribner's, 1937.

Tiryakian, E.A., 'Sociological Perspectives on the Stranger,' *Sounding*, 1973a, pp. 45-58.

Tiryakian, E.A., 'Perspectives on the Stranger,' in TeSelle, S. (Ed.), *The Rediscovery of Ethnicity*, New York: Harper and Row, 1973b.

Walsh, J., *Intercultural Education in the Community of Man*, Honolulu: University of Hawaii Press, 1973.

Williams, R.M., *Strangers Next Door: Ethnic Relations in American Communities*, Englewood Cliffs, N.J.: Prentice-Hall, 1964.

Wood, M.M., *The Stranger: A Study in Social Relationships*, New York: Columbia University Press, 1934.

Zajonic, R., 'Aggressive Attitudes of the 'Stranger' as a Function of Conformity Pressures,' *Human Relations*, vol. 5, 1952, pp. 205-216.

Figure 1.1: A Typology of Stranger-Host Relationships*

	Stranger's Interest in Host Community		
Host's Reaction to Stranger	Visit	Residence	Membership
Friendly (Learning to Positive)	Guest	Newly Arrived	Newcomer
Ambivalent (Indifference)	Sojourner	Simmel's Stranger	Immigrant
Antagonistic (Leaning to Negative)	Intruder	Middle-Man Minority	Marginal Man
General area of Research	Sociology of Tourism	Intercultural Adjustment	Acculturation/ Assimilation

*This is modified and expanded from Levine (1977).

PART II

LANGUAGE, EDUCATION AND MINORITY GROUPS

Chapter Four

MULTICULTURALISM AND EDUCATION:
PRELUDE TO PRACTICE

Gajendra K. Verma

This chapter is addressed primarily to those well-intentioned educationalists, particularly in Britain, who seem to show their concern for the education of children from ethnic minority groups.
During the last two decades a number of models and strategies have been presented to deal with the changed characteristics of British society and in this paper I wish to raise issues and problems with regard to the concepts of multiculturalism and education. It is time to take a new look at the various conceptualizations and ask ourselves whether the reality of contemporary Britain requires a different response than the ones we have been pursuing or developing since the 1950's.

THE LABELS OF MULTICULTURAL EDUCATION

In our everyday interaction sometimes we use certain words or terms which have no clear-cut meanings; these have blind-alley implications which not only take us away from moral and social realities, but direct us towards conceptual confusion. One such term is 'multicultural education'. This phrase has a number of meanings which vary from one society to another.

Multicultural education in one form or another has begun to emerge around the globe as a field of study since the 1950's. Other apparently synonymous terms like 'multiracial', 'multiethnic', 'multicultural' and 'multilingual' have also been in constant use for some years now, particularly in Britain, Canada, United States, Australia and more recently in Sweden. Yet, the nature and process of these terms have not been fully explained to practitioners. Because of the confusion over the terminology the terms have become a form of shorthand for describing away issues faced in a practical situation such as the classroom. As a result, the one thing about multicultural education that seems certain is its uncertainty. For example, does the attainment of multiculturalism mean the education of children whose parents come from different cultural backgrounds? Are we talking about educating all pupils about different cultures? Perhaps Black Studies, Asian Studies, Ethnic Studies, Mother-tongue Teaching, celebration of ethnic minority festivals and such activities are what multicultural education is about! Closely related to this labeling is the anxiety on the part of some people that multicultural education will become a euphemism for minority education. Whatever it may mean, the terminology has featured increasingly widely in research reports and in the media, and then into the everyday language of those interested in the educational process.

In Britain, the number of advisers to Education Authorities responsible for the vaguely defined area of multicultural education has grown steadily over the past decade. Such a step is based upon the premise that all education should be multicultural, reflecting the ethnic diversity and structural complexity of British society. Accounts from many of these facilitators of 'change' suggest that there is less clarity over their role and the exact meaning of this label for policy development. I would argue that because of confused thinking about multicultural education there is an absence of a national policy, and although teachers and teacher educators are beginning to accept the existence of 'multicultural education', what it really means in practice is far from clear. The term 'multiculturalism' today comes readily to the lips and pens of those who wish to be seen as 'progressive', in the fields of education, media, social welfare and police- community relations. The label of multiculturalism is also being used in a fragmented and superficial way at all levels from primary to higher education, without having any regard as to whether the particular strategy is relevant to the needs and aspirations of the overall community. Thus Eggleston (1983), in a comment on 'ethnic naivety', urges teacher educators, with regard to multicultural education, to "avoid premature emphasis on difficulty, differentiation and disadvantage especially when they are presented in a theoretical way that seems unrelated to the classroom."

The confusion over the terminology and implementation is not peculiar to Britain alone. Considering multicultural education in the United States, Gibson (1976) remarked:

> "The literature on multicultural education lacks clarity with regard to key concepts and abounds with untested and sometimes unsupportable assumptions regarding goals, strategies and outcomes."

In Australia, educators have attempted to relate multicultural education in terms of a "problem" to be overcome rather than a desirable aspect of society. The philosophy of the 1950's and early 1960's was that the traditional homogeneity of Australian society would be maintained by the effective adaptation of all newcomers to the Australian way of life. The arrival of ethnic minority groups was therefore seen as a potential threat to national cohesion and unity. The term which has increasingly become synonymous with multiculturalism in Australian curriculum planning is 'Ethnic Studies'. Thus in devising educational programmes, all too often 'Ethnic Studies' is confused with compensatory programmes for 'migrant' children. Writing about the Australian situation, Chipman (1980) comments that: "It is pretty obvious, and agreed by many if not most multiculturalists, that Australia is at present, in operational terms, a highly assimilatory society". There is a clear implication that so-called 'ethnic studies' are merely a device for subordinating the needs and aspirations of minority groups to those of the majority. Somewhat similar criticisms of Canadian 'multicultural' policy have been made by Buchignani (1980). The issue here as in other countries is that an ill-defined 'multicultural' policy is an obfuscating ideology which obscures the real class and race-based inequalities and exploitations of Western societies.

Given the difficulties in both conceptualizing and putting into practice a policy which addresses the real inequalities of society, it is not surprising that the concept has become confused and often lacking in credibility and has created confusion for many policy makers, theorists and practitioners. It presents a challenge to educators, administrators and researchers.

Commenting in the context of the Canadian situation, Burnet (1975) writes that multiculturalism is a misleading and inacccurate term because most ethnic groups do not retain entirely their traditional culture; neither do they remain separate and distinct groups. According to Baptiste (1976), Americans too are now beginning to increasingly realize that they are multicultural, not only in the sense of racial and cultural mix, but also in terms of identifying common needs, interests and concerns which cut across different ethnic and cultural groups. The model which is emerging is of different ethnic groups with complementary and interlocking needs, rather than of groups united around class or economic needs. This is a Weberian model of social structure, with status rather than class groups as the major segments of society.

American education, however, does not seem to have come to any consensus with regard to approaches in the 'multicultural' area, and as a result, there is a 'distinctively American buzzing confusion' (Glazer, 1977). Given the lack of clarity over definitions and aims of multicultural education, the problem facing practitioners in the field is "the lack of clear delineation of the consequences of multiculturalism if the values underlying such a concept were manifested in human behavior" (Dolce, 1973).

At this point it may be useful to briefly examine evolution of specific processes underlying the idea of multicultural education.

EVOLUTION OF MULTICULTURALISM IN
BRITISH EDUCATION

Since the 1950's and throughout the 1960's and 1970's, the increased migration of a variety of ethnic groups, mostly from former British Colonies (e.g. the Caribbean, the Indian Sub-continent, East Africa) has generated discussion about the nature of British Society. As a result of that process, individuals of different and potentially conflicting cultures now inhabit the same country, town or classroom. The character of the school population, particularly in urban areas, has undergone considerable change in the direction of cultural, linguistic and religious diversity. Thus the need has arisen for a process of education which can be adapted to meet the needs of this changed society.

In response to this growing diversity of the population and the increasing complexity of British society, theorists have offered models and programmes to promote 'multiculturalism' in education.

Yet, so far there is no widely understood or accepted model of multiculturalism in education. Various explanations can be offered for the conflicting perspectives. Multicultural education was and is still perceived in terms of minority self-awareness programme. Usually these programmes focused on only one ethnic group, e.g. Black Studies, Asian Studies. The failure to have a clear national policy for all ethnic groups meant that institutions at the earlier stages of education were left to their own devices to understand and then respond to the issues and challenges of a changed society.

The efforts of the recent past and to deal with the changed characteristics of post-war Britain led to different and sometimes conflicting programmes and strategies, designed specifically to "deal with" children from New Commonwealth backgrounds. The Department of Education and Science (then called the Ministry of Education) in the 1960's adopted a cautious or timid approach in dealing with the education of "immigrant" children. Willey (1982) comments that:

> "Initial central government reaction to immigration....in the 1950's and early 1960's was to play down the implications, to suggest that no particular social policy response - or action by teachers - was necessary...."

However, teachers and schools in Britain had already been attempting to provide programmes for immigrant pupils for sometime without any guidance from the Ministry of Education. At first educational provisions were very much 'ad hoc' and the emphasis was on educational programmes for the acquisition of English. Teachers and schools soon saw, however symbolically and stereotypically, 'non-English-speaking children' (Asians) as a 'main problem', and the education system responded with what was regarded as appropriate provision (Meredith, 1971). The principle behind such a strategy was that the new groups of children would be assimilated into a relatively homogeneous British society, just as it was thought that previous groups of immigrants had been absorbed. This process has been described as the 'assimilationist' approach, though the word was neither defined nor challenged at the time.

As the scale of the supposed problem grew, other measures were felt necessary. For example, in

June 1965, the D.E.S. issues Circular 7/65 recommending that 'undue concentrations of immigrant children' in schools should be avoided. A solution suggested was to disperse the immigrant children. At the initiative of the D.E.S., a minority of the 64 Local Education Authorities with significant numbers of immigrant pupils adopted a "bussing" policy, where children from New Commonwealth backgrounds (usually children of South Asian origin) were transported from their home area to attend a more distant school. The practice of dispersal has been described as racist in that only children from immigrant communities were distributed - a one way process. Such a strategy clearly reflected the ideology of the time, namely to seek to assimilate or absorb different ethnic/cultural groups into the main stream of society. Such thinking and resultant policy decision are part of the 'dominant culture' model. The effect of this thinking on educational practice would supposedly be to make the children as 'British' as their native, white counterparts. In recent years, many writers (e.g. Bolton, 1979; Street-Porter, 1978; Willey, 1982) have criticised assimilationist policies as ethnocentric, culturally dominant and indeed racist.

In the early 1970's, there began a shift in thinking and policy, away from the assimilationist approach towards one of 'integration'. This approach was heralded by Roy Jenkins' (1966) definition of integration, "not as a flattening process of assimilation, but as equal opportunity, accompanied by cultural diversity, in an atmosphere of mutual tolerance". Thus, the focus in educational provision moved towards the design of programmes intended to promote unity while allowing for diversity; such programmes were to seek to meet the 'special needs' of ethnic minority children in the British educational system. Research conducted during this period shows that the education of ethnic minorities was perceived as 'problem oriented' (Verma and Bagley, 1975; 1979).

In the 1980's more diverse views of society prevail than in the 1960's, because of the fundamental socio-cultural ideological changes. Currently in fashion is the model of cultural pluralism, which is often confused with multiculturalism. This perspective regards each ethnic group as having the opportunity to develop and retain its distinct culture and traditions within the framework of the larger society. Pluralism, according to some writers (e.g. Street-Porter, 1978; Bolton, 1979), is the only policy which avoids racism. Cultural pluralism has been defined as "a system that accepts that people's values and life styles are different and works in such a way as to allow equal opportunity for all to play a full part in society" (Bolton, 1979). Bolton, like other multiculturalists, discusses assimilation, integration and cultural pluralism as three different responses to immigrant communities. As outlined earlier, language teaching was the main educational provision under the assimilationist perspective. Under the integrationist approach, educators had to take into account the cultural background of learners in order to make the educational programme more effective. In writing about an ideal pluralist society, Bolton (1979) asserts that efforts should be made to influence the attitudes of teachers and pupils, implying that current educational practices encourage negative attitudes towards ethnic minorities and promote unhealthy race relations. One of the major problems with interpretations such as those of Bolton and Street-Porter is that people not familiar with the multicultural literature may draw the conclusion that teachers should abandon teaching English as a second language and learning about minority cultures, since these are linked with assimilationism and integrationism.

The British government's support for multiculturalism or cultural pluralism appeared in the 1977 Green Paper, "Education in Schools". This Paper emphasised that the presence of ethnic minority groups in Britain has implications for the education of all children, and that all schools, whatever their ethnic composition, should give their pupils an understanding both of the multiethnic nature of British society and of Britain's place in an interdependent world. The Green Paper refers to "the needs of this new Britain" which should be reflected in school curricula.

The core of this emerging model of cultural pluralism is that the different ethnic, cultural and religious groups making up society, ought to have equal power, in terms of access to economic and political resources. If such equality of power is not provided, ethnic differentiation in society becomes a form of racism rather than pluralism (Bagley, 1972). The question arises as to whether society at large is ready to commit itself to multiculturalism to the extent of including ethnic groups in the power structure!

There has also been a recognition that many of the school practices concerned with race, culture and ethnicity have been damaging to the self-esteem of minority children. Such practices reinforce ethnic stereotypes and discriminatory behaviour both in schools and in society. Some progressive organizations, such as the National Union of Teachers in Britain have recently argued that much of the existing curriculum materials in schools is ethnocentric and inappropriate for a 'multiethnic' society. Studies have also revealed that children's perceptions and images about the outside world are created through school literature and texts which currently embody racial stereotyping, ethnocentrism, tokenism, etc. (See the chapter in this volume by Verma and Mallick on 'Children's books and ethnic minorities'). Thus, the unsuitability of the existing curriculum material and the need to produce new materials for classroom practice has been a continuing theme of multiculturalism in British education. This is a progressive trend in multicultural philosophy; but the general, confused policy of multiculturalism has also been espoused by groups in Britain who have been anxious to forestall ethnic conflict and unrest by certain palliative measures which left existing power balances and economic interests unaltered.

One issue in the evolution of multiculturalism in Britain is that its implementation is still localised. It could be seen, even with its present imperfections, to be a response merely to local needs, whether to those of the community as a whole or to those of particular groups within the community. As a result, those schools in areas where presently the number of ethnic minority children is negligible are not being offered any preparation for later participation, personal or political, in an ethnically diverse society. It is clear from the many multicultural philosophies, programmes and approaches that they are ad hoc and, in their confusions and lack of balance, reflect competing claims for political, social and economic power. The British educational system has so far failed to concern itself with the preparation of all individuals to live in a society composed of varied races, cultures, social norms and life styles, each different but interdependent. It has failed also in helping pupils to understand the nature of racism, and the gross inequalities of power in British society.

The question of ethnic and cultural diversity and the social and economic subordination of many ethnic 'minority' groups can no longer remain a private matter on the political agenda. It is now becoming apparent that powerless ethnic minorities in many countries are making it explicit that they wish to retain their cultural and religious differences within a framework of economic equality or opportunity.

It is also obvious that first generation immigrants to many Western countries tend to retain their native cultures and resist assimilationist trends; the degree to which their children wish to retain elements of their cultural heritage is a complex matter however. In the 1960's and early 1970's the expression 'culture shock' was often used by teachers (Lynch, 1981) in order to explain the alleged difficulties which immigrants from the New Commonwealth would experience on their arrival in Britain. This was also a ready explanation for the poor school performance of some immigrant children.

Anwar (1976) and Watson (1977) have both used the title 'Between Two Cultures' in reporting their work on minority groups in Britain to illustrate their supposedly marginal position. Watson concludes that minority children are "caught between the cultural expectations of their parents (the first-generation migrants) and the social demands of the wider society."

Returning to the concept of multiculturalism in education, all reviews since the later 1970's give a negative evaluation of the previous two decades of British policy and practice. In an attempt to provide a theoretical rationale for education in multiracial Britain, Street-Porter (1978) describes the educational response to the presence of minority racial groups in terms of three overlapping phases, based in turn upon the concepts of assimilation, integration and pluralism. She criticises the first two approaches and supports pluralism as the only approach which avoids racism. There is no mention, however, in the writing as to how this could be implemented, since there are even minorities within minorities because of religious, cultural and linguistic differences.

Nandy (1971) seemed to have a better understanding of the situation, and noted four issues facing teachers in a multiracial society: (a) English for non-English speaking immigrant children; (b) helping these children to adjust to a new society; (c) understanding what it meant to be a minority child; (d) recognising the educational needs of a multiracial society.

Few educationalists would disagree that language is the primary vehicle for the maintenance of one's own culture. Ghuman (1975), in comparing the qualities of thinking displayed by different cultural and ethnic groups in a multiracial context, concluded that:

> "If we accept the important role of language in the development of higher cognitive processes, further attention has to be paid to the improvement of the children's oral and written language."

One of the recommendations of Ghuman's research is that English as a second language should be taught from the age of three years, when children are most receptive to new linguistic experiences.

The most recent concept introduced in the field of multiculturalism is "Mother-Tongue" teaching. The term is currently popular amongst educators and administrators. The Council of the EEC (European Economic Community), on 25 July, 1977, adopted the directive that ethnic minorities have a right to the maintenance of their home language and culture through the school system of a member-state. It is interesting to note that a similar point was made by the Bullock Report (1975) recommending a positive attitude towards bilingualism in Britain:

> "Certainly the school should adopt a positive attitude to its pupils and whenever possible should help maintain and deepen knowledge of their mother-tongues."

The argument for and against mother-tongue teaching within the educational sector is still continuing. However, for some ethnic groups another language may have greater social prestige, for example, learning a community language. In spite of the negative reactions from certain sections of the British population, support for mother-tongue teaching has come from many writers and minority organisations. It is claimed that learning of mother-tongue (particularly for Asian children) will keep the child in contact with his other culture which is an important basis for a healthy self-concept. The issue is in fact much more complex than it is conventionally viewed.

At this point, another perspective concerning multiculturalism is how far language and cultural differences between minority and dominant groups can be seen in terms of deficiency. Cultural relativists would argue that no one culture or language is superior or richer to another, though a multilingual and multicultural (even bicultural) individual might be better equipped and informed for life in the world today.

Multiculturalism from this perspective implies that the issue is not only how to educate the majority group about the culture, language and ways of life of minority groups, but also how to educate minorities to know about and adapt to the culture of the majority. In other words, all ethnic groups should be educated for life in a complex multiethnic society.

A common ambiguity inherent in the concept of cultural pluralism is the confusion and interchangeable use of the concepts of 'ethnicity' and 'culture'. In any discussion concerning education in a culturally pluralist society, this is exemplified by the frequent use of interchangeable terms such as 'multicultural', 'multiethnic' and 'multiracial' indicating degrees of cultural differentiation. In such usage an ethnic group is usually defined on the basis of cultural criteria. Unlike the term 'race' which has its foundations in physical distinctiveness, the term 'ethnic group' is associated with social structures and shared values, implying the existence of an 'ethnic identity'. Thus, an ethnic group is a group of people with common values, customs, behaviours, beliefs and social norms. Ethnicity and culture, though part of an individual's identity, must be analysed more broadly than mere attributions of group membership, e.g. Asians, West Indians. Multiculturalism in education must include both inter-cultural and intra-cultural dimensions.

MULTICULTURAL MODELS AND IMPLEMENTATION

Given the lack of clarity over the nature and process of multicultural education, it is not surprising that there is a poverty of literature developing models of multiculturalism. Some writers have advocated strategies and approaches for achieving a multicultural society through the educational system, though their perspectives often differ significantly. Thus, the whole area is characterised by a wide variety of competing and conflicting approaches. In view of this reality it can be argued that multicultural education, as currently conceived, is no more than a loose heading for a collection of interests inspired by an awareness of the social and political significance which is popularly attached to a complex set of phenomenon.

Some educators and theorists have focused on the curriculum as the primary vehicle for attaining multiculturalism. In fact, a changed curriculum has become synonymous with multicultural education, though there is little agreement with regard to the nature and process of such a curriculum. It is therefore unfortunate that the theoretical framework seems to have little relevance for practitioners of such education. Bullivant (1981) aptly observed that:

> "Definitions and conceptual models compete with one another....and in general, a good deal of the curriculum is in a mess."

He further comments on the basis of his comparative studies of cultural pluralism in six countries that:

> "With so many knowledge/power managers, ideologists and counter ideologists with vested interests in plural education, it is little wonder that every case study demonstrates considerable confusion over how to make provisions for its ethnic groups and other features of pluralism."

One explanation may be that ideologies about the nature of the educational problem have little relevance to practice, as pointed out by Eggleston (1983). Lynch (1981) summarizes the position succinctly:

> "There is no theory of multicultural education, in the sense of an articulated body of valid knowledge with scientific characteristics and predictive capacity."

Nevertheless, in Britain, few teachers would reject out of hand the need for multicultural education by some model or other, though few would agree on the content and methods of a multicultural curriculum. The curriculum reform movement in response to the changed social and demographic characteristics of post-war Britain was at first conceived as a way of eliminating bias in curriculum materials and of countering ethnocentric stereotypes (Williams, 1979). Studies also showed the relationships between poor academic performance of minority children and an inappropriate curriculum (Verma and Bagley, 1979; 1982).

However, by the 1970's, there was some agreement amongst a range of educationists of the need at least to change the curriculum to reflect the changed socio-cultural characteristics of society. The main emphasis has been on ethnic minority traditions, cultural heritage, religion and other aspects of country of origin. That is to say, the approach attempted to meet the needs and aspirations of ethnic minority groups, rather than of all children.

Given the context of the curriculum reform movement it is difficult to ascertain the direction in which the current vehicle of multiculturalism in education is being driven.

Jeffcoate (1979) has expressed concern about the relationships between multicultural curriculum and classroom practice. He asserts that the current debates by theorists about the multicultural curriculum seem to have little relevance to practitioners, and proposes a curriculum model which goes beyond purely local concerns. One of the criteria in selecting learning experiences, according to Jeffcoate, should be to look towards the global and international scene which can provide relevant information about other races and cultures. He warns, however, that such information should not be judged against British norms and values. Such a perspective is similar to the one proposed by Stent, Hazard and Rivlin (1973), that cultural pluralism should be seen in terms of an international scale which goes beyond national boundaries. According to these writers the concept "must include basic ideas of equal opportunity for all people, respect for human dignity, and the power to control the signficant environmental and psychological forces impinging on people....Cultural pluralism includes recognition, acceptance and support of all cultures."

An apparent difficulty in developing an international perspective for intercultural education is the actual identification of the values and aspirations of the groups involved (Smolicz, 1980). Moreover, the 'subjective culture' of ethnic minority groups is likely to vary considerably from one group to another (Landis and McGrew, 1979).

Returning to the British situation, there has been rhetorical commitment, at least, to the ideology that multicultural education - by changing the curriculum - will enhance equality of opportunity for pupils from minority communities and increase their life chances. Educationalists have offered different types of justifications for such a curriculum. Some stress equality of opportunity for all children while others emphasise that teaching about other cultures will increase respect for those groups and will reduce prejudice and discrimination. Critics of these approaches point out that without coming to grips with the key issues of social and institutional change, mere tinkering with the periphery of the curriculum will have little impact. Cox (1974) suggests that no real change will occur until the whole educational system changes. Bullivant (1981), one of the strongest critics of multicultural education in Australia, argues that multicultural education could, in effect, be a strategy of controlling minorities, rather than enhancing their self-determination.

Williams (1979) identified three perspectives for justifying a multicultural curriculum - technicist, moral and socio-political. The technicist approach is described as a compensatory concept, and stresses equality of opportunity for all children. Those who believe in this approach see curriculum change as a basis for enhancing children's self-concept. The moral perspective also aims at all pupils in a school and attempts to improve self-understanding and as a result fosters cooperation, and diminishes prejudice and discrimination. The socio-political perspective implies that "internal colonial cultural domination will cease". Those advocating this idea would like to see the permeation of the whole curriculum. In order to help minority pupils to overcome problems of identity, various curriculum programmes have been attempted in practice using this model. However, Williams' analysis of the three approaches to multicultural education clearly shows that there is no easy solution to the issue of multicultural curriculum.

Mullard (1981), a radical, black, academic, rejects the whole concept of multicultural education on the grounds that the idea is based on racist assumptions. He comments that "racism is not only a permanent, structural, ideological and political feature of British society, but is also a permanent feature of our educational system in general and of our schools in particular". Mullard admits that his model may be oversimplified. On one hand he advocates that teachers and administrators should develop "practices based on a deeper understanding of racism", while on the other hand he considers that educational policy might have shifted from assimilationism to cultural pluralism. There is no suggestion or guideline in his model as to how his strategies might be implemented by practitioners.

A report from a Schools Council Research Project, conducted by Little and Wiley (1981), recognised that, "Authorities reported considerable work on the appropriate nature of curriculum development in multiracial schools". It is apparent from this survey that very little action has been taken in this respect in British schools with few or no ethnic minority pupils. This report contains 66 recommendations for action by the D.E.S., L.E.A.s, schools, parents, community groups, professional associations and examination boards. The report has made it clear that immigration is no longer of great significance, although many New Commonwealth families, particularly South Asians, retain close links with their country of origin.

Stone (1981) regards multicultural education as a form of compensatory education based on models of the 1960's. She suggests that equality of attainment for black children can be best achieved by giving them traditional English education using formal methods of the highest quality.

A recent publication by the Schools Council (1982) proposes that, "In terms of educational practice, this means that all school lessons need to employ curriculum materials and examinations which include examples drawn from a wide range of cultures and which avoids presenting a solely Anglocentric view of the rest of the world, which may often be condescending". Such a perspective is common rhetoric in the literature of multiculturalism which is based on an uncritical acceptance of British society as 'multicultural'. In this document there is the naive, implicit suggestion that curriculum can change fundamental aspects of social structure and bring social stability.

One of the theoretical aspects which has given rise to muddled thinking is the whole notion of defining culture primarily in terms of ethnicity. Such a definition assumes that there are single Indian, Pakistani, West Indian or English cultures. Such a definition does not allow for two important factors. Firstly, a 'culture' (whatever it is) is not a static entity. It is dynamic and it changes over time in interaction with political and ecological factors. Secondly, a 'culture' is not objective; any attempt to describe it must allow for the way in which it is perceived by different individuals living in that particular culture. Personal experience may well dictate a different attitude to or perception of some particular aspect of a shared culture. Collectively, these differences may well be of considerable importance to individuals or sub-groups within those having what seems superficially to be a 'shared' culture.

Thus, one of the crucial problems relating to multiculturalism in education is the misuse of the concept of culture. Most of the writings consider it as an institutionalised group phenomenon, assuming a homogeneity within a given cultural group. Such homogeneity does not exist! Thus, the definitions of culture on which models or conceptualisations of multiculturalism are based are inadequate and out of date (Bullivant, 1981). Furthermore, multiculturalism in education should also have as its focus the individual in a culturally pluralistic society. Ethnicity and culture must be viewed more broadly than as mere labels of group membership. Pedagogically, multiculturalism should include both ethnic and pluralistic concepts in an educational environment that encourages an analysis of cultural similarities and compatibilities. It must also include both intercultural and intracultural dimensions.

Turning to the higher education sector there seems to be little information of changed paractices in a multicultural direction. Some work, however, has been done in teacher education, particularly at Colleges of Education. In 1979 Cherrington and Giles (1981) surveyed multicultural aspects of teacher training in Britain. The findings of this survey showed that even the limited development in teacher education was so fragmentary that it has had very little impact on teachers' attitudes and their professional skills. Only 14 colleges had a total of 26 different courses in multicultural education and of these, only four were compulsory. Data from Polytechnics showed that 18 different courses were offered by nine different Polytechnics, and of these only four were described as compulsory. Within the University sector only 4 courses labelled as multicultural education were offered by four universities.

The researchers also obtained information concerning course design and content of multicultural education programme. An interesting finding was that, "The terms multicultural and multiethnic education were used in a very limited way. Without exceptions, these terms were employed to develop approaches for equalising educational opportunities for children presumed to be disadvantaged because of cultural and/or linguistic differences; or for teaching about the culture of ethnic minority groups, either to members of those groups in order to improve self-image, or to other groups and the wider population in order to create cultural awareness and to improve race relations" (Cherrington and Giles, 1981).

The survey also indicated that all the courses and elements of courses described as multicultural or multiethnic in teacher training institutions were concerned with cultural content focussed almost exclusively on the background and heritage of New Commonwealth groups to the exclusion of all other cultural groups. The findings of this study raise questions about the aims, strategies and outcomes of education in a plural society, which has been the main concern of this paper.

Quite apart from the theoretical and practical issues which have already been discussed, there are a number of research issues relating to multiculturalism. The pre-eminent problem is the myriad of applications given to many of the key concepts in the area. Research work in the field is the product of many different disciplines, adopting different perspectives. Nonetheless, research in the area of multiculturalism is accelerating, and as a result methodologies and strategies are also being refined.

The problems and issues outlined in this paper will not go away overnight, but a more unified, rational conceptual model may emerge in this research. Even a model employing "plural methodologies" or several different disciplinary approaches unified in an overall conceptual model about what kinds of knowledge are required, would be acceptable. Within this unified perspective there would be room for the present range of disciplines to tackle the problems, but the concepts would be defined within an intercultural framework rather than reflecting traditional orientations, as they do presently. There is then, a need to generate a firm framework of <u>interculturalism</u> in education, looking not only on the nature of ethnicity, culture, and power in relation to a changing social structure in which children of all ethnic groups have new and changing needs, but also at an educational philosophy, method and practice which will be international, fostering interaction and understanding between ethnic groups both within and between different social systems across the world.

CONCLUSIONS

It is clear from the above discussion that there is a great diversity of cultural, ethnic and social patterns in British society and hence, there is simply no one model which is either desirable or acceptable to all ethnic groups. In other words, multiculturalism in education must allow for considerable variations within any ethnic group, since it is likely that some individuals are more 'ethnic' or culturally retentionist than others. Social, cultural, linguistic, religious, socio-economic, class and personal characteristics all contribute to the particular educational aspirations of ethnic groups, which can range from education for assimilation to education for cultural autonomy. This freedom of educational aspiration is qualified in a number of ways: any particular educational model adopted by the majority in any particular ethnic group should allow for any individual in that group to opt for a different model without sanction; the education should impart to the individual advanced cognitive skills for maximum cultural participation and upward social mobility; and the education should be fundamentally non-sexist and non-racist. There is, of course, a danger that some ethnic groups will opt for educational models which perpetuate ethnocentrism and the subordination of women.

The issue of curriculum design is also a difficult one. However, curriculum innovations must reflect a real sense of purpose; aims should be easily translated into practice. Materials, activities and experiences that are inter-disciplinary, multi-dimensional, comprehensive, meaningful and trustworthy should be part of the whole curriculum. It should be emphasised that many of the principles of multiculturalism currently being practised in schools at present are devices, implicit or explicit, which encourage ethnic separation without tackling fundamental issues of racism, sexism and economic exploitation.

The ultimate aim of multiculturalism in education must be to facilitate the social and scholastic development of young people who have a cognitively complex view of the world in which they live (Bagley and Verma, 1983). While they retain a sense of pride in their personal and cultural identity, children of all ethnic groups should also have developed a sufficient degree of empathic awareness of those around them without a continued "masking" of alienative and exploitive forces in social structure. In effect we are proposing the development of a particular attitude or approach for individuals or groups which would ideally permeate the whole educational system.

Intercultural education should meet the cultural, affective and cognitive needs of groups, and individuals from all ethnic groups in society. It is a continuous and dynamic process which must broaden and diversify as it adapts to changing circumstances. Such education seeks to promote parity of educational achievement between groups and between individuals, and mutual respect and tolerance between different groups. Multiculturalism is not about exotica but about all the people in a society and about the interdependent nature of the world. This orientation of intercultural education recognises that a wide range of alternative strategies exists within any society, and that it should be possible for young people to operate from a broad spectrum of interacting cultural bases.

REFERENCES

Anwar, M., Between Two Cultures, Commission for Racial Equality, London, 1976.

Bagley, C., 'Pluralism, Development and Social Conflict in Africa', Plural Societies, Summer, 1972, 13-32.

Bagley, C. and Verma, G.K. (eds.), Multicultural Childhood: Education, Ethnicity and Cognitive Styles, Gower Publishing, Aldershot, U.K., 1983.

Baptiste, H.P., Jr., Multicultural Education: A Synopsis, College of Education, University of Houston, Texas, 1976.

Bolton, E., 'Education in a Multiracial Society', Trends in Education, vol 4, 1979, 3-7.

Buchignani, N., 'Culture or Identity? Addressing Ethnicity in Canadian Education', McGill Journal of Education, vol 15, 1980, 79-93.

Bullivant, B., The Pluralist Dilemma in Education, George Allen and Unwin, Sydney, 1981.

Bullock, A., *A Language for Life*, H.M.S.O., London, 1975.

Burnet, J., 'The Policy of Multiculturalism in a Bilingual Framework: An Interpretation' in A. Wolfgang (ed.), *Education of Immigrant Students: Issues and Answers*, Ontario Institute for Studies in Education, Symposium Series 5, Toronto, 1975.

Cherrington, D. and Giles, R., 'Present Provision in Initial Training' in M. Craft (ed.), *Teaching in a Multicultural Society*, Falmer Press, England, 1981.

Chipman, L., 'The Menace of Multiculturalism', *Quadrant*, vol 24, no 10, 1980, 3-6.

Dolce, C., 'Multicultural Education - Some Issues', *Journal of Teacher Education*, 24, 1973, 282-3.

Ghuman, P.A., *The Cultural Context of Thinking*, N.F.E.R., Windsor, 1975.

Gibson, M.A., 'Approaches to Multicultural Education in the United States: Some Concepts and Assumptions', *Anthropology and Education Quarterly*, 7, 1976, 7-18.

Glazer, N., 'Public Education and American Pluralism', in J.S. Coleman et al (eds.), *Parents, Teachers and Children: Prospects for Choice in American Education*, Institute for Contemporary Studies, San Francisco, 1977.

Jeffcoate, R., *Positive Image Towards a Multicultural Curriculum*, Chameleon Books, London, 1979.

Jenkins, R., Speech made on 23 May, 1966, to a meeting of the National Committee for Commonwealth Immigrants, quoted in *Essays and Speeches* by Roy Jenkins, Collins, 1967, 267.

Landis, D. and McGrew, P., 'Subjective Culture and the Perceptions of Black and White Urban School Teachers' in Verma, G. and Bagley, C. (eds.), *Race, Education and Identity*, MacMillan, London, 1979.

Little, A. and Willey, R., *Multi-Ethnic Education: The Way Forward*, Schools Council, 1981.

Lynch, J. (ed.), *Teaching in the Multi-Cultural School*, Ward Lock Educational, London, 1981.

Meredith, G., 'The Changing Response of a Secondary Modern School in Handsworth, 1958-70', in McNeal, J. and Rogers, M. (eds.), *The Multi-Racial School*, Penguin, Harmondsworth, 1971.

Mullard, C., 'The Social Context and Meaning of Multicultural Education' in Davies, B. (ed.), *Educational Analysis*, Carfax Publishing, Oxford, 1981.

Nandy, D., 'Foreword' in McNeal, J. and Rogers, M. (eds.), *The Multi-Racial School*, Penguin, Harmondsworth, 1971.

Schools Council, *Multicultural Education*, Schools Council, London, March, 1982.

Smolicz, J., *Culture and Education in a Plural Society*, Curriculum Development Centre, Adelaide, 1980.

Stent, M.D., Hazard, W.R. and Rivlin, H.N., *Cultural Pluralism in Education: A Mandate for Change*, Appleton-Century Crofts, New York, 1973.

Stone, M., *The Education of the Black Child in Britain*, Fontana, Glasgow, 1981.

Street-Porter, R., 'From Immigrant to Briton - The Change in Educational Attitudes' in Unit 12-13 *Race and the Urban Child* (E 361, Education and the Urban Environment), Open University Milton Keynes, 1978.

Taylor, J.H., *The Half-Way Generation*, National Foundation of Educational Research, Windsor, 1976.

Verma, G.K. and Bagley, C. (eds.), *Race and Education Across Cultures*, Heinemann, London, 1975.

Verma, G.K. and Bagley, C. (eds.), *Race, Education and Identity*, MacMillan, London, 1979.

Verma, G.K. and Bagley, C. (eds.), *Self-Concept, Achievement and Multicultural Education*, MacMillan, London, 1982.

Watson, J.L. (ed.), *Between Two Cultures*, Basil Blackwell, Oxford, 1977.

Willey, R., *Teaching in Multicultural Britain*, Longman for the Schools Council, York, 1982.

Williams, J., 'Perspectives on the Multicultural Curriculum', *Social Science Teacher*, vol 8, no 4, April, 1979.

Chapter Five

EDUCATION, LANGUAGE AND ETHNIC GROUPS IN BRITAIN

Olav A. Rees

In setting out to reconsider the notion of a multicultural curriculum for children entering school in Britain during the next decade, there seem to us to be at least two points which might be regarded as central to the enterprise. In applying these, in conjunction with ideas derived from research on educational provision for bilingual (1) children in the Mother Tongue and English Teaching Project, it seemed to us likely that different kinds of multicultural curricula were possibly more appropriate than those currently being used in British schools. That this was so reflected the tendency to neglect or to misconceive linguistic elements in the expression of cultural background among children from ethnic minorities and to plan curricula from a primarily assimilationist (2) standpoint.

The two points we have in mind are these. First, the expectation that each child will have educational provision which is appropriate to his or her age, aptitude and ability; a point incorporated, of course, in the British 1944 Education Act. The second point is that cultural identity, values and aspirations of a child's own ethnic group should be fairly represented in the form and content of the curriculum available at a local school. Clearly there will always be a variety of ways, both as to form and content, which such points might be implemented for any given child. But it is worth considering how far, or in what sense, existing patterns of provision, particularly for younger children, are consonant with them.

Some recent developments in curriculum research (Bedfordshire Education Service, 1980; Rees, Fitzpatrick, Sharma and Nasser, 1981) and in the formulation of a policy for the education of bilingual children have a bearing on the application of these points and we shall outline these first.

If there is one factor which seems more than any other to have driven recent research and policy development on education of children from linguistic minorities it seems to be the draft directive adopted by the Council of the European Economic Community (E.E.C.) on 25th July 1977. This provides for children of migrant workers to have, as of right, provision for the maintenance of their home language and culture through the school system of a member state. The directive assumes, of course, a particular view of the relationship of 'migrant workers' (and their children) to the dominant cultural/linguistic patterns of the host community. This relationship is necessarily a transient one in the sense that migrant workers are temporary residents and that provision for their children is designed to facilitate their return to the country of origin. This in turn tends to lead to a particular kind of curricular provision according to the methods and styles of the country of origin; this has been reflected in the pattern of European curriculum research related to these provision of the draft directive.

As a general influence the draft directive in Britain has been substantially resposible for three major research projects, funded either by the E.E.C. directly or by the Department of Education and Science. Further developments through the School Council are also beginning to ensure the development of curriculum materials for use with children from linguistic minorities. The projects already well in progress or completed are the Bedford Project (Italian and Punjabi speakers), the Mother Tongue and English Teaching Project (Punjabi speakers) and the Linguistic Minorities Project.

The force of the directive in turning attention to educational provision for bilingual children from linguistic minorities does not mean, however, that its terms fit the real nature of the situation in Britain. Rather few linguistic minority groups are temporary residents; the vast majority are permanent settlers and need therefore to be considered from a very different standpoint. They and their children are consumers, like any other residents, of the national educational system.

The adoption of such a draft directive has to be seen against a general background of development in practical and research interest in bilingual education for linguistic minorities in countries which had traditionally adopted monolingual patterns of education (for example the U.S.A., Australia and Canada). In fact, as long ago as 1953 a UNESCO conference published a monograph on "The Use of Vernacular Languages in Education" in which it was considered axiomatic that the best medium for teaching was the pupil's mother tongue. Similar points have been made more recently by other writers (Savile and Troike, 1971).

In the U.S.A., where the position of minority ethnic and linguistic groups can be considered in some ways like that of Asian groups in Britain, the growth of interest and of practical action on bilingual education has been marked. Under political and educational pressure there has been some change from a monolingual and assimilationist approach towards a pluralist (3) policy involving bilingual education programmes where these are appropriate. Much attention has been devoted there to the meaning of the principle of 'equality of provision' in a multilingual and multicultural society and the problem has been the subject of legal debate. As a result of social and political pressures there have been two Bilingual Education Acts and a variety of related legal decisions. Many school boards have evolved programmes of bilingual education and policy guidelines which define what is called 'Bilingual-bicultural' education. Similar changes have also taken place in, for example, Sweden (Lasonen and Toukomaa, 1978), Australia (Claydon et al., 1977) and Canada (Lambert and Tucker, 1972). Recent economic changes, however, have tended to make such programmes vulnerable.

All this represented a developing awareness of the linguistic characteristics of new migrants and settlers in many Western European and North American countries. One of the earliest indications of British interest in bilingualism and its educational significance in English schools was the conference in 1975 on "Bilingualism in British Education" convened by the Centre for Information of Language Teaching and Research in collaboration with Leicestershire Education Authority and other Midlands Education Authorities (CILT, 1976). Given the lack of experience with bilingualism in the English context discussion focussed on other (indigenous) models for bilingual education. In retrospect, these seem not to be wholly appropriate bases for considering the bilingual education of, for example, Asian children in English inner city areas.

The Department of Education and Science's interest in formulating a policy on the education of children whose home language is not English is related to the provision of the draft directive. This means in practice a policy which can apply to children from a wide variety of ethnic backgrounds and of linguistic skill. The Mother Tongue and English Teaching Project was part of their research response to this problem.

The Mother Tongue and English Teaching Project originated from the interest of the Bradford Education Authority in providing for the educational needs of young children of Asian ethnic origin. Many of these speak an Asian language at home and come to school with little or no knowledge of English. Existing practice in the district follows one of two major patterns. In the city area many non-English speakers initially attend Infant Centres where they can acquire sufficient command of English and preliminary educational skills to be able to cope, with assistance, in an ordinary First School. They tend to be transferred to a First School, as soon as they acquire this basis, after between one and six terms from entry to the Infant Centre. In the rest of the district children go immediately to First Schools where provision is made for special help in second language learning.

As a result of discussion with the research directors and with other interested parties, the project was planned so as to mount a one year bilingual education programme, (4) to describe the context in which it took place and to provide information about its progress and outcome. The programme was intended for rising five year olds whose parents were of Asian origin and who attended school in the Bradford area. The children involved were speakers of Punjabi (Mirapuri variants) who entered school in September 1978. At that point they were judged to have little or no knowledge of English. Some seventy children were involved in both the bilingual education programme and in the control groups.

One Infant Centre in the Bradford City area and one First School outside the city were identified as having a sufficiently large intake of Punjabi speakers for the research design. They also met other criteria (Rees, Fitzpatrick et al., 1981). Through Punjabi-speaking liaison teachers, evidence of the general acceptability of a bilingual education programme was obtained; virtually all parents of entrants to the schools were willing to allow their children to participate. This may, however, reflect their sense of trust in the schools rather than a clear conception by parents of the implications of such a programme. Subsequent interviews with parents have revealed support for a bilingual education programme on cultural and instrumental grounds, but there has been little evidence, as one might expect, of an understanding of the educational or developmental justification for such a progamme.

The intention behind the project was to provide information on teaching through both mother tongue and English in a bilingual progamme. Substantial use of a child's mother tongue (i.e. home language) in the classroom, as well as English, was planned. The curriculum was to consist of a programme of general education in the first year of school which could facilitate the child's adaptation to school, promote linguistic and cognitive development and facilitate the acquisition of English. The children entered the two schools in September 1978 and the bilingual programme ran until July 1979. During the course of the year a comparison was made between children who worked according to existing practices (i.e. almost wholly through the medium of English) and children taking part in the bilingual education programme. The attainment of the children, their cognitive and linguistic development and their use of Punjabi and English in the classroom were monitored using a variety of relatively unobtrusive techniques.

At the same time the research team collected information about the context in which the programmes took place. This included a study of teachers' attitudes to the use of Asian mother tongues in school, an intensive investigation of the background of the children, and research into parents' attitudes to bilingual education, to education and schooling generally, and into their aspirations for their children. The results from this field study have been linked with the classroom data in the interpretation of the study.

There are a considerable number of problematic issues which the experience of this and other research projects suggest need to be part of any reappraisal of the multicultural curriculum as it applies to children from linguistic minorities. In considering briefly some six of these we wish to comment on the force of the points we started out with, and any implication of research for particular views of each issue. Briefly these issues concern the meaning of the term multicultural, the heterogeneity of ethnic groups, the assumption of assimilation underlying existing curricula, the range of effective curricula for young Asian children, the acceptability to teachers of alternative curriculum models, and the aspirations and expectations of parents.

One immediate question, then, is to say what we might mean by 'multicultural' when applied to a particular curriculum. The cultural distinctions which have up to now been the most generally recognized in English schools are those which focus on matters of dress, of food, of material artefacts of the country of origin and so forth. There is little indication of the perceived salience of language differences, except in a trivial sense. And it seems that the cultural background referred to with ethnic groups is of the country of origin rather than that actually experienced by them in their communities. The range of cultural elements used, too, are all ones which may be experienced by children from every ethnic or social background with little or no difficulty. But cultural identity and cultural values are necessarily expressed through a particular language and it is arguable that linguistic differences are often the most culturally salient, certainly as between different ethnic groups. But taking account of these brings forward the difficulty that children cannot readily share the same curriculum when home language becomes an integral part of the process.

A second concern is that there is a prevailing assumption, at least in the form of the curriculum for bilingual children in English Primary schools. This is that children of, for example, Asian origin are a broad but rather homogeneous group. The effect of this is to minimize perceptions of cultural and religious variation and effectively to ignore the potential educational relevance of different languages dialects and patterns of bilingualism.

It is also becoming clearer as time passes that the expectation that a monolingual curriculum for second language learners would prove a successful instrument of assimilation (at least of linguistic assimilation) has proved to be misplaced. Our own conceptions, as indicated earlier, are that such a policy in any case is not consonant with a 'multicultural curriculum'. Experience in many bilingual societies suggests that ethnic identity and religious affiliation, for example, are bound up with language use and will tend to ensure the survival for long periods of time of the bilingual language of ethnic minorities.

If we turn to the question of the possible range of effective curricula suitable for young children from linguistic minority groups there seems to be one factor which might inhibit reappraisal. This is the assumption, even a widely held belief, that effective control of English as a means of access to educational opportunity depends on spending the whole or even the bulk of each school day working through the medium of English. It is not necessary to dispute the usefulness of English within the wider society while questioning this convention. The argument that international experience and research does not support this assumption about the range of effective curricula (in terms of language strategies) (Spolsky, 1977; Mitchell, 1979) does not carry much weight. Research in the Mother Tongue and English Teaching project in Bradford does however suggest strongly that this assumption is unwarranted (Rees, 1983). Children in the bilingual education groups showed equal or greater progress in a range of intellectual tasks than did children in the control groups.

In the course of the Mother Tongue (MOTET) project we asked teachers working in the schools where Asian languages might be usefully employed as part of school activity. In general the majority of such uses represented an instrumental orientation and did not indicate that they thought the home language of the children, even where Asian teachers were available, was a suitable educational medium. Whether this is a reflection of insufficient opportunity to become aware of possibilities from other educational systems, or of a fundamental unwillingness to accept languages other than English in schools, is a difficult point to clarify. Whichever it is any reappraisal of curricula for children from ethnic minorities will presuppose a substantial attempt to inform and widen views on questions of this kind.

Finally it is often said that Asian parents have no wish to see their home language introduced into the school and that they want the child to use only English there. While this may have been true at one time (Khan, 1980) recent research in this country (Bedfordshire Education Authority 1980; Rees, Fitzpatrick et al. 1981) suggests that this is no longer true in a simple fashion. There is clearly room for parent and teacher understanding of the issues involved in the use of more than one language within the school.

Thus the representation in a real sense of cultural characteristics of an ethnic group in the curriculum and the provision of education appropriate to a child's aptitude and ability implies a serious reappraisal of the place of children's home language in the curriculum and as a vehicle for the curriculum where the language is not English. Given the variety of languages in many areas of urban Britain this may prove difficult except for a limited number of concentrated linguistic minorities within the state school system (5).

NOTES

1. <u>Bilingual</u> - i.e. those who have at least minimal skill in using two languages.
2. <u>Assimilationist</u> - refers to educational programmes where members of a minority language group are intended to become indistinguishably full members of the majority culture and where there is no institutional support for their culture.
3. <u>Pluralist</u> - in educational terms refers to a system where a minority language community can count on institutional support or tolerance for the maintenance of their culture (including language).
4. A 'bilingual education programme' is taken to be a complete programme of work during the school week through the medium of two languages and which is planned as a whole. Work in both languages is not simply directed at learning the language but a general educational function. Note here that a 'bilingual' child is taken to mean one who has any discernible level of commuicative performance available in two languages.
5. This is a revised version of a paper presented to the Third Annual Intercultural Conference, University of Bradford, July, 1981.

REFERENCES

Bedfordshire Education Service, <u>E.C. Mother Tongue and Culture Pilot Project 1976-80</u>; Report for the Colloquium at Cranfield Institute of Technology, 1980.
C.I.L.T., <u>Bilingualism and British Education: The Dimensions of Diversity</u>, 1976.

Claydon, L., Knight, T. and Rado, M., *Curriculum and Culture*, Allen and Unwin, Australia, 1977.

Khan, V.S., The 'mother tongue' of linguistic minorities in multicultural England, *Journal of Multi-lingual and Multicultural Development*, I, 1980.

Lasonen, K. and Toukomaa, P., *Linguistic Development and School Achievement Among Finnish Immigrant Children in Mother-Tongue Medium Classes in Sweden*, Research Report No. 70, University of Jyvalkyla, Dept. of Education, 1978.

Lambert, W.E., and Tucker, G.R., *Bilingual Education of Children*, Newbury House, Rowley, Mass, 1972.

Mitchell, R., *Bilingual Education of Minority Language Groups in the English Speaking World: Some Research Evidence*, CORE 3 (2), Fiche 13D2, 1979.

Rees, O.A., 'Ethnic group, bilingualism and attainment' in C. Bagley and G. Verma (eds.), *Multicultural Childhood: Education, Ethnicity and Cognitive Styles*, Gower Press, Aldershot, U.K., 1983.

Rees, O.A., Fitzpatrick, F., Sharma, S. and Nasser, S., *Digest of Volumes I and II of a Report to the Department of Education and Science on the Mother Tongue Project*. University of Bradford School of Research in Education, Bradford, 1981.

Savile, M.R., and Troike, R.C., *A Handbook of Bilingual Education*, TESOL, Washington D.C., 1971.

Chapter Six

LANGUAGE, DISADVANTAGE AND MINORITY EDUCATION

John Edwards

Minority education is a topic of considerable current interest. It is a reflection of larger issues of majority-minority contact involving such matters as government policy, the assimilation-cultural pluralism debate, desires of both minority and segments of the population, social disadvantage and reactions to varieties of group distinctiveness. All of these important features, which impinge upon any informed discussion of minority education, have been quite extensively treated in the literature, but with varying degrees of objectivity. Particular interest groups put forward particular claims; research findings are tossed about with some abandon; historical analyses and precedents are invoked when they seem likely to buttress a given case. This aura of polemics and the selective use of evidence is not, in itself, surprising in an area lying at the junction of social science and social policy. Nor can we hope to eliminate subjectivity entirely from our discussions -- the notion of value-free social science is a myth. However, I would argue that many discussions of minority education have offered confused minglings of relative objectivity and subjectivity, and that writers are often less than honest with readers inasmuch as they do not make their own value preferences clear (Edwards, 1976 to 1981). In this chapter I wish to deal briefly with a number of the important aspects of minority education, attempting to establish the necessary strands in realistic arguments on the topic.

THE MINORITY GROUP

To begin with, it is as well to define what is signified by the 'minority' in minority education.

Generally, of course, minorities can arise in many ways and may be delineated by many different types of distinctiveness (or, perhaps, by none at all). In the sense used here, however, <u>minority</u> reflects ethnic group membership. Among the possible categories (see Royal Institute of International Affairs, 1963), the most relevant are indigenous minorities and, especially, immigrant populations (which can include the rather permanent 'migrant' workers groups in Europe; see Widgren, 1975). Within these groupings, the specifics of majority-minority relations obviously vary immensely; there is, however, the general feature of <u>separateness</u>, which in turn presumes some degree of group distinctiveness (colour, religion, language, etc.). This separateness is not, of course, a static entity. Groups, or group members, may become assimilated; also, some types of separateness may eventuate in an elite, which then may vigorously resist change.

Minority status need not always be a function of numbers; groups holding subordinate economic, social or political positions within a larger society may also reasonably be seen as minorities (see e.g. Rose, 1972). In fact, regardless of numbers involved, minority-majority issues are mainly ones of relative status and power. This in turn indicates how important is the <u>comparison</u> process. And, it is the consequences of intrasocietal comparison, especially those of a psychological and linguistic nature, which are of direct relevance here. This is a useful point to clarify -- after all, an ethnic minority in one context may be a majority group elsewhere. It is when groups stand in such a relation to one another that at points of contact, that one may be judged inferior in some sense to the other, and minority issues cause concern. This implies that other groups (e.g. social class groups) which have received much attention under the heading of <u>disadvantage</u> can also be included in this discussion.

DISADVANTAGE

Disadvantage, in the educational and psychological literature, signifies a relatively enduring condition descriptive of certain groups -- including ethnic minorities and working classes -- whose "knowledge, skills and attitudes...impede learning" (Passow, 1970, p. 16). Three major explanations

have been offered for the aetiology of disadvantage.
(1)

The first view is that some groups are inherently less able than others. Historically, this has wide popularity, and it is certainly extant today. Within the academic community it has had its most recent support in Jensen's work (see e.g., Jensen, 1969). As his thesis has achieved great publicity, I shall be very brief here. Jensen's position is that certain groups suffer a genetic inferiority in intelligence, that this can be demonstrated through appropriate ('culture-free') tests, and that it necessitates different educational treatments. Each of these points is debatable and, in fact, there is no good evidence for any of them (especially for the first which, if successfully challenged, eliminates the others). Jensen has maintained his position in the face of strong criticism (see Jensen, 1980; see also Van den Berghe, 1981), but it is not a likely explanation for educational and social disadvantage. It is interesting to note, in fact, that even if Jensen's claims about racial and class variations in intelligence were granted, there would appear to be no practical significance to them anyway, in terms of the proportion of any achievement differences explained.

The second major view of disadvantage holds that children from certain groups are deficient because of inferior physical, social and psychological environments. These deficiencies, it is argued, can be eliminated or reduced through programmes of 'resocialisation' or compensatory education (see e.g., Bereiter and Engelmann, 1966; Deutsch, 1967; Hess and Shipman, 1968a, 1968b) (2). However, this environmental position also has its difficulties. For example, whenever characteristics of the deprived environment are noted, it is assumed that these are related to such things as lack of school success, general inability to learn, etc. It is, in fact, almost always impossible to verify such links; many children from poor environments do well at school, and Wiseman (1968) has remarked that there are many 'good' homes in poor neighbourhoods and vice versa. Characteristics considered to be deficits, or to lead to deficits, are usually so judged from a middle-class standpoint which assumes the correctness of its own standards and behaviour.

If this last point is accepted, then group differences in achievement are essentially cultural in nature, not substantive or innate. This does not make them any the less important, because the comparative process which identifies them is a fact of life for social subgroups, but it is a vital philosophical distinction. This is the standpoint of the third major perception of disadvantage -- that so-called disadvantage arises from difference and not from deficit. It argues that just as it may be unfair to compare, say, the French and Fijian child because their environments are so dissimilar, so it is unfair to compare the middle-class child with his working-class counterpart, or the immigrant with the native. This is a viewpoint which surely commends itself to us here; for, if we acknowledge that caution is always needed when dealing with cross-cultural matters, then it is also likely that cross-<u>sub</u>cultural circumspection is warranted. Disadvantage arises when groups which share certain elements of life, by virtue of proximity if nothing else, and yet which also differ in some respects, come into contact with each other. If such contact did not exist then disadvantage as considered here would not exist; it is when contact leads to comparison that disadvantage takes form. And this, of course, happens constantly. Minority group members come into contact with majority society, are forced to do so and, indeed, often wish to do so. Consider the following observation of Wax and Wax of American Indian disadvantage (for 'Indian child', we might also read 'black child', 'immigrant child', 'lower-class child', etc.).:

> If the Indian child appears as "culturally deprived", it is not because he is lacking in experience or culture, but because the educational agencies are unwilling to recognize the alienness of his culture and the realities of his social world. It is not that the child is deprived culture, it is that the culture which is associated with his parents is derogated because they are impoverished and powerless. (1971, p. 138)

LANGUAGE

So far I have pointed out that an understanding of minority-majority relations and of disadvantage requires, at core, an awareness of the power of social comparison and it implications. This is of specific importance when one considers linguistic issues - often the most visible and most discussed features of group distinctiveness. The debate between the environmental and 'difference' positions on disadvantage generally has been seen, in the linguistic context, in terms of the substandard-nonstandard issue.

The realisation that <u>languages</u> differ from one another, and cannot be seen in terms of 'better' or 'worse', has been current for some time; thus, for example, Gleitman and Gleitman (1970) and Lenneberg (1967) reject completely the notion of 'primitive' languages. It is only relatively recently, however, that this sort of acknowledgement has been extended to dialectal variation <u>within</u> language.

Given the generalities discussed previously it is completely unsurprising that certain ethnic minority and social class dialects have been seen as inferior, deficient and essentially substandard approximations to standard dialects. This view has more and more given way to one which holds that dialects are different but not deficient varieties (e.g., Trudgill, 1975); therefore, to the extent to which group speech patterns can be seen as valid dialects they may be accorded <u>non</u>standard status -- nonstandard being a non-pejorative term which simply acknowledges the differential social status of dialects which are, linguistically, neither better nor worse than one another. The most well-known example -- of a variety long considered substandard, but now more correctly seen as nonstandard -- is the Black English Vernacular (BEV) of the United States. The work of Labov (e.g., 1973, 1976) and others has demonstrated that BEV has its own rulegoverned structure which, although differing in certain ways from the standard, is clearly of dialectal status.

Dialectal variation is the linguistic issue of most relevance to disadvantaged speakers of the national language. While it might be argued that this is not quite the main concern for minorities who speak a different language altogether, it has a wider relevance than may first be supposed. First, many ethnic minorities <u>are</u> speakers of the national language (for example, the West Indians in Britain). V. Edwards (1979) has pointed out that difficulties experienced by West Indians in Britain are similar to those encountered by black speakers in the United States. She also notes that apart from social prejudice, there may exist real dialect interference which compounds the problems. Second, perhaps more important in the sense that it affects <u>all</u> minority members at some point in their relationship with the larger society, is the fact that, when the national language has been learned to a degree permitting participation in regular classrooms, it is in many instances a non-standard variant of that language which is used (see e.g., Giles and Bourhis, 1975). Many black children born in Britain to non-English-speaking parents may, for example, sound just like white natives having broad Cockney or Liverpool accents/ dialects. Such black speakers may suffer more because of nonstandard use than do white non-standard speakers, that is, they may be seen as approaching too closely a group which does not welcome them. Of course, even if immigrants learned standard English this would not necessarily endear them to the native population, especially if there remained other, non-erasable marks of distinction.

THE EDUCATION OF MINORITIES

Speakers of Nonstandard Varieties
The thrust of what has been discussed is that there are no linguistic grounds upon which to reject language variation. Consequently, the problem is one of social prejudice and convention. While this is not necessarily any easier to deal with than substantive linguistic deficiency, it is important to understand the difference, since it implies altered 'treatment'.

I put 'treatment' in quotation marks since, in fact, no remediation or intervention is called for, at least not with regard to oral language (written language may require direct instruction, but this applies to all children regardless of the dialect they use). What is required is sensitivity of teachers and schools to language variation, so that non-standard varieties will not become stigmatised and children may be allowed to express themselves without constant 'correction' towards the norms of another dialect. This does not mean that non-standard speakers will not find expansion of their linguistic repertoire useful, but it does imply that active instruction may well be counter-productive. Children are surrounded by standard dialect speakers, of whom one of the most important is often the teacher. There is ample evidence that non-standard speakers are usually well able to comprehend standard dialect by an early age. The use of this variety must ultimately depend upon the speaker's own wishes and needs. The role of the school here is passive, but vital -- to foster a tolerant atmosphere in which such usage is not stifled through assaults to psychological identity made in the name of 'correct' language, 'proper' language, and the like. Given some freedom in the matter, speakers will become bidialectal to the degree required.

Speakers of Foreign Languages (3)

There has been a great deal of recent interest in bilingual, multilingual and culturally pluralistic education as a response to the needs of those not speaking the national language. Until fairly recently, for example, Englishspeaking countries including the United States, Britain and Canada did not provide public education in languages other than English; those desiring 'foreignlanguage' (4) schooling had to provide their own. Such private education has had a long and interesting history, and is still existent -- although general patterns are ones of decline with increasing assimilation over generations.

The current interest, on the other hand, has to do with provision of non-English education in publicly-supported schools, and is a complex and controversial matter. If such education were advocated only as a transitional measure it would not be so hotly debated and could even be seen as hastening and smoothing the assimilation process. The transitional variety of bilingual education in the United States is, indeed, the most prevalent today.

However, the transitional variety of bilingual education does contribute to cultural pluralism -- the condition favoured by most writers on the topic. Ethnic diversity, permanent pluralism, the 'new ethnicity' -- these are the goals of those supporting a <u>maintenance</u> form of bilingual education (which is to become an integral part of education generally). The endorsement of cultural pluralism, and the rejection of assimilation are, it may be argued, reflections of an enlightened, liberal attempt to rectify past injustices, to reinstate rendered ethnics and to somehow promote a more egalitarian society. There are some difficulties, however.

1. Cultural pluralism and assimilation are terms of some ambiguity, carrying strong emotional connotations. There is reason to suppose that they are <u>not</u> polar opposites but rather exist in some state of symbiosis. For example, a society like the United States may be originally pluralistic (by necessity), then may achieve some degree of homogen-

eity, and then -- in groups now relatively secure -- may show some desire for greater uniqueness. There is a sense here of cultural pluralism appealing most to the most secure and, in fact, most assimilated of 'ethnics' (see Higham, 1975; Sowell, 1978).

2. Cultural pluralism may be seen as an elitist phenomenon which does not reflect very well the views of the masses. Many 'ethnics' appear generally assimilationist in outlook, unlike those who presume to speak for them (Drake, 1979).

3. Cultural pluralism appears to be a curiously static perception of society, with a naive reliance upon ethnic solidarity, commitment and boundaries. This is belied by history generally and, more specifically, by the social movements creating ethnic mixtures in the first place.

4. Cultural pluralism may keep people within boundaries, which does not seem particularly praiseworthy (see Drake, 1979). In this connection, Fishman (1980) has made a curious statement:

> Stable bilingualism and biculturalism cannot be maintained on the basis of open and unlimited interaction between minorities and majorities. Open economic access and unrestricted intergroup interaction may be fine...but they are destructive of minority ethnolinguistic continuity. (p. 171).

This implies that a very high price must be paid for stable pluralism -- a price that is more than most, perhaps, would be willing to pay. Here, Van den Berghe (1967) and others have noted that cultural pluralism is not always conducive to democracy.

These points are mentioned only to emphasise that conceptions like assimilation (bad) and cultural pluralism (good) are naive. It is also easy to see that this naivete may have quite profound implications for educational policy.

CONCLUSION

The foregoing points, in my view, must be considered dispassionately in discussions of minority education. People are entitled to their opinions but they must be wary when it comes to translating these into policy. The obvious statement to make next is to call for attention to the needs and wishes of minorities themselves. Yet, such is the nature of the topic that we have hardly any specific information from minorities themselves. Thus, Fishman (1977) notes that "the only aspect of bilingual education that has been even less researched than student attitudes and interests is that of parental attitudes and interests" (p. 45). Despite much propaganda, we do not have unequivocal evidence of widespread support for active policies of maintenance bilingual education and cultural pluralism. In fact, such information as may be gleaned from historical perspective leads to the conclusion that active support may not be broad; trends of immigration and assimilation (people voting with their feet, or their actions at any rate) seem to indicate much more assimilationist sentiment than one would gather from the academic literature.

We need more information from 'ethnics' themselves. What are their views of the essential aspects, as well as the dispensable ones, of group identity? What do they want from education, and who should support it? My own prediction is that if we could assess such feelings at a grassroots level, we would not find support for many of the things asked for in the name of ethnic groups. This is, admittedly, speculation on my part -- but at least it is speculation which offers some alternative to much of the literature which is itself speculation suffused with personal values, however 'objectively' it is presented.

Let me end by giving three non-objective ethnic statements, followed by one academic appraisal of minority education in the United States which depart from the usual line.

1. (From Larry Zolf, a well-known Canadian journalist): "I want to be Jewish on my own time and on my own money...I don't need a multiculturalism grant to be Jewish either" (1980, p. 6).

2. (From S. Hayakawa, the Japanese-American semanticist): "We've got too many ethnic groups who are pushing for their own...I believe in bilingualism but I don't want to see it subsidized by the taxpayer...insofar as politicians make a point of their ethnicity and push their own ethnic group at the expense of all other interests, it's a divisive force" (1980, p. 12).

3. (From Richard Rodriquez, Mexican-American writer): "The bilingualists oversimplify when they scorn the value and necessity of assimilation... they equate mere separateness with individuality... It is not enough to say that such schemes (i.e., bilingual education) are foolish and certainly

doomed..." (1980 a, p. 34 & p. 39; see also Rodriquez, 1980 b).
   4. (From Diane Ravitch, writer on minority education): "To assume today that immigrants who accepted and furthered Americanization had been indoctrinated is to credit the immigrants with little intelligence or self-interest. It is more likely that they took from Americanization programs what they wanted and ignored what they did not want" (1976, p. 218).

NOTES

   1. <u>Disadvantage</u> is often associated only with the environmental position; this has resulted in some confusion over whether it is a useful term (Edwards, 1981c).
   2. A useful recent criticism of intervention programmes may be found in Raven (1980).
   3. See further details in Edwards (1976, 1977, 1980b, 1981a).
   4. The only exception has been the teaching of Welsh in a small section of the British Isles.

REFERENCES

Bereiter, C. and Engelmann, S., <u>Teaching Disadvantaged Children in the Preschool</u>, Prentice-Hall, New Jersey, 1966.
Deutsch, M., <u>The Disadvantaged Child</u>, Basic, New York, 1967.
Drake, G., 'Ethnicity, Values and Language Policy in the United States', in Giles, H. and Saint-Jacques, B. (eds) <u>Language and Ethnic Relations</u>, Pergamon, London, 1979.
Edwards, J., 'Current Issues in Bilingual Education', <u>Ethnicity</u>, vol. 3, 1976, pp. 70-81.
Edwards, J., 'Ethnic Identity and Bilingual Education', in Giles, H. (ed.), <u>Language, Ethnicity and Intergroup Relations</u>, Academic, London, 1977.
Edwards, J., <u>Language and Disadvantage</u>, Edward Arnold, London and Elsevier North-Holland, New York, 1979.
Edwards, J., 'Bilingual Education: Facts and Values', <u>Canadian Modern Language Review</u>, vol. 37, 1980 (a), pp. 123-127.

Edwards, J., 'Critics and Criticisms of Bilingual Education', Modern language Journal, vol. 64, 1980 (b), pp. 409-415.

Edwards, J., 'The Context of Bilingual Education', Journal of Multilingual and Multicultural Development, 1981 (a), in press.

Edwards, J., 'Psychological and Linguistic Aspects of Minority Education', in Eltis, K., Megarry, J. and Hoyle, E. (eds.), The Education of Minorities, (World Yearbook of Education, 1981), Kogan Page, 1981 (b), in press.

Edwards, J., 'Disadvantage: Guilt by Association', Educational Psychology, 1981 (c), in press.

Edwards, V., The West Indian Language Issues in British Schools, Routledge & Kegan Paul, London, 1979.

Fishman, J., 'The Social Science Perspective', Bilingual Education: Current Perspectives, Centre for Applied Linguistics, Arlington, Virginia, 1977.

Fishman, J., 'Minority Language Maintenance and the Ethnic Mother Tongue School', Modern Language Journal, vol. 64, 1980, pp. 167-172.

Giles, H. and Bourhis, R., 'Black Speakers with White Speech: A Real Problem?', paper presented to the Fourth International Congress of Applied Linguistics, Stuttgart, 1975.

Gleitman, L. and Gleitman, H., Phrase and Paraphrase, Norton, New York, 1970.

Hayakawa, S., 'Pay for Your Own Tongue', Maclean's, vol. 93, no. 29, p. 12.

Hess, R. and Shipman, V., 'Maternal Attitudes Towards the School and the Role of the Pupil: Some Social Class Comparisons', in Passow, A. (ed.) Developing Programs for the Educationally Disadvantaged, Teachers College Press, 1968 (a).

Hess, R. and Shipman, V., 'Maternal Influences Upon Early Learning: The Cognitive Environments of Urban Pre-School Children', in Hess, R. and Bear, R. (eds.), Early Education, Aldine, Chicago, 1968 (b).

Higham, J., Send These to Me, Atheneum, New York, 1975.

Jensen, A., 'How Much Can We Boost IQ and Scholastic Achievement?', Harvard Educational Review, vol. 39, 1969, pp, 1-123.

Jensen, A., Bias in Mental Testing, Free Press, New York, 1980.

Labov, W., 'The Logic of Nonstandard English', in Keddie, N. (ed.), Tinker, Tailor...The Myth of

Cultural Deprivation, Penguin, Harmondsworth, 1973.

Lenneberg, E., *Biological Foundations of Language*, Wiley, New York, 1967.

Passow, A., *Deprivation and Disadvantage: Nature and Manifestations*, UNESCO Institute for Education, Hamburg, 1970.

Raven, J., 'Intervention As Interference', *Scottish Education Review*, vol. 12, 1980, pp. 120-130.

Ravitch, D., 'On the History of Minority Group Education in the United States', *Teachers College Record*, vol. 78, 1976, pp. 213-228.

Rodriguez, R., 'Aria: A Memoir of a Bilingual Childhood', *American Scholar*, vol. 50, 1980 (a), pp. 25-42.

Rodriguez, R., 'An Education in Language', in Michaels, L. and Ricks, C. (eds.), *The State of the Language*, University of California Press, Berkeley, 1980 (b).

Rose, A., 'Minorities', in Sills, E. (ed.), *International Encyclopedia of the Social Sciences*, (Volume 9-10), Collier-Macmillan, New York, 1972.

Royal Institute of International Affairs, *Nationalism*, Frank Cass, London, 1963.

Sowell, T., 'Ethnicity in a Changing America', *Daedalus*, vol. 107, 1978, pp. 213-237.

Trudgill, P., *Accent, Dialect and the School*, Edward Arnold, London, 1975.

Van den Berghe, P., *Race and Racism*, Wiley, New York, 1967.

Van den Berghe, P., 'Review of: Bias in Mental Testing', *Social Forces*, vol. 59, 1981, pp. 837-840.

Wax, M. and Wax, R., 'Cultural Deprivation as an Educational Ideology', in Leacock, E. (ed.), *The Culture of Poverty: A Critique*, Simon & Schuster, New York, 1971.

Widgren, J., 'Recent Trends in European Migration Policies', *International Review of Education*, vol. 21, 1975, pp. 275-285.

Wiseman, S., 'Educational Deprivation and Disadvantage', in Butcher H. (ed.), *Educational Research in Britain*, University of London Press, London, 1968.

Zolf, L., 'Mulling Over Multiculturalism', *Maclean's*, vol. 93, no. 15, p. 6.

Chapter Seven

THE EDUCATION OF CHILDREN OF IMMIGRANT GROUPS:
A COMPARATIVE PERSPECTIVE OF BRITAIN, FRANCE,
THE NETHERLANDS, THE FEDERAL REPUBLIC OF GERMANY
AND SWEDEN

Arpi Hamalian and
Joti Bhatnagar

INTRODUCTION

This paper will examine the education of immigrant children in five industrialised countries of Western Europe: Great Britain, France, the Netherlands, the Federal Republic of Germany and Sweden. These countries have recently received large waves of immigrants from different sources. The tradition of race relations and minority accommodation patterns differ from one country to another. However, rapid industrial growth has created comparable problems in these countries. Recently, through their association in the European Community structures, they have been trying to find new solutions to common problems. These countries were once relatively homogeneous in terms of ethnicity (pluralism such as that in the Netherlands was mainly on religious-sectarian basis). The influx of many different ethnic, religious and cultural groups has turned them (at least in the urban centres) into heterogeneous, multi-ethnic societies. An ever growing number of persons with diverse backgrounds claim integration rights in the host countries of Europe while retaining their cultural identities based on the countries of origin of their parents or grandparents. This reality has not been openly acknowledged so far and is not yet well documented. Therefore, policy measures in all areas, but especially in the area of education are neither realistic nor effective, since they do not address the needs of the changed contexts of the industrialised nation - states of Europe.

The first part of the paper outlines briefly the different waves of post World War II migrations and the movements of 'guestworkers' in Europe. The consequences for the formal educational systems are highlighted at the end of this section. The second part of the paper presents a summary review of the structures of the immigrant population in the United Kingdom, France, the Netherlands, the Federal Republic of Germany and Sweden. In each country, the main orientations of the educational policies adopted for the immigrant children are presented. The third part of the paper examines some of the consequences of the educational policies in existence and describes the situation of immigrant children in the educational system of the host countries. An account of recent pedagogical action is presented at the end of this section. The conclusion examines the concept of multicultural education in the context of industrialised nation states and its uses and usefulness in practice and policy.

POST WORLD WAR II MIGRATIONS AND THE MOVEMENT OF GUEST-WORKERS IN EUROPE: CONSEQUENCES FOR THE FORMAL EDUCATIONAL SYSTEM

After the end of World War II, Western Europe experienced unanticipated and rapid economic progress. The industrialised countries of Europe were faced with a high and pressing demand for labour. The shortage of workers was created partly because of demographic problems as a result of the war, and partly as a result of a secular economic upswing. Natives were generally able to avoid unpleasant and poorly paid jobs. Therefore, these countries resorted to the importation of workers from less developed countries of the mediterranean region. This solution took the form of the temporary recruitment of 'guest-workers' (from the German designation of 'Gastarbeiter') brought into the 'host' country for a limited period of employment (Bauer, 1970; Bagley, 1973; Bohning, 1972, 1974, 1978; Castles and Kosack, 1973; Freeman, 1979; Gonzales-Paz, 1971, 1973; Kayser, 1971; Kubat, 1979; Kuhn, 1978; Mayer, 1972; Morokovasic, 1972; Petersen, 1978; Power, 1979; Rist, 1978; Salt and Clout, 1976; Verkoren, 1973; Werner, 1974, 1977; Whyte, 1972).

At the same time, another wave of immigrant workers started coming into Europe. This wave was composed mainly of citizens of the former colonies of Britain, France and the Netherlands (Adler, 1977; Bagley, 1973; Freeman, 1979; Power, 1979). A further wave of migrants resulted from the formation of the European Economic Community (EEC). Free movement of workers within the European Community was laid down by the treaty of Rome (1957) and came into force in 1968 (Collins, 1975; Kayser, 1977; Lebon and Falchi, 1980; Mayer, 1975). The work permit which is essential to taking a job, gives the community a practical method of preventing permanent settlement of non-Community immigrants. However, especially until the recession of the middle 1970s, more workers were brought in from outside the Community than had moved across the borders of the member states under the free movement provisions.

Today, almost fifteen million immigrants, approximately half of them economically active, are living in the industrialised countries of Western Europe. Their share of the total population varies from 5 to 15 percent in the major immigration countries (Werner, 1977; Lebon and Falchi, 1980; for updated information see SOPEMI - Organization of Economic Cooperation and Development, Directorate for Social Affairs, Manpower and Education - Continuous Reporting System on Migration). These figures exclude illegal migrants (Bender, 1970; Power, 1979), refugees (Holborn, 1975; Rideau, 1980) and the naturalised immigrants or non-indigenous immigrants from former colonies who hold the nationality of the immigrant country. Illegal immigrants are sometimes estimated at 10 percent of the officially registered immigrants. The number of naturalised immigrants can amount to about 50 percent of the non-naturalised foreigners in countries with a comparatively liberal naturalisation policy like France. In the Netherlands and France too, many citizens of the former colonies automatically have full citizenship of the metropolitan country, and are not counted as 'immigrants'.

For a long time, and as a matter of policy, most industrialised countries of the European Economic Community regarded the migrant workers from the less developed countries as "economic goods available to the exchange market like other commodities" (Birindelli, 1976; Blitz, 1976; Bohning, 1978; Kindelberger, 1967; McDonald, 1969). Furthermore, since the immigrants were concentrated in jobs rejected by the natives, the availability of the foreign workers helped the social promotion of the native working class (Castles and Castles, 1971; Schiller and Diefenbach, 1975; Sheehan, 1973). This led to the creation of an underclass described by

Hoffman-Nowotny (1976) as the process of Unterschichtung:

> This stratum is ethnically different, its members have no political rights and with regard to stratum characteristics, they do not conform to the general development level of the immigration country. This means first that the social distances existing in the society increase and second that a highly developed society has again to deal with problems specific to different i.e. lower levels of development, problems which were believed to have been resolved long ago.

On the other hand, the guestworker movement probably exacerbated the underdevelopment of the sending countries and therefore created economic and political barriers to the return home of the guestworkers (Bohning, 1972; Griffi, 1976; Paine, 1974; Provost, 1970; Schiller, 1975; Bovenkerk, 1978). As a consequence, the expected high rate of rotation of guestworkers did not materialise. Instead, by the late 1960s, rotation was replaced by increased length of residence and family migration and settlement. As recession began to effect the worker importing countries of Western Europe (between 1971-1978), they all enacted laws severely curtailing or totally restricting further in-migration (Bernard, 1976; Lohrmann, 1976; Rocheau, 1978).

Gradually, the manpower importing countries had to face the political reality that the guestworkers were 'human beings' and their settlement was more or less permanent. This was due mainly to the economic realities of the individual guestworker and those of the sending and receiving countries. As 'human beings' the guestworkers brought with them an added social burden (Ball, 1973). They had associated costs in housing and children (Menendez-Aguirre, 1972). These children needed education (Johannesson, 1975; Widgren, 1975; Egger and Boillat, 1975). The receiving countries also found that their freedom of manoeuvre against these workers was limited by a growing human rights movement (Bohning, 1978; Maggs & Lee, 1976; Granier & Marciano, 1975). Still, the Western European countries continued to propagate the 'buffer theory', trying to justify their temporary migration policies directed to the maintenance of a flexible quota of 'foreign' workers as 'cushions for the economy/Konjunkturpuffer'.

However, with a tighter labour market, the 'bufferclass', the 'underclass' became the target of increasing discrimination and racial conflict. Racist attitudes and incidents became more open and spread generally throughout Western Europe, culminating in ugly incidents even in Sweden (N.Y. Times, June 20, 1977; Oberg, 1974; and Wadensjo, 1975); in Switzerland where 'unberfremding'/ Hyperzenie'/ Hyperforeignization' became a major issue in several elections and referenda (Kuhn, 1978; Macheret, 1969; Mayer, 1972; Petersen, 1975); and in the Netherlands (Bagley, 1973).

Therefore, by the mid 1970s, the Western European classrooms had a significant minority of children who spoke the indigenous language hardly or not at all. Colour cuts across the variable of language difficulty: many 'immigrants' from Asia, Africa and the Caribbean in Britain, France and the Netherlands speak excellent English, French or Dutch, and have higher status than guestworkers from the Mediterranean, who are usually lighter in colour than the colonial migrants. In France particularly, prejudice and discrimination is more likely to be expressed against Arabs (from Algeria and other parts of North Africa) than against black people from the overseas Departments in Africa and the Caribbean (Bagley, et al., 1979). In some European countries, the third generation of 'immigrants' has started school already. However, since these countries refuse to acknowledge themselves as immigrant receiving countries, the notion of 'immigrant born here' corresponds to an educational reality experienced by teachers in European classrooms. The attitude of citizens of former colonies is, in addition often confused, and the educational provision for children of colonial migrants is plagued with similar problems encountered in finding a just and adequate policy for children of guestworkers (see Bagley, 1983 for a case study of the Netherlands).

For two decades, the immigrant receiving countries of Europe operated almost in a vacuum of policies and guidelines when dealing with the education of immigrant children. However, as these countries realised in the mid-1970s that the problem had become quite acute, they tried to coordinate their collective experiences in search of viable recommendations and directives. The Council of Ministers of the European Communities issued their first report in 1974 (followed by updated reports every year). The topics examined include: Reception systems and methods; ways of teaching the mother tongue and of carrying out basic and further training of teachers; pre-school education; educational and vocational guidance; international schools and national schools located abroad; pre-vocational and vocational training for young migrants. The actual work related to the education for migrant workers' children is being pursued on two fronts: the implementation of action programmes (social and educational) and the application and drafting of regulations. Pilot programmes are being initiated. For example, a scheme to develop reception systems for foreign children entering the first year of primary education was implemented in Limburg, Belgium in 1976/77. In the same year in Paris and Bedford, England, a scheme for instruction of mother tongue in primary schools' curriculum was started. In France and the Federal Republic of Germany, programmes for training teachers for immigrant students were inaugurated at the same time.

Although the respective Ministeries of Education try to compile a bank of information, the findings of these experiments are limited so far since they must operate for several years before some trends become apparent. Furthermore, empirical studies although increasing in number and sophistication are not cumulative and the results are most of the time inconclusive and contradictory. Since the socio-political context of the research, as well as ideologies and attitudes towards immigrants are changing--with the realisation that the children of migrant workers are real immigrants who will settle in the receiving countries--the assumptions and, therefore, the theoretical framework and domain used in these studies are in constant fluctuation. As far as the political action is concerned, the directives issued by the Conference of Ministers have a very limited field of application as coercive legal instruments in the member countries.

The Commission of the European Communities published a study (1977) compiling the results of several pilot studies and the experiences of the member communities. The following important facts emerge:

1. The number of native children at primary schools is diminishing whereas the number of children of foreign born parents is increasing sharply.

2. The ratio of foreign children completing secondary education is significantly lower than that of foreign children in primary education, and there is hardly any sign of improvement.

3. The ratio of foreign pupils is usually between 5 and 10 percent but it is much higher in the industrialised regions where immigrant children out-number national pupils in many schools located in working class districts.

4. 1,500,000 foreign children up to the age of 16 are registered at schools in the Community; but at least another two million children who are nationals but are treated to some measure like immigrants (children of immigrants from former colonies) should be added to that number to get a picture of the magnitude of the resulting problems.

A general remark is in order at this point. The words 'guestworker,' 'immigrant,' 'foreigner,' 'alien,' are used interchangeably and broadly in this paper. This reflects the confusion existing in laws, literature and everyday usage in Europe. In Germany, for example, all immigrants are foreigners. In France, the immigrants from the Overseas Departments are technically not foreigners, and all statistics in France are given for foreigners only. The same is true in Britain, for the immigrants from the Commonwealth and those from Ireland. These immigrants are not considered foreigners, therefore, technically they are not included when referring to foreigners. On the other hand, in Britain, 'immigrant' has become synonymous with 'non-white'. In the Netherlands, guestworkers are regarded as potential settlers and are referred to as immigrants. Overall patterns of conflict differ also from one country to the other. In Britain, the conflict is mainly racially based. In France, race is an important factor but more general conflict is witnessed in social policy areas related to immigrants. In the Netherlands, non-conformity to the existing divisions in the social order creates conflict situations. Fear of 'overforeignerisation' and resistance to the integration of foreigners, specially in schooling, is at the forefront of conflict in the Federal Republic of Germany. Immigrant children are, therefore, children who are non-white, children who are born of parents who are guestworkers, children who come from homes where at least one parent has a home language different from the language of the receiving country, children who are born of immigrant non-white parents. Power (1966) points out that "'immigrant child' is a technical term applied to children with certain socio-cultural backgrounds and who may need special educational treatment". All these definitions and more should be kept in mind when interpreting different sets of statistics emanating from different sources in Europe.

THE STRUCTURE OF THE IMMIGRANT POPULATION AND THE POLICIES ON THE EDUCATION OF IMMIGRANT CHILDREN IN FIVE COUNTRIES OF EUROPE

United Kingdom
As a former Empire, Britain has primarily considered itself a country of emigration. Until recently, the British policy toward immigrants has traditionally followed a laissez-faire line. The recent pattern of immigration has often been conditioned by historical circumstances and the legacy of the 'Empire' status. Thus, Britain had the status of an emigrating country from 1950 to 1959, of an immigrating country from 1960 to 1965, and again of an emigrating country from 1966 to 1976.

Recently immigration controls have become more and more selective and the continuing hard core of racism and its representatives have advocated the suppression and eventual repatriation of non-whites (Bagley, 1970; Bagley, Mallick and Verma, 1979). Although there are many who hold an assimilationist policy and few others who advocate a pluralist society, there is continued structured rejection of even the best qualified immigrants, leading to their general alienation (Ballard & Holden, 1973; Bagley, 1976 and 1982).

According to official estimates, the total number of immigrants is in the region of 3 million. Of these about 50 percent are white immigrants and the other half have come from the West Indies, Asia, Africa and Southeast Asia (Asians - 618,000; West Indians - 236,000; Africans - 30,000). Nearly three-quarters of the coloured immigrants are concentrated in the West Midlands and Greater London (Verma and Mallick, 1981; Walker, 1978). Recently, the numbers of Chinese and Turkish immigrants has started growing as well (Garvey and Jackson, 1976). Therefore, today, there are several hundred thousand immigrant children belonging mainly to the visible minority group in the British school system. A survey by Townsend and Brittan (1972) showed that ethnic minority children constituted approximately 3.3 percent of the total school population in the country but their concentration in certain urban areas accounted for their presence in large numbers in many schools.

To promote the acceptance and the integration of 'coloured immigrant minorities' successive acts of protective legislation were passed, starting in 1968. Most attempts made in Britain in defining an 'immigrant child' have focused on these minorities. The Leeds Education Authority for example, defined immigrant children as: "Coloured children born in tropical countries of the Commonwealth, or children born in this country at least one of whose parents are from a tropical country" (Butterworth, 1967). The Plowden Report (1967) defined an immigrant child as "a child born abroad of immigrant parents or born in this country of parents who emigrated after 1958". By the 1971 census more than half of the population of West Indian or Pakistani ethnic origin (enumerated at 274,545) had been born in the United Kingdom.

For a long time, the general attitude of several schoolboards was to take a laissez faire position concerning the increasing number of immigrant children in their schools. This led to a vicious circle of unfavourable attitudes of immigrant children towards school and low motivation and achievement. By 1965, the Minister of Education, in circular No. 7, recommended a dispersal policy of immigrant children on educational grounds. The thinking at the time was that no school should have more than 30 percent of its enrollment as immigrant children. The Plowden Report (1967) recommended that the criteria used for dispersal should be linguistic and other difficulties at school and not factors such as ethnic group membership. By the 1970s, however, it had become clear to all parties concerned that dispersal did not serve any useful purpose educational or otherwise. More positive steps were taken by the establishment of an Educational Disadvantage Unit and a Center for Information and Advice on Educational Disadvantage (Department of Education and Science, 1974). But a draft directive of the EEC issued in Brussels, in 1976, and calling for the provision of mother tongue teaching within school hours, was opposed strongly by the British. The grounds advanced were that the Department of Education and Science had no power to require local education authorities to make the necessary curricular provisions. So long as many educational authorities rigidly hold to an assimilationist policy, on the implicit assumption that as long as the immigrant children are treated on the same footing as the local children, the problem will sort itself out, there is little hope that any positive steps will be taken to facilitate the accommodation of minority immigrant children into a basically racist and elitist school system.

France

France has a long tradition of demographic self-concern which was clearly stated in the third plan of economic development (1958-1961) advocating immigration for continued demographic growth. Therefore, after the end of World War II and until about 1974, France exercised a more or less open migration policy in order to solve its demographic problems.

The number of immigrants who came to France from its former colonies (not including Overseas Departments) and workers recruited from Mediterranean countries is estimated to be 3,900,000 - according to the 1975 census, there were 1,192,300 African immigrants (Algerians, Moroccans, Tunisians, Maltese, Senegalese) and 116,915 Asians of which 50,860 were Turks. Although the foreigners represent only about 8 percent of the total French population, they are concentrated in large numbers in special areas of France. According to the 1975 census, the cities most heavily populated by 'foreigners' are Paris (12 percent), Lyon (11.8 percent), Marseille (7.9 percent), Lille (8.1 percent) and Grenoble (12.8 percent).

According to the 1977-78 census by the Ministry of Education, there were 592,559 'foreign' children in the French public school system, representing 9.3% of the total school population. These children are distributed throughout the French school system from pre-school (where they represent 9.1% of the total preschool population) up to the age of 16 which is the end of compulsory school attendance. It is to be noted that these statistics do not include immigrant children with French passports such as the children of Algerian repatriates and the immigrants from the French West Indies. On the other hand, the rapid naturalisation process in France adds about 30,000 new Frenchmen annually. With the number of aliens at close to four million, this does not help too much in terms of solving the problem of substantial minorities in France.

Furthermore, it adds to the statistical problem of accounting for the true number of children of immigrants who need special attention in the school system.

Until the early 1970s, the French Ministry of Education operated on a laissez-faire and assimilationist assumption. As in Britain, it was hoped that the immigrant students would be absorbed in the system and eventually the problem will disappear. In France, it was claimed that the language problem faced by immigrant children is not as acute as in the other countries of Western Europe. The majority of those children were either born in France or arrived at a very young age. It is estimated that out of 85,000 foreign children in French schools, only 20,000 require help through introductory or adjustment classes in learning the language (Charlot, 1981).

Since 1970, the Ministry of Education has established and supported financially many special programmes for the education of children of immigrants. The aim of these programmes is to provide for their gradual integration in the regular classrooms. However, there is not much help available for children who arrive after the age of twelve who instead of opting for the regular school system, many have no choice but to go into professional and technical education for which they are largely unprepared. However, a 1978 ministerial proposal took a more positive stand in recommending measures of flexibility in each school to accommodate the needs of the immigrant children. Recently, several centers were opened to provide for specialised teacher training for 'immigrant' children (Charlot, 1981).

The problem of racism is as prevalent in France as in Britain. The portion of the French public that exhibits most virulent racism is the lower socio-economic class. Since most immigrants live in close contact with this portion of the population, minority children encounter the same racist attitudes in France as elsewhere in Europe. In addition to racism, the immigrant child has to face the barriers erected by a traditionally elitist system of education.

The Netherlands
Population growth in the Netherlands has always been very rapid and therefore, since World War II, the Netherlands has pursued an out-migration policy providing subsidies to those citizens who wished to

leave the country. Nonetheless, the Netherlands continued to receive important waves of immigrants. However, the proportion of those officially classified as 'aliens' has remained low because the former Dutch subjects are not included in the statistics. In 1975, the total alien population was estimated to be 370,000 persons.

Until 1970, the policy of the Dutch government towards migration was neutral. Since 1970, strict restrictive measures have been applied by limiting in-migration to those countries with which the Netherlands has a labour importing agreement: Greece, Morocco, Tunisia, Portugal, Spain, Turkey, Yugoslavia and the EEC Countries (Kubat, 1979).

Like Britain, the Netherlands has considerable colonial links with the Caribbean, and the immigrants from the Antilles and Surinam are very similar to the West Indian immigrants to Britain. Estimates put the total of the Surinamese immigrants in 1975 at 140,000, one-third of the total Surinamese population. The Netherlands had already absorbed some 300,000 Indonesians in the '50s and in the '60s had recruited some 300,000 'foreign' workers of which Turks and Moroccans formed a large part. Although the Dutch government put in place a very elaborate social policy for the reception and settlement of the Indonesian immigrants, the arrival of the foreign workers did not receive much attention since the authorities considered them as 'temporary' workers (Dincer, 1962). Treatment of the West Indian immigrants in general was often unclear, ambiguous; sometimes they were ignored or treated like the Indonesian 'repartriants'; and latterly they have been treated more like migrant workers. None of these policies has been particularly successful (Bagley, 1983). Although some of these migrant workers left after a short stay, many others brought in their families and planned to settle in the Netherlands. By the early '70s, the Dutch government started taking policy measures to facilitate the integration of these migrants while starting to control new migration waves.

It has been argued that the basically plural Dutch society and government have been more open to the integration of foreigners than their British counterparts. However, in spite of the positive action attempt by the official authorities, there were many racial incidents in the Netherlands similar to the British and French incidents (Bagley, 1973).

The Netherlands society is organised along four separate blocks, or pillars of society: Catholic, Dutch Reformed, Dutch Re-reformed and Secular. These communities co-exist in a pattern of accommodation, each having its own institutional completeness. The integration of immigrants has been the responsibility of the different pillars of society and has been organized on voluntary action basis. Bagley (1973) gives an example from The Hague. The immigrants are received into 'casas' - housing accommodations that group together immigrants of the same background. The transition to total integration is made gradually. Group 'individualism' is accepted, since it forms the basis of social organisation of the Dutch society. However, since there is a very delicate balance of power between the already existing blocks of society, conformity is emphasised in the integration process. In the rhetoric of comparative studies, the Dutch variety of racism is described as being ethnocentric (based on feelings of cultural superiority) rather than on colour discrimination as such. The same analysis probably has some relevance to the French situation (Bagley, et al., 1979).

According to statistics compiled by the Commission of European Communities in 1977 - there were 19,700 'foreign' pupils during the 1974/75 school year in the Dutch school system, all levels combined. This represented 1.3 percent of the total pupils in the system for that year. These statistics do not include children of parents from the former dependencies of Surinam, the Dutch Antilles and the Moluccan Islands. As a matter of official government policy, the children of immigrants are subject to the same schooling provisions as are the Dutch, but special language training and coaching is often provided. The overall aim of this education is to enable the children of immigrants to take their place in Dutch society in an industrious, conforming way, retaining a degree of ethnic identity. However, this 'plural' model has had profound difficulties in practice, and has led to significant alienation on the part of some sections of Moluccan and West Indian youth (Bagley, 1973 and 1983).

The Federal Republic of Germany
The Federal Republic of Germany has declared on several occasions that it is not an immigrant receiving country. Therefore, the official position remains that of 'temporary integration' of the

guestworkers. The government remains adament about not wanting any immigrants. By 1973, Germany started controlling in-migration more directly but it had already four million foreigners whose length of stay was increasing.

The number of guestworkers' children increased with the more and more restrictive policies of immigrant labour and the resulting family reunion policies in particular. Furthermore, the German birth rates continue to fall dramatically while immigrant birth rates have remained high. One-third of all births in cities like Stutgart, Frankfurt and Salsburg have been to foreign parents in recent years. Children born to foreign parents in Germany are not entitled to West German citizenship, and racism seems to be increasing with the mounting numbers of ethnic minority children. Thus, while there were only 2,000 children of guestworkers in German schools in 1954, by 1964 their number had reached 35,135 and by 1971 they numbered 165,000. In 1974/75, there were 53,000 foreign children in official preschools (schulkindergarten) representing .03 percent of the total pre-school population, and 203,500 children were found at the 1st level (4.6%) and at the 2nd level 159,000 students were registered (2.7%). By 1983, because migrants tended to be younger than the German population, and have higher birth rates, these ratios have increased dramatically.

The mandatory schooling for children of 'aliens' up to the age of 16 was introduced in 1964, after the number of children became substantial. A standing Conference of Ministers of Education, with powers only to recommend, has issued a series of specific recommendations in view of the integration of foreign children and making provisions for mother tongue instruction. However, since schools are administered directly by the individual German states (Lander), the situation of immigrant children varies from one state to the other (Rist, 1979).

Rist (1979) has described the German Government's position well:

> ...it should be evident that the policies governing the lives of guestworkers in Germany are confused and contradictory. The continual slippage between the pronouncements of a concern for integration and well-being of the foreign workers and the realities of policies that tend to produce opposite outcomes can only

reflect the deeper ambivalence of the Federal Republic towards the foreign worker.

Castles (1980) illustrates how government policies turned temporary into permanent migration while claiming the opposite. By placing the analysis in a class formation framework he concludes:

> In the years of rapid labour-intensive expansion of the 1960s, immigrant workers provided a relatively cheap and easily available source of flexible labour. Now that economic growth has slowed, automation has cut labour needs, and capital export to low-wage countries is replacing import of labour, the immigrant population is taking on a new function; it forms a sort of social buffer, cushioning the West German population against the worst effects of the restructuring of the economy. The immigrants bear much of the brunt of change, but educational underachievement appears to provide legitimation of this, while lack of political rights helps to contain protest. Although large-scale immigration has ceased, immigrants remain an important factor in the class structure of West Germany - and of Western Europe.

Nazi propaganda continuously referred to the foreign workers from 'friendly and neutral' countries as 'Untermenschen', the 'Subhumans'. As Rist points out, behind the new abstraction of 'Gastarbeiter,' there is the image of the guestworker as an 'unwanted but tolerated intruder' and the threshold of tolerance is getting lower and lower every year. The children of foreign workers or the so-called second and even third generation foreigners are the targets of intolerance fueled by racism and xenophobia.

Different sources estimate that between 50% and 90% of the children of foreign workers leave secondary school without a qualifying certificate (Wilpert, 1977). 'Illiterate in two languages' and without work permits during a period of high unemployment rates in Germany, these immigrants youths live their lives in a sociopolitical limbo as, well as increasing alienation. Indeed, they are referred to as Germany's 'social time bomb' and are viewed as presenting a real threat to the country's political stability (Castles, 1980).

Sweden

As a country receiving immigrants in the modern sense, Sweden's experience goes back only to the second World War period. Hammar (1980) has documented the events prior to World War II when Jews were prevented from coming to Sweden and the changes in the immigration policy that took place at the end of the War, when Sweden received large groups of refugees from Finland, Estonia, and Latvia.

Until 1966, immigrants coming to Sweden for work encountered a laissez-faire situation. In 1966, immigration to Sweden became regulated, although there is no regulation of migration between the Scandinavian countries. About 50 percent of the immigrants come from Finland. According to information provided by Ekstrand (1981), in 1975, the ten countries from which the most immigrants came, besides Finland, were Denmark, Norway, Yugoslavia, Greece, the U.S.A., Great Britain, Turkey, West Germany and Italy, in that order.

A Royal Commission on Immigration appointed by the Government articulated the goals and principles of the Swedish immigration policy. A bill based on the proposal was adopted unanimously by the Parliament in May 1975. One feature of the new policy is the linking of immigrant and minority affairs. This was based on the premise that a large number of immigrants will settle in Sweden permanently and form linguistic and cultural minorities. It is also presumed that many in-migrants will eventually return to their home country and therefore, they and their children should be given the opportunity to maintain their linguistic and cultural ties with their own country while being treated alike on an equal basis with Swedes.

According to OECD/SOPEMI sources, there were 424,200 foreign nationals residing in Sweden in 1978, representing 5.1 percent of the total population. The same course gives the number of foreign pupils in primary schools as 59,720 and in the secondary schools as 35,119 for the 1977/78 school year. Since the immigrants have a higher birth rate than Swedes, about 23 percent of all children born in 1978 have immigrant parents.

Officially, immigrant and Swedes enjoy an equal access to all educational services from the kindergarten to the University level. School attendance is mandatory until the age of 16. A Parliament resolution in 1968 provided for instruction of immigrants in their mother tongue. A bill passed in 1976 considerably increased the number of hours devoted to the immigrant's mother tongue. Furthermore, the State budget for 1976/77 shows a sum equivalent of about 60 milion U.S. dollars earmarked for education and other special programmes for immigrants and refugees. Some of this money is devoted to special instruction in Swedish and other subjects for a transitional period to help the integration of the immigrant child into the Swedish school system.

By comparison to Britain, France, the Netherlands and the Federal Republic of Germany, racism, xenophobia or ethnocentrism do seem to be less of a problem in Sweden, but as Ekstrand (1981) notes, "...the immigration of coloured people is very small indeed. There is much talk about discrimination against immigrants but, in an international perspective, the situation so far is rather idyllic."

ACADEMIC ACHIEVEMENT AND RELATED FACTORS INFLUENCING THE ADAPTATION OF IMMIGRANT CHILDREN TO THE EUROPEAN SCHOOL SYSTEM

Academic Achievement

On the whole, studies carried in this area in Europe, as elsewhere, indicate that immigrant children's attainment at school is considerably less than that of the children of the indigenous population. Bodenbender (1976) indicates that more than 60 percent of all children of foreign workers in Germany in the appropriate age group, do not complete any of the three alternatives for secondary education (Wilpert, 1977). Dungworth (1974) found that in German schools, immigrant children do considerably worse than the local children. In spite of positive teacher attitudes, achievement measures by grades do not correspond to the eagerness of children (Bayer et al., 1975). Similar findings have been reported for France (Lipkin, 1974), Sweden (Ekstrand, 1981; Halmstrand, 1978, 1979; Jansson & Linden, 1974; Johannesson, 1973; Persson, 1978) and Britain (Bhatnagar, 1970; Coard, 1971; DES, 1971; Little et al., 1968; Townsend 1971; Bagley, 1982).

However, there is added evidence in these studies that factors other than ethnicity or immigrant status as such accounted for the lower level of performance (Bhatnagar, 1976). Individual studies emphasise these other factors. Socioeconomic status was cited by Persson (1978) as well as all the others; social and personal adjustment by Bhatnagar (1970), length of education in the English school system by Little (1975) and Ashby et al. (1970). These studies found that with the passage of time, the performance of immigrant children improves, particularly among those groups whose culture places value on education as a measure of social mobility. Stanton and Shah (1974) found that quality rather than mere length of schooling was an important factor in the educational attainment of immigrant children.

Ability
It has been argued that lower educational attainment among immigrant children is primarily due to their lower level of potential ability (Eysenck, 1971). It is now well established that immigrant children, particularly those from non-European, Central and Southern European backgrounds tend to do worse than other groups on tests of intelligence and academic aptitude (Bhatnagar, 1970; Eysenck, 1971; Haynes, 1971; Jensen, 1969, 1973; McFie & Thompson, 1970; Vernon, 1969; Watson, 1973). However, it is also generally agreed among psychologists that there is no such thing as a culture free intelligence or aptitude test (Samuda, 1975). Cognitive styles valued and hence stressed in socialisation and education differ across cultures (Vernon, 1975; Bagley and Verma, 1983). Research evidence has demonstrated that even the non-verbal and performance tests are culture loaded (Verma and Mallick, 1981 a). Systematic studies controlling for a range of relevant variables have failed to demonstrate differences in the potential ability of various ethnic groups (Bagley, 1975).

Culture Shock and Culture Conflict
Many studies have argued that one of the major causes of lower educational achievement among immigrant children is the phenomenon of 'culture shock' and 'culture conflict' (Bhatnagar, 1970; Derrick, 1966; Edsen, 1966; Johannesson, 1973; Rogers, 1972). The children who arrived in a new country and new school system are confronted suddenly with different value systems and behavioral expectations. However, there is now evidence that culture conflict can be greater among children born in the country of immigration. The Plowden Report in Britain (1967) referred to this and illustrated

the fact that children are caught between the expectations of the school system and the parents. The confrontation of the two cultures and traditions seems to be more acute than in the case of the first generation immigrant child (Rex & Moore, 1966; Collins, 1973). Religious and sexual roles and expectations cause a high degree of conflict as well. The results in a minority of cases are severe social and psychological problems leading to maladjustment (Aurelius, 1980; Brazier, 1965; Charlot, 1981; Goldman & Taylor, 1965, 1966; Gaertner-Harnach cited in Raoufi, 1981; Haynes, 1971; Rijk, 1978). the effects of labelling and negative stereotyping by teachers and others should not be underestimated, however (Bagley, 1975 and 1982).

Results of recent studies tend to de-emphasise the problem of culture shock as a problem specific to immigrants groups. It has been argued that some behaviour problems are common in the passage from rural to urban conditions, from homogeneous to heterogeneous societies, and can also be associated with generational differences in experiences and expectations (Parker et al., 1969; Ekstrand, 1981). Ekstrand tested an alternative concept – 'culture squeeze'. The assumption here was that in the long run, cultural differences 'squeeze' immigrants. However, his data did not support this hypothesis. Furthermore, it is illustrated in the literature that tests of 'normal' behavior and 'adjustment' are often culturally biased, and are simply a means of stereotyping immigrants. This is brought out clearly in Bagley's research (1975 and 1982) which shows that black children in British samples were categorised negatively in their behaviour by teachers and positively by parents, completing the same behaviour check list.

School and Mental Conflicts
Several researchers have referred to behavioural deterioration of immigrant children in the school. They have illustrated extreme cases of maladaption as well as many variants of apparently unstable behaviour (Almeida, 1972; Berthelier, 1976; Eysenring, 1975; Munoz, 1975; Vasquez, Richard, 1978; Vinana, 1978). However, there is not sufficient information on the subject to demonstrate that such disorders are more frequent among migrant children than among children of the host country (Ekstrand, 1981; Eppink, 1979; Kloehn, 1978). The problem of bias and prejudice in teachers has to be

considered too, in interpreting such reports (Verma and Mallick, 1982).

Language
Language acquisition and social acceptability appear to play a larger role in the adaptation of immigrant children, in the development of positive self-concepts and integrated identity. Considerations related to these areas have generated several research studies.

The linguistic problems of immigrant children have dominated the research and action in the field of education since immigrant children cannot function in a school system unless they are competent in the language of instruction (Baker, 1965; Bell, 1966; Johanesson, 1973; Wallis, 1962). Goldman (1973) classified the linguistic problems of children of immigrants into three categories: a) total language deficiency; b) partial language deficiency; and c) dialect idiosyncrasy. Generally, the findings indicate that language learning problems result in school achievement difficulties (Alleyne, 1965; Bayer et al., 1975; Braun & Klassen, 1970; Gartner-Harnach et al., 1975) as well as emotional disturbances. However, recent studies have indicated that academic achievement of immigrant students seems to be a question more of social and cultural factors than of bilingualism (Ekstrand, 1981).

Based on inconclusive research results, the tendency among educational policy makers has been to move from a position where no language instruction was provided, to providing special instruction programmes for second language teaching, through to the present position of advocating and supporting instruction in the home language and the language used in the school of the host country simultaneously. There is no agreement about the best age at which to start instruction in either language, nor the best methods to be used. Ekstrand (1980) illustrates how myths supported by weak research results may form the basis for educational policy.

It is obvious that political reality and expediency affect decisions on policy about language teaching more directly than any other factors. Most immigrant-receiving governments of Europe who devote some attention and considerable financial support to this area, legitimise their expenditures with the argument that the immigrant children will one day return 'home' to their country of origin. Home governments provide language instruction in host countries since they hope to maintain an active and outspoken group of immigrants to put pressure in negotiations of bilateral agreements with the 'host' government or to gain internal political support by referring to a distant but loyal group of supporters.

Social Interaction, Self-Esteem and Self-Concept
Most psychologists agree that social acceptability is an important ingredient of adjustment to and/or assimilation into a new society. Research evidence shows, however, that minority children, particularly black and Asian children find social acceptability neither among peers, nor with teachers (Brown, 1973; Hubbard, 1965; Kawwa, 1965; Lederman, 1969; Pushkin, 1966). For example, foreign children in German classrooms, as elsewhere, are described to be in a state of communication isolation and ghettoism, leading to the formation of segregated groups and cliques (Harrant, 1976; Pommerin, 1977; Savvidis, 1975).
That such negative socialisation experiences may result in a low self-esteem and self-concept is amply illustrated and supported by research evidence in many countries (Ekstrand, 1981; Oktem, 1976; Raoufi, 1981; Verma and Mallick, 1978, 1981; Wilpert, 1977; Young and Bagley, 1982). In order to maintain adequate self-concept which is essential for satisfactory educational attainment at school, Handlin (1969) makes a case for maintaining strong ethnic identity. This case is being made now in all countries faced with the education of immigrant children (Verma and Bagley, 1979).

Lack of Appropriate Education
As illustrated in the discussion of educational policies of the separate countries, until the early 1970s few special provisions were available to improve the quality of the education offered the immigrant children. The fact that immigrants are concentrated in areas with poor housing with few community resources accounts for their high numbers in 'ghetto' schools with poor facilities and incompetent personnel. The effect of such education is well illustrated in the general literature: the staffing of the underclass. Presently, most countries attempt to do something towards improving the crisis situation resulting from this attitude of

benign neglect. Special teacher training programmes seem to be the measure most popular in addition to special language classes.

In England, curriculum units and special teacher training programmes were developed to enable teachers to familiarise themselves with the social and cultural background of immigrant children, to sort out factors related to prejudice and its effects (Butterworth, 1970; Community Relations Commission, 1974; Derrick, 1970; Mallick and Verma, 1981; Mee, 1970; Rudd, 1970). Similar special training mechanisms are developed and introduced in France (Charlot, 1981) and Sweden (Ekstrand, 1981; Swedish National Board of Education, 1977, 1978). Germany is gradually moving in this direction as well (Raoufi, 1981).

RECENT PEDAGOGICAL ACTION

Creches, Nurseries and Pre-School Institutions
Since most immigrants arrive into the host countries when they are under thirty of age, they bring with them very young infants or have their first children in the host country. Therefore, in Europe, the attendance of immigrant children in creches, nurseries and pre-school institutions of various types is being focused upon as an important mechanism in their adaptation. The major problem in using such a mechanism effectively, assuming it works, is the fact that a great number of these children have a clandestine status. Due to housing shortage and laws governing imported labour, the presence of family members is sometimes not declared officially. Therefore, children born to immigrant parents are quite frequently not registered at birth in the receiving country. In the same way, some parents buy addresses in areas other than the areas of actual residence and therefore their children cannot benefit from the existing facilities which are most of the time regionally administered (Castles and Kosack, 1973).

Attendance at creches and various forms of nursery and pre-school centres (day care, part time play groups etc.) is stressed as a mechanism to bridge the gap between the home culture and the host culture. It is argued that immigrant parents, because of poor education and lack of appropriate parenting skills do not provide a rich enough home environment. The research evidence is not definitive on this question. As far as the quality of care of children at home is concerned there are extra-family causes and intra-family causes reported. Poor housing conditions and, therefore, non-availability of adequate assistance from neighbourhood organisations is an example of extrafamily causes referred to quite frequently (Dumon, 1979).

As an example of intra-family causes, one can mention the argument that immigrant mothers apply child rearing methods that are functional in the country of origin but not in the host country (Baumgartner-Karabak and Landesberger, 1978; Cohen, 1975). In this respect there are many studies referring to the inadequacies of the traditional system of child rearing for purposes of adaptation to the host culture and others pointing to some advantages. The isolation of mothers, the differential sex-role socialisation patterns are other areas of concern (Dumon, 1979; Wilson, 1978). In Germany, children of immigrants are alleged to exhibit lack of manual dexterity, compared to their German peers; but it is also pointed out that the strong emotional support provided in the immigrant family is helpful for better adjustment and emotional stability as an adult (Wulfing, 1978; Dasberg, 1978).

While several studies (such as Castles, 1980) point out to the fact that not enough places are available to accomodate immigrant students as well as the hurdles encountered in making use of them, -- parents' ignorance of availability of services, administrative red tape, high costs, distrust of unfamiliar institutions -- other studies illustrate and document the fact that immigrants are even more likely to know and use the bureaucratic health and welfare organizations than the families of the host country (Dumon, 1977; Haavio-Mannila, 1976).

There is controversy in the literature about the language to be used in the pre-school institutions. While the new trend is to emphasise the importance of bilingual education, there are advocates of the position that the stress should be on the acquisition of the host country's language before learning the language of one's parents (Falchi, 1979). The problem here is that language is not learned in a vacuum and unless parents can reinforce the learning at school, a breach of communication will result. This could lead to a number of social and psychological difficulties. Furthermore, it has been suggested in the literature that the language acquired in a working class sociolinguistic environment often bears little relation to the standard linguistic forms used in school.

Therefore, several researchers advocate special support for language training for parents. This is being implemented at a wide scale in Sweden (Bhatnagar, 1980; Ekstrand, 1980).

The training of teachers for bicultural and multicultural pre-schools is another problem. First, there is the number of different backgrounds found in a classroom. Some countries are making efforts for homogeneous groupings where possible. Then there are the problems associated with different methods used by different cultures in non-verbal communication. The wisdom of using teachers who belong to the immigrant group or the host group is not resolved and there are financial and administrative problems related to this question. Differential quotas are a problem. It has been reported for example that in Berlin there is official discrimination against children of immigrants in allocating pre-school places. On the other hand, Ekstrand (1980) reports that immigrant children receive preferential treatment in Sweden. However, in spite of this positive measure with strong financial backing, the situation is far from being ideal even in Sweden.

In France, since it is claimed that only about 20,000 of the foreign children need special language training, there is no particular concerted policy on providing specialised pre-schools (Charlot, 1981). In the Netherlands, up to 1964, children of foreign workers were sent to Dutch schools appropriate to their age. Most special efforts in pre-school education are made by special voluntary agencies and organisations who specialise in the integration of immigrants into Dutch society. However, it is acknowledged that reception possibilities for these children are insufficient in the Netherlands (Rijk, 1978).

Statistics in Germany indicate that every third baby has a foreign nationality. In Frankfurt, every second child has foreign parents. Four-hundred thousand foreign children, or 10.3 percent of all foreigners are below the age of six (Statistiches Bundesmat, Sept. 1976). Up to 95 percent of the 95 percent of the foreign children under the age of six remain at home. Only five percent attend kindergarten (Raoufi, 1981; Mehrlaender, 1974). As elsewhere, the number of kindergartens is quite insufficient for accomodating German children. As a result, about 15 percent of immigrants send their children to relatives during working hours. Most of the socialisation is done on the street, in 'ghetto' situations since there is mutual distrust for interaction and play due to prejudices of parents of both immigrants and German children (Raoufi, 1981).

Low attendance rates manifested among immigrant children at the pre-school level have their repercussions at the later stages of schooling. In Britain, there is research evidence that a high proportion of West Indian mothers rely on help from outside the home for the care of their children (Bagley, 1975a). The commercial day care facilities chosen are often poor ones, because of financial concerns. Therefore, the West Indian children find themselves in poor stimulation situations both intellectually and emotionally (Bushell, 1974; Verma and Mallick, 1981). As a consequence, they are often described, along with many children of immigrants discussed in this paper, as having 'lost the race long before starting school' (Pringle, 1971). This is dramatically illustrated in the evidence from the British National Child Development Study reported by Bagley (1982).

Preparatory Classes

A large number of children of immigrants arrive in the host countries after the age of six. These are in general children who were left behind when the parents first came to the host country. Failure of the rotation system of guestworkers, high birth rates, and various family reunion policies increased their numbers in the countries of in-migration. Therefore, various forms of preparatory classes emerged to prepare for their integration in the regular school system.

Some preparatory classes are formed by withdrawal, either partial or total. In these classes, immigrant children are taught separately on a full time basis with emphasis on language instruction and cultural orientations. When partial withdrawal is practiced the minority children are reintegrated into the regular classrooms for activities such as art and physical education. Another alternative is the reception centre. These centres are separate from the regular schools. Once the children demonstrate the necessary competence in the language of the host society, they are allowed to cross over to the regular school system. Presumably, these separate schools follow the same curriculum as the local schools and therefore, in addition to gaining competence in the new language the children will pick up all the knowledge necessary to be transferred into regular classrooms.

Many Asian and African immigrant children to Britain have sufficient knowlege of English. What is most difficult in this case is the fact that the school system, the curriculum and the testing methods are totally unfamiliar. By sending older children to a reception center for a few weeks, the education authorities expect to find out their educational level and familiarise them with their new surroundings. When there is no reception centre the burden of determining the amount of help needed by the child falls on the shoulders of the regular class teacher.

When the first language resembles the mother tongue, the provision is a few week's instruction in the new language. This is the case in France for Italian, Spanish and Portugese children. After an intensive three months course in French, they usually have a sufficient command of the spoken language to follow the normal course of studies in regular classrooms (CEC, 1977).

When the first language bears no relation to the mother tongue, special arrangements are made. These are usually of three types (CEC, 1977):

a) A short reception class: The most successful ones have a small group of homogeneous students with respect of age and background, although most often one finds children of different ages grouped together. The main emphasis is on teaching the new language (or one of the two languages - like French or German in Luxemburg), as soon as possible, and integrating the children into regular classes. The average length of these classes is about six months.

b) Two year reception classes: These classes do not concentrate on language alone. The mother tongue is used for preparing the children in all the subjects necessary for integration into regular classes of their own age group and the new language is taught for a few periods each day. The class teacher is usually of the same origin as the children and the new language is taught by a native speaker. These classes are being experimented with in the Netherlands and some of the German Lander. Once they have completed their two year reception class, the children go to their local school.

c) The four to six year reception classes: In these experimental situations found in the Federal Republic of Germany, especially in Bavaria, the first four years of primary education are taught in the child's mother tongue. German is taught five hours a week in the first two years and eight hours a week in the third and fourth years. However, this system is feasible only if there are enough children of the same ethnic group and enough foreign teachers competent in the host language. Furthermore, the children should begin such a course before the end of the third year of elementary school.

The many problems with this approach are illustrated by the Bavarian experience. Although the children are grouped by nationality of origin, the mother tongue they are supposed to speak is not always the same. One may find several different dialects and different languages, for example, in the case of Kurds and Turks from Turkey. Therefore, children from the same nationality grouped together may be assigned a teacher of the same nationality whose language they cannot understand. Furthermore, while they are being taught high German at school, on the street the German they practise is very different. Difficulties in preparatory classes are increased by the wide variation in the age of children grouped together which leads to discipline problems in addition to problems of selfconcept. This situation makes it impossible to follow a regular school curriculum so that it becomes impossible to prepare the children for integration into regular classrooms even if the language barrier is overcome.

The continued isolation and the increasing number of years spent in preparatory classes have a further cause: the uncertain status of the foreign teachers employed. Even when one finds competent foreign teachers, the conditions of work offered to them are inferior compared to their German counterparts. However, since the employment may be the only way the foreign teachers can justify their stay in the host country, they may slow down the transition process. When the number of children in a special class is below 15, the teachers lose their jobs. Therefore, they sometimes try to maintain large numbers of students in their classes. Preparatory classes often become synonymous with ghetto schools (Castles, 1980; Rist, 1978).

Dispersal is another method used. This was recommended in the 60's in Britain and is still practised in Berlin and elsewhere. The assumption is that there should be 20-30 percent of minority children allowed in each school and/or school class. The argument is that dispersal allows maximum 'rub-off' effect of both language and customs. The host country parents are afraid that their children will be disadvantaged and therefore the schools in cities where immigrants are found in large numbers become more and more immigrant schools only. Busing has been attempted in various of the European countries, but with no positive results (Plowden, 1967; Rist, 1978; Raoufi, 1981).

Classes in the Mother Tongue

Mother tongue classes are offered by special arrangements with the consulates of the countries of origin from where immigrants were recruited. These classes are most of the time placed completely in isolation of many other experiences that the immigrant children have in the host country and therefore their effectiveness in the integration process is in doubt.

In summary, all five European countries discussed in this paper have adopted various means and methods to increase their help to minority children, to improve the conditions of their schooling. It should be noted, however, that these measures if they work at all, alleviate the problem on a temporary basis and do not constitute policy measures to ensure that every child in school has an equal opportunity to put his or her hands on the levers of power.

CONCLUSION

The five case studies presented in this paper have highlighted the following common points:

1. Immigrants are welcome at the initial stage as staffers of the underclass in each country.

2. Immigrants often have linguistic problems. Belonging to the underclass, the educational facilities accessible to them are not adequate for their special needs. Therefore, their school experience results in underachievement.

3. The educational underachievement provides legitimation for the continued confinement of these immigrants in the underprivileged positions of the social structure.

4. Historical variables and developments such as traditional, colonial, hegemonic relations, racism and relitism, constitute further stumbling blocks and hurdles on the road to socio-economic success and upward mobility-the main mechanism for integration in stratified, industrialised societies.

5. The formal educational systems in these five countries are still deeply rooted in traditional elitist ideologies reflected in the curriculum and in selection mechanisms embedded in the schooling process. Therefore, upward mobility is extremely difficult in general and more so for 'foreigners'.

6. Recent policies aimed at the accommodation of minority children in school systems are heavily based on psychological research and therefore have the tendency to magnify, for purposes of illustration, the individual problems of particular children. The result is to describe minority pupils as 'problems'. Such an approach will have negative effects on decisions by policy makers who search for generalizations to form the basis of uniform legislation. For example, it is a common practice to make provisions for second and third language teaching in most traditional European curricula. However, making a similar provision for mother language instruction to minority children is considered a major problem and imposition, or is subject to strong resistance by policy makers.

7. The recent trend in immigrant education is toward 'separate' but 'equal' facilities at least for a certain portion of the compulsory schooling years. On the other hand, many immigrant groups have tended, in the reaction to inferior and demeaning education, to organize independent schools from their own resources. These trends are encouraged and are praised as indices of a more 'liberal', 'integrationist,' and 'pluralist' orientation on the model provided by the 'multicultural' nations of the 'new world', and by the proponents of multiculturalism in education. A warning is in order at this point. As educators however we should be careful not to become the champions of mechanisms that will further legitimize the perpetuation of an underclass constituted mainly of certain racial and ethnic minorities. We shall, therefore, participate actively in the clarification of some of the

concepts involved in multi-culturalism and education.

The 'new nations' which have official ideologies of multiculturalism are not clear on the meaning of the concept. Canada has an official policy on 'bilingualism and multiculturalism'. Official publications in Hawaii refer to a multicultural society setting it in contrast to the United States in general. In the United States, a multi-ethnic perspective has been officially endorsed since 1976 by the National Council for the Social Studies. The American Association of Colleges of Teacher Education still hold the view that the United States is multicultural or culturally pluralist or culturally diverse, while the multi-racial classification of the society is illustrated by the census system which enumerates nine major groups (1970 Census). Australia is adopting an official ideology of multiculturalism along the Canadian lines. All these countries are relatively 'new' nations based mainly on recent immigrant populations. The normative ideal they want to achieve is one of true institutional pluralism in the socio-political sphere. However, given the pre-dominance of a certain core group in the central power positions of each of these nation states, policy statements about multiculturalism, cultural pluralism, multiethnicity, multiracialism and polyethnicity become ideal ways of mystifying the nature of pluralism and perpetuating the political dominance of a certain group over others.

Multiculturalism in education is interpreted in various ways. Gibson (1976) has identified four common programmatic approaches to multicultural education in the United States: a) Education of the Culturally Different or Benevolent Multiculturalism; b) Education About Cultural Differences or Cultural Understanding; c) Education for Cultural Pluralism; d) Bicultural Education. In Gibson's classification, education is equated to schooling. Education for Cultural Pluralism seems the most realistic model since it takes into account the socio-political context of formal education.

Instead of applying the third model of Education for a Plural Society, all these countries take refuge in programmes that may be best described as 'compensatory,' implying that cultural differences are the root of the problems children from racial or ethnic minority groups face in school and that these will be remedied through education.

Cultural differences, therefore, become identified with race or ethnic group identity. It is to be noted, however, that in the technical sense, neither race nor ethnicity are synonymous with a specific and easily identifiable culture.

According to Bullivant (1981), multiculturalism is a version of an ideology of pluralism which "...may well be a political panacea, amounting almost to a conspiracy, with the implicit aim of maintaining a degree of ethnic hegemony to perpetuate the power of the dominant ethnic group or Staatsvolk (Connor, 1973) vis a vis other ethnic groups..."

In this paper we surveyed five European countries who do not have official policies of multiculturalism or multicultural education. This choice of comparative case studies is to highlight features of the educational policy of each nation state vis a vis various and different racial and ethnic groups who settle within their boundaries. Although these immigrants did not arrive with the aim of permanent settlement, economic and political conditions have made their settlement semi-permanent and permanent in most cases. It is interesting to note, however, that the methods and mechanisms used in the formal educational sphere are quite similar within the five European countries and are comparable to measures taken by 'nation states' who have officially adopted some version of multicultural ideology.

In summarising the results of the Survey of Teacher Education for Pluralist Societies conducted between June 1978 and June 1979 in Britain, Canada, United States, Hawaii, Fiji and Australia, Bullivant (1981) concludes that:

> ...the net result is the same - ethnic hegemony prevails, within a general socio-historical ideological climate of prejudice and ethnocentrism against ethnics, which is apparent in each case study...Ideologists and knowledge managers construct and attempt to legitimate multicultural models of society that do not match socio-economic, cultural and demographic 'reality'. The routes to a fair share of power are obscured in education by emphasis on life style, rather than life chances.

Like most modern states, the five European nation-states used as case studies are characterised by a central authority which exercises power through a bureaucratically organised administration over the population of a well specified territory. Although through the process of industrialisation and immigration these modern states have become polyethnic, the tendency is for the national core to identify with one particular, traditional ethnic unit. However, the power core is maintained through an industrial culture. The curriculum of the school serves to maintain and transmit the competencies necessary for the survival of this particular culture. Since the institutions of formal schooling are "the instruments by which people control access to more specialized micro-cultures and to the power and privilege they confer," (Goodenough, 1971), policies for the education of immigrant children and/or any true policy of multiculturalism in education should strive towards equal opportunity of access to and progress in these formal educational institutions for each and every individual child irrespective of social, racial or ethnic origin.

REFERENCES

Adler, S., *International Migration and Dependence*, Farnborough, U.K.: Saxon House, 1977.

Almeida, Z., 'Aspects Psychosociaux et Psychopathologiques de la Transplantation,' *Sante des Migrants, Droits et Liberte*, Paris, 1972, pp. 103-128.

Alleyne, M.H., 'Research on the Effects of Bilingualism on Education,' in Jones, J. (Ed.), *Linguistics and Language in Multicultural Society*, London: Unwin, 1965.

Ashby, B., Morrison, A. and Butcher, H.J., 'The Abilities and Attainment of Immigrant Children,' *Research in Education*, no. 4, 1970, pp. 73-80.

Aurelius, G., 'Children of Migrant Workers in Sweden - Adjustment and Behaviour at School,' *ICMC Migration News*, nos. 3-4, 1980.

Bagley, C., *Social Structure and Prejudice in Five English Boroughs*, London: Institute of Race Relations, 1970.

Bagley, C., 'The Background of Deviance in Black Children in London,' in Verma, G. and Bagley, C. (Eds.), *Race and Education Across Cultures*, London: Heinemann, 1975 (a).

Bagley, C., 'On the Intellectual Equality of Races,' in Verma, G. and Bagley, C. (Eds.), *Race and Education Across Cultures*, London: Heinemann, 1975 (b).

Bagley, C., Mallick, K. and Verma, G., 'Pupil Self-Esteem: A Comparison of Black and White Teenagers in British Schools,' in Verma, G. and Bagley, C. (Eds.), Race, Education and Identity, London: MacMillan, 1979.

Bagley, C., 'Sequels of Alienation: Social and Psychological Factors in the Adjustment of Young West Indians in Britain,' in Glaser, K. (Ed.), Case Studies on Human Rights and Fundamental Freedoms, The Hague: Nijhoff, 1976.

Bagley, C., Verma, G., Mallick, K. and Young, L., Personality, Self-Esteem and Prejudice, Farnborough, U.K.: Saxon House, 1979.

Bagley, C., 'Achievement, Behaviour Disorders and Social Circumstances in West Indian Children and Other Ethnic Groups,' in Verma, G. and Bagley, C. (Eds.), Self-Concept, Achievement and Multicultural Education, London: MacMillan, 1982.

Bagley, C. and Verma, G. (Eds.), Multicultural Childhood: Education, Ethnicity and Cognitive Styles, Aldershot, U.K.: Gower Press, 1983.

Bagley, C., 'Dutch Social Structure and the Alienation of Black Youth," in Bagley, C. and Verma, G. (Eds.), Multicultural Childhood: Education, Ethnicity and Cognitive Styles, Aldershot, U.K.: Gower Press, 1983.

Barker, G., 'The Language Problems of Immigrant Children in Junior Schools." Unpublished study, Diploma in Primary Education, University of Nottingham, Institute of Education, 1965.

Ball, R., 'How Europe Created Its 'Minority' Problem,' Fortune, 1973, pp. 130-142.

Ballard, G. and Holden, G., 'The Employment of Coloured Graduates in Britain,' New Community, no. 4, 1975, pp. 325-336.

Bauer, E., 'Die Jugoslawischen Gastarbeiter in Westeuropa,' Donauraum, vol. 15, 1970, pp. 140-151.

Baumgartner-Karabak, A. and Landesberger, G., Die Verkauften Braute. Turkische Frauen Zwischen Kreuzberg und Anatolien, Reinbek bei Hamburg, Rowohlt, 1978.

Bayer et al., Fakaltat Fur Philosophie, Psychologie und Erziehungswissens-chaft der Universitat Mannheim, Zur Situation der auslandeischen Schuler in der BRD, Bericht uber den 29 Kongress der Deutschen Gesellschaft fur Psychologie, 1975.

Bell, R., 'The Grammar of the English Spoken by Indian Immigrants in Smethwick.' Unpublished M.A. dissertation, University of Birmingham, 1966.

Bender, E., 'Asylum in the Federal Republic of Germany and Some Problems Connected Therewith,' International Migration, vol. 8, 1970, pp. 167-173.

Bernard, W.S., 'Immigrants and Refugees: Their Similarities, Differences and Needs,' International Migration, vol. 14, 1976, pp. 267-281.

Berthelier, D., 'Les Enfants de Travailleurs Migrants: Problemes Psycho-pedagogiques et Medico-Sociaux,' Journees d'Etudes sur les Problemes Poses par la Scolarisation des Enfants de Travailleurs Migrants, Lyon, Avril, 1976.

Bhatnagar, J.K., Immigrants at School, London: Cornmarket, 1970.

Bhatnagar, J.K., 'Education of Immigrant Children,' Canadian Ethnic Studies, vol. 8, no. 1, 1976.

Bhatnagar, J.K., 'Linguistic Behavior and Adjustment of Immigrant Children in French and English Schools in Montreal,' International Review of Applied Psychology, vol. 29, 1980, pp. 141-158.

Birindelli, A.M., 'The Post-War Italian Emigration to Europe, in Particular to the EEC Member Countries,' Genus, vol. 32, 1976, pp. 179-193.

Blitz, R.C., 'A Benefit-Cost Analysis of Foreign Workers in West Germany, 1957-1975,' Unpublished manuscript, Nashville, Tenn.: Vanderbilt University, 1976.

Bodenbender, W., 'Zwischenbilanz der Auslanderpolitic,' paper presented to the Conference on Bildungsprobleme und Zukunftserwartungen der kinder Turkischer Gastarbeiter, Munich: Sudosteurope Gesellschaft, 1975.

Bohning, W.R., The Migration of Workers in the United Kingdom and the European Community, New York: Oxford University Press, 1972.

Bohning, W.R., 'Immigration Policies of Western European Countries,' International Migration Review, no. 2, 1974, pp. 155-163.

Bohning, W.R., 'International Migration and the Western World: Past, Present, Future,' International Migration, no. 1, 1978, pp. 11-23.

Bovenkerk, F., 'The Fable of Suleiman,' Netherlands Journal of Sociology, vol. 14, 1978, pp. 191-201.

Braun, C. and Klassen, B.A., 'Transformational Analysis of Oral Syntactic Structures of Children Representing Varying Ethno-Linguistic Communities,' ERIC Report, ED # 063316, 1970.

Brazier, D.B.,' Tears are Colourless: Handling the Young Immigrant,' The Times Educational Supplement, June 18, 1965.

Brown, G.A., 'An Exploratory Study of Interaction Among British and Immigrant Children,' British Journal of Social and Clinical Psychology, vol. 12, 1973, pp. 159-162.

Bullivant, B.M., 'Multiculturalism, Pluralist Orthodoxy or Ethnic Hegemony,' Canadian Ethnic Studies, vol. 13, no. 2, 1981, pp. 1-22.

Bushell, W., 'The Immigrant (West Indian) Child in School,' in Varma, V.P. (Ed.), Stresses in Children, Leicester: Unibooks, 1974.

Butterworth, E., 'The Presence of Immigrant School Children: A Study of Leeds,' Race, vol. 8, 1967, pp. 246-262.

Castles, S. and Castles, G., 'Immigrant Workers and Class Structures in France,' Race, vol. 12, 1971, pp. 303315.

Castles, S. and Kosack, G., Immigrant Workers and Class Structure in Western Europe, New York, London, Toronto: Oxford University Press, 1973.

Castles, S., 'The Social Time-Bomb: Education of an Underclass in West Germany,' Race and Class, vol. 4, 1980, pp. 369-387.

Charlot, M., 'The Education of Immigrant Children in France,' in Bhatnagar, J. (Ed.), Educating Immigrants, London: Croom Helm Ltd., 1981.

Coard, B., How the West Indian Child is Made Educationally Sub-Normal in British Schools, London: New Beacon Books, 1971.

Cohen, M., 'Experience de Travail de Groupe Aupres de Femmes Jeunes du Maghreb Recemment Installees en France,' Sauvegarde de l'Enfance, vol. 30, 1975.

Collins, D., Social Policy of the European Economic Community, New York: John Wiley & Sons, 1975.

Collins, J., 'The Social Background of Children from Immigrant Groups,' Education for Teaching, vol. 90, 1973, pp. 15-23.

Commission of the European Communities, Studies - Education Series, 'The Children of Migrant Workers,' Brussels and Luxembourg, 1977.

Community Relations Commission, A Bibliography for Teachers: Education for a Multicultural Society, 3rd. Ed., London: CRC, 1974.

Connor, W., 'The Politics of Ethno-Nationalism,' Journal of International Affairs, vol. 27, 1973, pp. 1-21.
Dasberg, L., 'Leren Samenleven: Ontwikkeling van Gedrag in de Eerste Levensfase,' Cahiers Biowetenschappen en Maatschappij, vol. 5, no. 1, 1978.
Deakin, N., 'The Dutch Experiment Revisited,' Institute of Race Relations Newsletter, March 1968, pp. 121-123.
Department of Education and Science, Potential and Progress in Second Culture: Education Survey, No. 10, London: HMSO, 1971.
Derrick, J., Teaching English to Immigrants, London: Longman, 1966.
Diaz-Plaja, G.L., La Condicion Emigrante: Los Trabajadores espanoles en Europa, Madrid: Ed. Caud. Dialogo, 1974.
Dincer, N., 'Emigration and Immigration in Holland: Policy and Organization,' Dissertation, The Hague: Institute of Social Studies, 1962.
Dumon, W.A., 'Educational Adaptation of Permanent Migrants,' International Migration, vol. 3, 1974, pp. 270-300.
Dumon, W.A., 'The Activity of Voluntary Agencies and National Associations in Helping Immigrants to Overcome Initial Problem,' International Migration, vol. 15, no. 2/3, 1977, pp. 113-126.
Dumon, W.A., 'The Situation of Children of Migrants and Their Adaptation and Integration in the Host Society, and Their Situation in the Country of Origin,' International Migration, vol. 12, nos. 1/2, 1979.
Dungworth, D., 'Gastarbeiter Pupils 'Half-Educated,'' The Times Educational Supplement, September 6, 1974.
Edsen, P., "East and West Meetings in Education for Integration,' Institute of Race Relations Newsletter, 1966.
Egger, E. and Boillat, J.M., 'L'Education des Enfants des Travailleurs Migrants en Suisse,' International Review of Education, vol. 21, 1975, pp. 323-334.
Ekstrand, L.H., 'Home Language Teaching for Immigrant Pupils in Sweden,' International Migration Review, vol. 14, no. 3, 1980.
Ekstrand, L.H., 'Unpopular Views on Popular Beliefs About Immigrant Children: Contemporary Practices and Problems in Sweden,' in Bhatnagar, J.

(Ed.), Educating Immigrants, London: Croom Helm Ltd., 1981.

Eppink, A., 'Socio-Psychological Problems of Migrants' Children and Cultural Conflicts,' International Migration, vol. 17, nos. 1/2, 1979.

Eyserck, H.J., Race, Intelligence and Education, London: Maurice Temple, 1971.

Eysenring, A.J., 'Op Weg Naar Een Transkulturele (ortho) Pedagogiek. Inzichten in de problematiese Opvoedingssituatie van kinderen en Jeugdigen uit Alloctitone Milieus in Nederland,' Den Haag, 1975.

Falchi, G., 'Education of Migrant Children Including Guidance and Language Training,' International Migration, vol. 17, nos. 1/2, 1979.

Freeman, G.P., Immigrant Labour and Racial Conflict in Industrial Societies: The French and British Experience, 1945-1975, Princeton, New Jersey: Princeton University Press, 1979.

Gaertner-Harnach, V., 'Bericht Uber den 29,' Kongress der Deutschen Gesellschaft fuer Psychologie, cited in Raoufi, 1981.

Garvey, A. and Jackson, B., 'Chinese Children,' cited in BBC/Runnymede Trust, Ethnic Minorities in Society: A Reference Guide, London, 1976.

Gibson, M., 'Approaches to Multicultural Education in the United States: Some Concepts and Assumptions,' Anthropology and Education Quarterly, vol. 7, 1976.

Goldman, R. and Taylor, F.M., 'Coloured Immigrant Children: A Survey of Research Studies and Literature on Their Educational Problems and Potential in Britain,' Educational Research, vol. 8, 1966, pp. 163-183.

Goldman, R., 'Education and Immigrants,' in Watson, P. (Ed.), Psychology and Race, Harmondsworth: Penguin, 1973.

Gonzales, Pas, J., 'La Emigracion Espanola,' De Economia, vol. 24, 1971, pp. 41-60.

Gonzales, Pas, J., 'El Futuro de la Emigracion Espanola,' Rev. Econ. Polit., vol. 63, 1973, pp. 103-122.

Goodenough, W.H., Culture, Language and Society, Reading, Mass.: Addison Wesley Modular Publications, No. 7, 1971.

Granier, R. and Marciano, J.P., 'The Earnings of Immigrant Workers in France,' International Labour Review, 1975, pp. 143-165.

Griffin, K., 'On the Emigration of the Peasantry,' World Development, vol. 4, 1976, pp. 353-361.

Haavio-Mannila, E., 'Social Linkages Used by Migrant and Non-Migrant Families in Solving Health, Work and Economic Problems,' Acta Sociologica, vol. 19, no. 4, 1976, pp. 325-398.

Hammar, T., 'Immigration Research in Sweden,' International Migration Review, no. 1, 1980, pp. 93-115.

Harant, S., 'Schulprobleme von Gastarbeiterkinder,' in Reimann, R. and Reimann, H. (Eds.), Gastarbeiter, Munich: William Goldmann, 1976, pp. 149-168.

Handlin, O. (Ed.), Children of the Uprooted, New York: George Grosset & Dunlop, 1968.

Haynes, J.M., Educational Assessment of Immigrant Pupils, London: NFER, 1971.

Hoffmin-Nowotny, H.J., 'European Migration After the Second World War,' paper presented to the Conference on Migration, New Harmony, Indiana, April 14, 1976.

Holborn, L.W., Refugees: A Problem of Our Time. The Work of the United Nations High Commissioner for Refugees 1951-1972, Methuen, N.J.: Scarecrow, 1975.

Holmstrand, L., 'Effekterna pa Allmanna Fardigheter och Attityder i Skolan av Tidigt Paborjad Undervisning i Engelska (The Effects on General Skills and Attitudes in School of Early Teaching of English), Department of Education, University of Uppsala, 1978.

Holmstrand, L., 'De Langsiktiga Effeckterna pa Allmanna Fardigheter och Attityder i Skolan av Tidigt Paborjad Undervisning i Engelska (The Long Term Effects on General Skills and Attitudes in School of Early Teaching of English), Department of Education, University of Uppsala, 1979.

Hubbard, J., 'Racial Attitudes in Young Children and Their Parents' Attitudes to Children Rearing and Social Problems,' Unpublished report for Diploma in Child Development, University of London, Institute of Education, 1965.

Jansson, K. and Linden, Y., 'Social Backgrund och Skilpresetationer hos Invnadrarbarn Vasteras (Social Background and School Achievement Among Immigrant Children in Vasteras), Department of Education, University of Uppsala, 1979.

Jensen, A., 'How Much Can We Boost I.Q. and Scholastic Achievement?,' Harvard Educational Review, vol. 39, no. 1, 1969.

Jensen, A., Educability and Group Differences, London: Methuen, 1973.

Johannesson, I., *Models for Bilingual Instruction of Immigrant Children*, Stockholm, Sweden: National Board of Education, 1973.

Johannesson, I., 'Bilingual-Bicultural Education of Immigrant Children in Sweden,' *International Review of Education*, vol. 21, 1975, pp. 347-355.

Kawwa, T., 'A Study of Interaction Between Native and Immigrant Children in English Schools with Special Reference to Ethnic Prejudice,' Unpublished Ph.D. Thesis, University of London, 1965.

Kayser, B., *Manpower Movements and Labour Markets*, Paris: OECD, 1971.

Kayser, B., 'European Migrations: The New Patterns,' *International Migration Review*, 1977, pp. 232-240.

Kindleberger, C.P., *Europe's Postwar Growth - The Role of Labour Supply*, Cambridge, Mass.: Harvard University Press, 1967.

Kloehn, E., *Verhaltensstorungen*, Munichen, 1977, cited in Eppink, 1979.

Kubat, D., *The Politics of Migration Policies*, New York: Center for Migration Studies, 1979.

Kudat, A., 'Stability and Change in the Turkish Family at Home and Abroad: Comparative Perspectives,' Berlin: Science Center, 1975.

Kuhn, W.E., 'Guest Workers as an Automatic Stabilizer of Cyclical Unemployment in Switzerland and Germany,' *International Migration Review*, no. 2, 1978, pp. 211-234.

Lebon, A. and Falchi, G., 'New Development in Intra-European Migration Since 1974,' *International Migration Review*, vol. 4, 1980, pp. 539-579.

Lederman, S., 'The Social Acceptance of Immigrants,' *Race Today*, 1969.

Lipkin, J., 'Le Sort des Immigrants en France,' *Canadian Society for the Study of Education Newsletter*, vol. 2, no. 1, 1974.

Little, A., 'The Educational Achievement of Ethnic Minority Children in London Schools,' in Verma, G. and Bagley, C. (Eds.), *Race and Education Across Cultures*, London: MacMillan, 1975.

Lohrmann, R., 'European Migration: Recent Developments and Future Prospects,' *International Migration*, vol. 14, 1976, pp. 229-240.

Macheret, A., *L'Immigration Etrangere en Suisse a l'Heure de l'Integration Europeenne*, Geneva, 1969.

Maggs, P.B. and Lee, L.T., 'North African Migrants Under Western European Law,' *Tex. Int. Law J.*, 1976, pp. 225-250.

Mallick, K. and Verma, G.K., 'Teaching in the Multi-Ethnic, Multi-Cultural School,' in Verma, G.K. and Bagley, C. (Eds.), *Self-Concept, Achievement and Multicultural Education*, London: MacMillan, 1982.

Mayer, K.B., 'International Migrations of European Workers,' *New Community*, no. 3, 1972, pp. 1-10.

Mayer, K.B., 'Intra-European Migration During the Past Twenty Years,' *International Migration Review*, no. 4, 1974, pp. 441-447.

McDonald, J.R., 'Labour Immigration in France, 1946-1965,' *Ann. Am. Assoc. Geog.*, vol. 59, 1969, pp. 116-134.

McFie, J. and Thompson, J., 'Intellectual Abilities of Immigrant Children,' *British Journal of Educational Psychology*, vol. 40, 1970, pp. 348-351.

Mee, E.C., 'Audio-Visual Media and the Disadvantaged Child,' *ERIC Reports*, ED # 053545, 1970.

Mehrlaender, U., 'Soziale Aspekte der Auslanderbeschaeftigung, Verlag Neue Gesellschaft Bonn-Bad Gotesberg, 1974.

Menendez, A.J.M., 'Children of Spanish Migrants in West Germany,' *Migration News*, vol. 5, 1972, pp. 3-8.

Morokovasic, M., 'Des Migrants 'Temporaires': Les Yougoslaves," *Sociologie et Travail*, vol. 14, 1972, pp. 260-277.

Munoz, M.C., 'Aspects Psychologiques de l'Adaptation des Enfants Migrants,' *Education et Developpement*, 1975.

Oberg, K., 'Treatment of Immigrant Workers in Sweden,' *International Labour Review*, 1974, pp. 1-16.

Oktem, O., 'Sprachdifizit, Pseudo-Oligophenien and Legasthenic bei Kindern Turkischer Gastarbeitern in Deutschland' paper delivered June 1976 at the Third Giessoner Woche, University of Istanbul (mimeo).

Paine, S., *Exporting Workers: The Turkish Case*, Cambridge, England: Department of Applied Economics, 1974.

Parker, S., Kleiner, R.J. and Needelman, B., 'Migration and Mental Illness,' *Social Science and Medicine*, vol. 3, 1969.

Persson, G., 'School Achievement of Immigrant Children: The Impact of Social Class and

Nationality,' *International Migration*, vol. 31, 1978, pp. 23-29.

Petersen, W., 'On the Sub-Nations of Western Europe,' in Glazer, N., Moynihan, D.P. (Eds.), *Ethnicity: Theory and Experience*, Cambridge, Mass.: Harvard University Press, 1975, pp. 177-208.

Petersen, W., 'International Migration,' *Annual Review of Sociology*, vol. 4, 1978, pp. 533-575.

Plowden Report, *Children and Their Primary Schools*, London: HMSO, 1967.

Pommerin, G., 'Deutschunterricht mit Auslaendischen und Deutschen Kindern,' Kamp, Bochum, 1977.

Power, J., 'Immigrant Childrent: Search for Policy II - Who is an Immigrant Child,' *Education*, December 9, 1966.

Power, J., *Migrant Workers in Western Europe and the United States*, Oxford: Pergamon Press, 1979.

Prevost, G., 'Comment et Pourquoi les Travailleurs Senegalais Viennent en France,' *Hommes Migr.*, vol. 115, 1970, pp. 91-119.

Pringle, K., *Deprivation and Education*, 2nd. ed., Longman in association with the National Children's Bureau, London, 1971.

Pushkin, I., 'An Investigation into the Development of Prejudice in Young Children,' Unpublished Ph.D. Thesis, University of London, 1966.

Raoufi, S., 'The Children of Guest-Workers in the Federal Republic of Germany: Maladjustment and Its Effects on Academic Performance,' in Bhatnagar, J. (Ed.), *Educating Immigrants*, London: Croom Helm, 1981.

Renner, E., 'Erziehungs-und Sozialisationsbed - Ingungen Turkischer Kinder,' Ein Vergleich Zwischen Deutschland und der Turkei, Rheinsletten: Neuburgweirer, 1975.

Rex, J. and Moore, D., *Race, Community and Conflict*, London: Oxford University Press, 1966.

Rideau, R., 'Europe: Crossroad in the Search of Asylums,' *ICMC Migration News*, vol. 3, 1980, pp. 16-21.

Rijk, J.T., 'The Problem of Second Generation Migrants in the Netherlands,' *Migration News*, vol. 27, no. 1, 1978, pp. 8-14.

Rist, C.R., *Guestworkers in Germany*, New York: Praeger Publishers, 1978.

Rocheau, G., 'Some Aspects of Intra-European Migration,' *Migration News*, July-December, 1979, pp. 13-18.

Rocheau, G., 'Ten Years' Migration in Europe,' Migration News, January, March, 1978, pp. 3-8.

Rocheau, G., 'The Crisis of intra-European Migration,' Migration News, January, March, 1979, pp. 3-9.

Rodgers, M., 'The Education of Children of Immigrants in Britain,' Journal of Negro Education, vol. 51, 1972, pp. 255-265.

Rudd, E.M., 'Language for Immigrant Children,' English Language Teaching, vol. 24, 1970, pp. 260-269.

Salt, J. and Clout, H., Migration in Post-War Europe, London: Oxford University Press, 1976.

Samuda, J.R., 'Cultural Discrimination Through Testing,' in Yetman, N.R. and C. (Eds.), Majority and Minority: The Dynamics of Racial and Ethnic Relations, Hoy Steele (eds.), Boston: Allyn & Bacon, Inc., 1975.

Savvidis, G., 'Zum Problem der Gastarbeiter Kinder in der BRD, Jugend und Volk, Wien und Meunchen, 1975.

Schmitter, B.E., 'Immigrants and Associations: Their Role in the Socio-Political Process of Immigrant Worker Integration in West Germany and Switzerland,' International Migration Review, no. 2, 1980, pp. 179-192.

Schiller, G., 'Chanelling Migration: A Review of Policy with Special Reference to the Federal Republic of Germany,' International Labour Review, 1975, pp. 335-355.

Schiller, G. and Diefenback, 'Technischer Wandel und Austanderbeschaftigung,' in Kudat, A. and Ozkan, Y. (Eds.), International Conference on Migrant Workers, Berlin: Athenauns Verlag, 1976.

Sheehan, E.R.F, 'Europe's hired poor,' New York Times Mag., December 9, 1973, pp. 36ff.

Simons, M.S.M., 'Italiaanse arbeiders in de Limburgse Mijnstreek in Twente,' Mens en Maatschappij, vol. 37, 1962, pp. 223-246.

Stanton, M. and Shah, G.H., 'Assessment of Non-English Speaking Immigrants,' Remedial Education, vol. 9, 1974, pp. 105-108.

Townsend, H.E.R. and Brittan, E., Organization in Multi-Racial Schools, Slough, NFER Windsor, 1972.

Townsend, H.E.R., Immigrant Pupils in England, the L.E.A. Response, Slouth, England: National Foundation for Research in Education, 1971.

Vazquez, Ana, Richard, G., 'Problemes d'Adaptation en France des Enfants Refugies de Cote Sud de l'Amerique Latine,' Institut des Sciences de l'Education, Universite de Caen, janvier-febrier, 1978.

Verkoren, N., 'Foreign Workers in Western Europe: A Regional Approach,' Europ. Demogr. Inf. Bull., vol. 4, 1973, pp. 129-134.

Verma, G. and Bagley, C. (Eds.), Race, Education and Identity, London: MacMillan, 1979.

Verma, G. and Mallick, K., 'Self Esteem of Black, Asian and White Adolescents in Multi Ethnic Schools,' The New Era, July, 1978.

Verma, G. and Mallick, K., 'Tests and Testing in a Multi-Ethnic Society,' in Verma, G. and Bagley, C. (Eds.), Self-Concept, Achievement and Multicultural Education, London: MacMillan, 1982.

Verma, G. and Mallick, K., 'Social, Personal and Academic Adjustment of Ethnic Minority Pupils in British Schools,' in Bhatnagar, J. (Ed.), Educating Immigrants, London: Croom Helm Ltd., 1981.

Verma, G. and Bagley, C., 'Issues in Multicultural Education,' in Verma, G. and Bagley, C. (Eds.), Self-Concept, Achievement and Multicultural Education, London: MacMillan, 1982.

Vernon, P.E., 'Intelligence Across Cultures," in Verma, G. and Bagley, C., (Eds.), Race and Education Across Cultures, London: MacMillan, 1975.

Wadensjo, E., 'Remuneration of Migrant Workers in Sweden,' Int. Lab. Rev., 1975, pp. 112-114.

Walker, S., 'The Immigrants: Yes We Can Live in Peace," Reader's Digest, 1978.

Wallis, B., 'English for Immigrant Children in Batley,' Unpublished dissertation for Post-Graduate Diploma in English as a Second Language, University of Leeds, 1962.

Watson, P., 'Race and Intelligence Through the Looking Glass,' in Watson, P. (Ed.), Psychology and Race, Harmondsworth, Middlesex: Penguin, 1973.

Werner, H., 'Migration and Free Movement of Workers in Western Europe,' International Migration, vol. 72, 1974, p. 311-327.

Werner, H., 'Some Current Topics of Labour Migration in Europe - Some Post Facts and Figures,' International Migration, 1977, pp. 300-307.

Whyte, G.E., 'The Economic Aspects of European Labour Migration,' European Demogr. Inf. bull., 1972, pp. 146-152.

Widgren, J., 'Report on the Educational Situation of Immigrants in Sweden,' (paper UNESCO meeting 22-26 Oct. 1973).

Wildgren, J., 'Recent Trends in European Migration Policies,' *International Review of Education*, vol. 21, 1975, pp. 275-285.

Wilpert, C., 'Children of Foreign Workers in the Federal Republic of Germany,' *International Migration Review*, 1977, pp. 473-485.

Wilson, A., 'A Burning Fever: The Isolation of Asian Women in Britain,' *Race and Class*, vol. 20, no. 2, 1978, pp. 129-142.

Wulfing, S., *Turkische Vorschulkinder in Koln*, 1978.

Young, L. and Bagley, C., 'Self-Esteem, Self-Concept and the Development of Black Identity: A Theoretical Overview,' in Verma, G. and Bagley, C. (Eds.), *Self-Concept, Achievement and Multicultural Education*, London: MacMillan, 1982.

Chapter Eight

USING A MULTICULTURAL CONTEXT AS A BASIS
FOR A CORE CURRICULUM: CULTURAL DIFFERENCE
AS EDUCATIONAL CAPITAL (1)

James Lynch

This paper proposes a holistic definition of multiculturalism, based on both expressive and instrumental definitions of culture, seen as a socio-ecological coping strategy. The definition is applied to the contemporary debate concerning the curriculum of British Schools. A distinction is made between multiculturalism and other terms such as polyethnicity, multiracialism, bilingualism and biculturalism. Multiculturalism is seen as a powerful marshalling ideology, descriptive of existing British society, also having prescriptive implications for the pursuit of multicultural education, which is regarded as a process having both core curriculum and whole curriculum, as well as pedagogical and wider school-community implications.

The dilemma of the balance of common and alternative values is focussed onto the issue of the core curriculum. The wider representation of the British multiculture in the current school curriculum is highlighted and reference made to the inadequacy in this respect of recent British official curriculum publications. The Australian Curriculum Development Centre document on the Core Curriculum is then used as an example of a potential approach to multicultural education: common culture and multiculture of British society are viewed as necessitating concommitant responses in the curriculum. Three major cognitive and socio-affective areas of culture are put forward as guiding principles for the design of such a curriculum and a series of critical questions proposed which could help to test the context of such a curriculum for its multicultural validity. The paper ends with an initial list of aims for the core curriculum in a multicultural society and a plea for the full acceptance of multicultural education as a correction for current crises in British society.

Perhaps the most pressing contemporary problem facing British education is how to respond to the compelling, but educationally largely ignored, 'fact' of the multicultural nature of British society in the 1980s (2). In that society, hundreds of language and dialect groups are represented, dozens of different religions, scores of different ethnic groups and all major racial families. The fabric of British society is thus irreversibly and inevitably multicultural. It might be argued that such a wealth of evidence surely poses imperatives for British education. Yet one seeks in vain those official marks of recognition and acceptance of this fact, which can be seen in such other countries such as the United States, Canada and Australia: no legislative measures such as the Bilingual Education Act, no official policy commitments such as that of the Canadian government to a policy of 'multiculturalism within a bilingual framework', no structural arrangements such as the establishment in Australia of the National Institute of Multicultural Affairs (3). One might be forgiven for thinking that the educational system, or at least those in control of the system, were deliberately refusing to take cognizance of the 'facts' and were rather content to continue sublimely with the age-old traditional commitment to producing good middle-class 'Angloids'.

There is certainly provision in some schools which tackles partial aspects of the issue. The Humanities Curriculum Project and the use of material from MACOS focussing, in its curricular design on pupil and teacher ethnocentrism, has provided considerable impetus and progress. Ethnic studies courses too have been initiated in some institutions of higher education and a few teacher education institutions have attempted to tackle some facets of teaching in the multicultural school (4). Some of the results of national projects addressed to one aspect of multiculturalism, namely the racial dimension, have appeared, some were due to appear in mid-1981, although other aspects would appear to have been swallowed irretrievably into a black hole (5). And, whilst such strivings are not to be dismissed or taken lightly, and some kind of 'ethnic' provision such as Black or Asian studies is likely to be necessary as long as some cultural groups are excluded from legitimate and equal access to the common culture, they tackle only partial aspects of the problem, and provide little basis for a holistic and coherent policy. Moreover they rarely come to grips with the real 'power' implications of accepting multiculturalism as a central, i.e. core value of our society: an ethical imperative which needs to be translated into the fabric of educational provision, both curricular and organisational. For multicultural educational provision of the kind cited above, without complementary access to core mainstream culture, may be an 'educational ghetto', an efficacious means of legitimating the status quo with its in-built discrimination against the underprivileged community groups (6). It may even be seen by such groups themselves as soaking up social and political unrest and dissent, without fundamentally changing the distribution of power and resources in society (7).

To avoid this pitfall, I suggest a holistic definition of multiculturalism is necessary, based on a view of culture which is both expressive and instrumental, and therefore politically 'power-sensitive' in order to achieve purchase on the need to formulate educational response to the contemporary 'fact' of multiculturalism in British society which is both descriptive and prescriptive. To link these definitions and policies to the currently popular issue of the core curriculum, its epistemological shape and complementary support, I draw on the work of Lawton and his colleagues, seeing curriculum as cultural transmission, and particularly his most recent work on the extrascholastic ramifications of curriculum development, seen as the selection, organisation and implementation of valued cultural capital (8).

As its touchstone, the paper takes the well-known and much quoted statement by Bernstein that:

> How a society selects, classifies, distributes, transmits and evaluates the educational knowledge it considers to be public, reflects both the distribution of power and the principles of social control. (9)

The statement quite clearly locates the power relationship between educational knowledge and social control as one of fundamental importance. Embedded in this is the idea that the one cannot change without the other and, if this is the case, there can be no introduction of 'real' effective multicultural education without disturbing the current distribution of power in society.

At the base of that issue, however, is the question of what is meant by multiculturalism, for much confusion arises, because the term remains undefined and it is unclear whether the word is being used as a word descriptive of a social 'fact' or prescriptive of an ideal world to be aimed at, or both. In this essay, multiculturalism is seen as a powerful marshalling ideology: a pattern of values and concepts, factual and normative used to explain social phenomena and to guide and influence political choices at individual, group and national levels (10). It can thus be descriptive (of the multicultural society which exists now) and prescriptive (in the sense of being used to justify a rather better and more equal distribution of resources and access to rewards in the multiculture of our children's society).

But the basic component of the word 'multicultural' is the word 'culture'; again a word subject to many interpretations, which may have many meanings and forms and may be manifest or implicit. Yet whether a society, prescribed or described, will be, or is, multicultural depends crucially on the definition of culture used. For the purposes of this essay, therefore, culture is defined as an interdependent network of ideals, values, conceptions, methods of thinking and communicating, customs and sentiments, used as a socio-ecological coping strategy by individuals and groups. In sum, it is society's nonmaterial socio-historical capital, furnishing mechanisms to interaction with the social and natural environment so as maximally to ensure the survival of the individual and the group of which he/she is a member. Culture is thus not only a message but, to use a well-worn dictum, it is also the communication and interaction medium. All accretions to the stock of culture, including ways of accruing, are effected through the membrane and operant of the existing stock and media. Valued selections of this cultural capital are considered so important as to merit special agencies for their preservation, supervision and transmission, and all new members of society are expected to acquire a basic capital: a process which is called enculturation.

Such definition of culture necessarily implies the existence of barriers as an integral part of culture. Just as an organism needs a barrier that we call a membrane to remain alive, so does a culture in order not to be diluted and then totally absorbed into the surrounding medium, and thus to cease to be an independently identifiable culture having well-defined limits. This is not to imply that the barrier, or membrane to continue the analogy, has to be totally impermeable. For, just as no barrier leads to the death of the culture, so does a totally impermeable one. Thus what is necessary for cultural evolution is the right balance of permeability: a balance which is crucial to effective long-term multiculturalism.

Seen in this light, multiculturalism takes on the descriptive meaning of alternative sets of the above stocks and media within separable, permeable membranes. Some of this capital of stocks and media will be held by only some of the members. Put simply and descriptively, multiculturalism means that there are many cultures existing within the same nation-state in permeable interaction with one another, absorbing from each other, evolving but without becoming so diluted as to cease to exist independently altogether. In such a context, a balanced cultural permeability is a predicate to survival.

But how does multiculturalism differ from other terms currently in use such as multiracialism and polyethnicity? The term multiculturalism may be considered to comprehend the two terms above as it also comprehends bilingualism and biculturalism. These latter are more restricted in meaning, perhaps even more precise in their way: the one, multiracialism refers to the existence within the one social system (it may be the nation-state) of several different races: caucasoid, negroid, etc. (examples of such societies would be the United States, Canada, Fiji, Australia and the United Kingdom). Polyethnic refers to the existence in the same social system (nation-state) of members of different national groups: in Australia, the Italians, Greeks, Jugoslavs, all of the same race, but deriving from different ethnic backgrounds. Within these ethnic groups there may well be further cultural differentiation based on language or religion as is manifest in the Jugoslav group in particular. Thus Britain is described as a multicultural - and not solely multiracial or polyethnic society, because the latter terms would exclude from recognition distinct cultures which are as legitimate, viable and functional as those based on race or ethnicity, and there are similar reservations about the terms bilingualism and biculturalism.

But is not multiculturalism within a single nation-state a contradiction in terms at best, or at worst a fundamental threat to the overall cultural cohesion and balance of a nation-state? This powerful argument has been too often neglected or even dismissed by advocates of multiculturalism (11). The concept of social cohesion generated by defined common values and characteristics and made explicit for analysis and critical appraisal, appear to be a potential seedbed, from which a closer understanding of both expressive and instrumental multiculturalism may grow. From that concept a link may be established to issues of the selection, transmission and evaluation of valued knowledge in society, and in this way, an understanding achieved of the role of schooling and school knowledge in the form of a core curriculum, in responding to and furthering multiculturalism.

But multiculturalism can also be a danger, for too high or rigid a barrier, too impermeable a membrane, too much multiculturalism in the sense of the pursuit of sectional culture to the neglect or exclusion of access or interaction with other cultures (and in particular that which is common within the multiculture, i.e. the common or core values of society), will set up a centrifugal tendency, leading to the disintegration of society. On the other hand, too much emphasis on a common culture will lead to the dilution and eventual absorption of other cultures in a centripetal tendency which will inevitably bring with it alienation and a reduction of the overall diversity of cultural capital available to society. This latter tendency would be considered also to bring with it a reduction in the economic capital available to society and may cause intolerable social and political tensions in the very fabric of society and particularly in the very fulcrum of its cultural transmission: the educational agencies including schools. Thus, the response to the question lies in achieving a cultural trade-off, analagous to a biological balance in the membranes of organisms, that will permit interaction without total absorption.

The dilemma is how to achieve an astute, sensitive and genuine balance of both core and alternative cultures, whereby each individual in society is at least bicultural in the sense of broadly embracing the core values (albeit in a democracy that one of these values will be that of critical questioning of those core values) and one or more sets of alternative values (12). This happens already in the vocational sphere, insofar as espousing the values of a particular occupational group (craftsman, technician, doctor, manager) does not exclude remaining within the mainstream culture. The important point, of course, is that in the cases quoted, the alternative cultures offer a functional mode, not just an expressive one, which as Bullivant points out, is a matter of life chances as well as life styles (13).

But here lies a further dilemma, and one which again is a nodal point for educational and epistemological innovation: namely how to provide for cultural transmission of both core and alternative values in a functional way, and thus avoid the trap of a 'folksy tokenism' which will in any case be the death of the alternative culture, in spite of strenuous lip-service to the contrary. One major response to this dilemma would appear to be found in arranging for that institution which par excellence has the function of cultural transmission, to be allocated the function of transmission of both a selection from the core culture (including components of the multiculture) and from complementary alternative cultures: a core curriculum with complementary alternative curricula (14).

Thus one answer to the question of what kind of educational response may be appropriate to the acceptance of the 'fact' of a multicultural society, is to be found in an appropriate process of cultural transmission where both descriptive and prescriptive accounts of multiculturalism are focussed on education. Such a multicultural education has inevitably to address itself to the consciousness of all participants in the nation-state, to dominant and dominated cultural groups, and the power relationships between them. Otherwise, it will remain a chimera of slender factual, *i.e.* descriptive import.

Whilst the clientele will be multicultural, and thus part of the cultural context which influences learning, the influence will be seen as illicit and will remain 'unrecognised'. Multiculturalism will be seen as being for 'ethnic minority groups' only and the acceptable culture will thus continue to be transmitted by the knowledge of production-line supervisors and chargehands (teachers) who are themselves committed officially to the transmission solely of the dominant culture. This indeed is the situation which, by and large persists in Britain at the moment, and it is referred to as cultural monism (15).

Sometimes schools and colleges have attempted to pursue multicultural education by attacking economically, socially and politically unimportant areas, either because they honestly believe that this is the easiest and safest entree to multicultural education, or because they are unaware of the power-political context in which educational knowledge is generated, legitimated and transmitted. Such tokenism is often supported by the knowledge-managers (in institutions of higher education and elsewhere) for it holds little danger for them and their charge: the transmission of the socially, economically and politically consequential knowledge, which affords access to mainstream rewards.

Herein lies a further problem in the construction of multicultural education in a democratic society. For democracy in education has come to mean equality of educational opportunity. This ideology has been well legitimated, in spite of the manipulation of the pursuit of this goal so that the majority population (proletariat) in western market economies have been sold the pass. In those societies, structural inequalities have remained stubbornly unbending throughout the period of ascendancy of the ideology of 'equality of opportunity' (16).

If we juxtapose one of the declared component values of democracy, namely equality of opportunity, with the reality of the definition of curriculum implicit in today's formal schooling, the mismatch becomes apparent. Democracy may be seen as the right to freedom of choice within the law, whereas the knowledge and values preferred by educational institutions represent a highly eclectic version of available contemporary culture: neither democratically arrived at nor balanced - and certainly not as measured against the contemporary, technological and multicultural society in Britain (17). The selection is presided over by high priests of epistemology, and the result is, for many, exclusion and, to many, a lopsidedness to the point of capsize.

It is worthy of note that one of the major reasons why there has been so much activity in the last few years in the field called the 'core curriculum', has been the increasing and by now critical difficulty in legitimating the present curricular situation in a technological, urban, industrialised and multicultural society. To use Habermas' terms, a mounting rationality crisis arises because an increasingly large number of people become aware of the contradiction between the ideology claimed and the state's actions (18). Thus the need arises from pressing social exigencies to lock the concept of multicultural education firmly onto the core curriculum.

Given that we live in a highly technological, industrial, multicultural politico-economy which places heavy emphasis on a market economy, demanding high levels of skill not least in such basic fields as literacy and numeracy and needing to generate new knowledge and products to continue to exist, one would have expected, as a visitor of logical mind from another planet, an emphasis in the school curriculum on polytechnical education, on economics, on a knowledge at the very least of the cultures represented in our society, on capitalising on the languages of those cultures in a way which would yield economic results, on newer technological skills and on a basic minimum level of technological and scientific skills for all. Yet the vast majority of children have no access to any kind of economic skills, they relinquish their science at 16+ or even earlier, they do not speak any foreign language, they have little if any technological expertise and many, many of them leave school with extremely low levels of numeracy and literacy. Above all, they know little or nothing of the 'British multiculture'. There are other anomalies too: the sexist nature of schools, continuing recognition for dead languages but none for bilingualism (except in Wales), denominational education for some cultural groups but not for others, state financed religious education for some but not for others, etc. All of these, and more, deficiencies seem to point to the compelling logic of a new core curriculum with complementary alternatives as being appropriate for a multicultural society. Central to this task is the definition, and not solely in cognitive or even subject matter terms, of what the core should provide in a democratic industrial, multicultural, market politico-economy, formulated in cultural power-process terms.

Surprisingly, a number of official documents in Britain have recently come close to recognition of the problem even if not of its intricacy. The Consultative Document published in 1977 spoke of the aims of schools as including "to instil respect for moral values, for other people and for oneself, and tolerance of other races, religions, and ways of life" (19). Rather passive perhaps and old-fashioned, even Victorian, in the concept of 'to instil' but a broader outlook is provided by the next aim: "to help children understand the world in which we live and the interdependence of nations" (20). Unfortunately, however, the active components of interdependence, interpersonal skills, of intercultural competence and learning are missing, as is the process dimension, although the text does continue to probe towards the need for a core.

Then too, the HMI document is peppered with references, the implications of which are a multicultural education as a determinant of the core curriculum (21). Whilst 'lumped' with disadvantaged and handicapped pupils, pupils from ethnic minorities are recognised as existing and they "may have learning difficulties which require special help" (22). Schools are noted as having, "for example, to consider the curricular implications of the racial and cultural diversity of contemporary society" (23). For the curriculum of the primary school, it is noted that the mother tongue of new entrants may not be English. Studies of "the beliefs and ways of life of historical characters and of people and communities, who live today in other parts of the world or indeed elsewhere in Britain", are advocated and a little later the admission is made that these studies are valuable in their own right. This is especially so in a country that is multicultural (24). There are also further relevant references to "Britain's role overseas today and in former times", the "conditions under which children live in other parts of Britain and abroad", the influence of "the major world faiths" and to helping children to understand (sic) our multicultural society (25). Whilst the recent Schools Council publication on the curriculum is muted on such a 'practical' issue (26) the DES Framework for the Curriculum (27) and its successor document do at least manifest an explicit recognition that "our society has become multicultural; and there is now among pupils and parents a greater diversity of personal values" (28). But what about developing the intercultural competence, the skills, expertise and commitment to make the multicultural society work and improve it?

Perhaps it is unfair to expect the concept of a holistic and instrumental understanding of multicultural education, seen as a central aspect of cultural transmission, to emerge from official documents at this stage. And yet others seem to be tackling that problem.

A publication of the Curriculum Development Centre in Canberra, for instance, sets out what it terms "Universal Aims of Education" and it is worth repeating them here for they have a very loud and clear message for curriculum developers in Britain. The document states: "Among the most fundamental aims of education are:

> the nurturing and development of the powers of reasoning, reflective and critical thinking, imagining, feeling and communicating among and between persons;
>
> the maintenance, development and renewal (and not merely the preservation) of the culture; that is of our focus and systems of thought, meaning and expression - such as scientific knowledge, the arts, languages and technology;
>
> the maintenance, development and renewal (and not merely preservation) of the social, economic and political order - including its underlying values, fundamental structures and institutions;
>
> the promotion of mental, physical, spiritual and emotional health in all people. (29)

As a point of departure for curriculum planning as applied to the British core, it would be interesting to seek to improve on them, but, as it is, they provide us with a useful set of bench marks for a core curriculum within a multicultural educational context, attentive both to the need for social cohesion and the acceptance of cultural pluralism. They offer a set of aims (with inherent values) which can be measured against the defined characteristics of the contemporary socio-ecological context and its needs. Cultural aims themselves, they can be used as systems for the selection and transmission of culture - or by extrapolation multiculture - as one of the major defined characteristics of British society. The document tries to define what a core curriculum ought to do, including: "acknowledge the plural, multicultural nature of our society and seek a form of cultural social integration which values interaction and free communication amongst diverse groups and subcultures, i.e. the common multiculture" (30), and as one of the core learnings of the core curriculum it sets 'interpersonal and intergroup relationships' (31). Nine areas of knowledge and experience are proposed and multicultural education, no doubt, draws on a number of 'domains'.

The gist of the argument is that, as society itself has a common culture and a multiculture, these should both be represented in the common core for all pupils. This would then be complemented by 'alternatives' and 'specials' from the multiculture for those who wished them. These could focus on particular aspects of the multicultural society's cultures in the form of provision for ethnic studies, for community languages, for English as a second language, etc. The pitfall to avoid is seeing such contributions as merely dealing with the frills. They have to be functional and to be seen to be socially valued to be merited for inclusion.

To be effective a core curriculum, responsive to the needs of a multicultural society, will need to foster for all children as a minimum three major cognitive and socio affective areas of culture seen instrumentally (as well as major expressive dimensions):

> A conceptual map of the pluralist society (including the development of understanding and awareness of the multicultural nature of society) (32);

> The development of intercultural competence and commitment (including an understanding of the nature of prejudice and its genesis from social, historical, economic, political and cultural macro- and micro-contexts);

> The ways in which a democratic market politico-economy seeks to provide equality of access to social rewards and economic resources (including a knowledge of the power-conflict situations in which intolerance and exploitation emerge).

The consequence of the acceptance of such guiding principles as being one element against which the core curriculum may be designed, will be that other areas of the core curriculum, such as literature, music, dance, crafts, cooking, games, sports, folktales, etc., will need to be tested for their sensitivity to our multiculture (33). The 'core' programme would need to respond to the above imperatives in an inter-cultural and inter-disciplinary way, in the sense of taking account of, but not being structured solely on, separate and distinct racial or ethnic groups or subjects, for such an 'apartheid' approach may actually strengthen stereotypes and prejudice rather than promote respect and acceptance (34). This process will inevitably involve the construction of instruments to evaluate 'multiculturally valid' materials and content (35).

Because multicultural education is a process, it cannot be pursued through a single unit, module, subject or programme (36). Rather its form will be inherent, expressed and active in the policies and aims, socialisation processes, structures, individual intergroup and community relationships and control mechanisms of institutions and the system as a whole, as well as in the core and other content.

The 'hidden curriculum' of curricular processes and situations thus needs to be explored, mapped and implemented in a way which is compatible with multiculturalism or it will covertly flaunt the high ideals of a 'cognitive core' (37). The core has to have a socio-affective as well as a cognitive dimension in the sense, for example, that it aims to develop not just the knowledge, understanding, awareness but also to provide the predispositions, skills and expertise to act in ways which are conducive to multicultural education: in short, not just cross-cultural awareness but cross-cultural competence and commitment. For such competence to be functional it has to be seen as a core value of society, one which gives access to mainstream access to mainstream rewards, so that, in this way, the preservation and development of biculturalism is seen to be recognised and supported by society in the allocation of symbolic and material resources and rewards. This is one of the keys to open up the dilemma of common culture, which is functional, and multiculture which is seen as expressive and non-functional; to overcome the problem of a declared commitment to preservation of community identities, language and cultures masking the operative value of their disregard and neglect.

But the penetration of multiculturalism as a core value into the fabric of the educational system raises another aspect of the curricular situations referred to above, namely the contextual, or more specifically organisational dimensions, both internal to the school and in terms of relationships with the community. In this respect, progress on the very modest baseline provided by the Taylor Report in 1977 has been poor (38). It is simply contradictory to include such intercultural knowledge, awareness and competence in the core curriculum, if they are not backed up by appropriate processual and organisational practices. The development of anything other than a bland cognitive lip-service to multicultural education means a fundamental change in the balance of power in schools and in their relationships with their communities (39). (It also implies a change in power relationships in other sectors too, for instance in higher education and not least teacher education, for the teacher force or most of it will have to be gradually retrained to enable it to undertake the new tasks and develop the new competence. The concern in this paper is, however, with the school and it is there that the main thrust of the argument must remain.)

What, we may ask, are the organisational practices and teaching-learning processes which may culturally reciprocate the core values of multiculturalism? An initial list might be provided if we were to ask questions such as:

1. How is the basic data about the multicultural society of Britain in the 1980s presented? What kind of a conceptual map of the multiculture is provided? How?

2. Are the teaching methods consciously aimed at developing intercultural competence and the concept of cultural inter-learning amongst staff, students and with the community?

3. Does the organisation recognise different cultural 'qualifications' and capital? In which ways?

4. What part does the local community play in influencing the organisation and curriculum of the institution?

5. How culturally sensitive is the climate of the institution?

6. How far is the style of governance of the institution organic, how far bureaucratic, closed and mechanistic?

7. Does the organisation implicitly disadvantage certain cultural groups for no other reason than their culture?

8. How far is the institution open to client and community evaluation?

9. In what ways is that community potently involved in decisions concerning the institution and its programmes.

Such is a no doubt incomplete and initial list of questions intended to be no more than indicative of some of the issues, to which each institution will need to address itself in the pursuit of a multicultural education appropriate to a multicultural society as present fact and future (improved) aspiration. The responses will quite healthily differ from institution to institution and from locality to locality, for in the multicultural society there are no monolitic solutions (40). They will require a recognition, as in the Australian document, of different means to universal ends, common certification from different settings, (41) but will exclude the subconscious drift approach to curriculum development as a response to financial crises in education revealed by a recent survey (42).

A modest list of initial principles for the core curriculum might include those which enable students: to recognise, understand and value the culturally diverse nature of society; to develop a critical appreciation of their own culture; to gain an understanding of cultural backgrounds different from their own; and, to acquire the necessary values, predispositions, skills and expertise to function positively, productively and with cultural sensitivity in a pluralist society (43). The important need is for the full acceptance of multicultural education as an instrumental survival strategy for contemporary British society in correcting for current individual, group and societal crises, and its function in the selection, organisation and implementation of the core curriculum.

NOTES

1. An earlier version of this paper was published as "Multicultural Education and the Core Curriculum', Curriculum in March, 1982. I am grateful to the Editor of that journal for his permission to reproduce the bulk of that paper here.
2. In Department of Education and Science, Local Authority Arrangements for the School Curriculum, (London: HMSO, 1979), it was revealed that on answering the question "what about promoting racial understanding?" almost one third of LEAs said that this was not a major problem. Only one in ten of the authorities said that they encouraged the appointment of teachers and other staff who themselves came from ethnic minority communities.
3. Apart perhaps from Section 71 of the 1976 Race Relations Act.
4. The results of surveys available by early 1982 were depressing to say the least. See, for example, Giles, R. and Cherrington, D. (1982), Multicultural Teacher Education in the United

Kingdom: A Survey of Courses and Other Provisions in British Institutions of Higher Education, London: Commission for Racial Equality.

5. See inter alia Sikes, P.J., Teaching About Race Relations, (Norwich: CARE, 1979). Two books from the Schools Council Project "Education for a multiracial Society" were due for publication in June, 1981: a main book and an evaluation study.

6. This point was made by a Parliamentary Select Committee which reported in mid 1981. See House of Commons, Home Affairs Committee, (1981) Fifth Report: Racial Disadvantage, London: HMSO, p. LXVI.

7. See Stone, M., (1981) The Education of the Black Child in Britain, Glasgow: Fontana.

8. See, for example, Lawton, D. (1975), Class, Culture and the Curriculum, London: Routledge and Kegan Paul.

9. Bernstein, B. (1971) "On the Classification and Framing of Educational Knowledge" in Young, M.F.D., Knowledge and Control (New Directions for the Sociology of Education), London: Collier Macmillan, p. 47.

10. See Gould, J. and Kolb, W.L. (eds.) (1964), A Dictionary of the Social Sciences, London: Tavistock, p. 315, adapted.

11. A number of documents and publications abroad have recently addressed themselves to this problem, however, see Australia, Commonwealth Education Portfolio (1979) Discussion Paper on Education in a Multicultural Society. Canberra (1979) and an unpublished report to the Canberra Curriculum Development Centre Council, Interim Advisory Panel to the Curriculum Development Centre Council (1979) "Education for a Multicultural Society: Concept and Implications". Canberra: CDC. Amongst the areas included were parliamentary democracy, economic opportunity for betterment of the individual, the English language, equality before the law and freedom of the individual to a private sphere.

12. Linton, R. (1936) The Study of Man, New York: Appleton-Century.

13. Bullivant, M.B. (1979) "The STEPS Case Against Multicultural Education: Some Cross National Findings", in Rowley, G. (ed.) Proceedings of the 1979 Annual Conference of the Australian Association for Research in Education, Melbourne: AARE. I am also indebted to Dr. Bullivant for providing me with much useful and stimulating information during my stay in Australia and particularly in discussions at

Monash University in Melbourne, where he outlined his case against Multicultural Education. A summary of his arguments is contained in Bullivant, B.M., "Multiculturalism: No", Education News (1980) Vol. 17, No. 2, June, pp. 17-20.

14. Some recent English and Scottish official publications seem to increasingly favour the idea of a 'core' and elective areas, albeit from a subject-centred point of view. See Department of Education and Science and Welsh Office (1980) A Framework for the School Curriculum, January and Scottish Education Department Consultative Committee on the Curriculum (1977) The Structure of the Curriculum in the Third and Fourth Years of the Scottish Secondary School, Edinburgh: Her Majesty's Stationery Office. Note that Circular 14/77 on local authority arrangements for the curriculum "did not directly approach this problem" DES (1980), op. cit., p. 5. Lawton points out however, that the secret "Yellow Book" appeared to herald DES conversion to the idea of a common core curriculum, that the Great Debate document Educating Our Children took up the issue in paras. 2.1 to 2.18 and that the Curriculum 11-16 document takes up the question of the distinction between common and core curricula. See Lawton, D. (1980) The Politics of the School Curriculum, London: Routledge and Kegan Paul.

15. These points have recently been discussed in Jeffcoate, R. (1979) Positive Image: Towards a Multicultural Curriculum, London and Richmond: Readers and Writers Co-operative in Conjunction with Chameleon Books.

16. In a recent lecture, Lawton has envisaged democracy as one of the two most important features of contemporary British society; the other being industrialization, and democracy is certainly one facet of the current ideological profiles of British society. (An equally important feature of contemporary British society is its multiculturalism). See Lawton, D. (1979) Curriculum Planning and Technological Change, (The Stanley Lecture) London: Royal Society of Arts.

17. Lawton rightly identifies technology as being one of the missing pieces, Lawton (1979), op. cit.

18. Habermas, J. (1976) Legitimation Crisis, London: Heinemann. Whilst it is beyond the scope of this article to pursue the issues involved, it must be pointed out that Habermas sees occurrences in market economies as issuing from just such problems in steering the economy as Britain is experiencing

at the moment and sees identity crises as connected with these steering problems, creating secondary problems that affect consciousness in such a way as to endanger social cohesion. See Habermas, op. cit., p. 4. The implicit argument of this article is that multicultural education, manifest in both core and complementary components of a reformed school curriculum, is needed both for reasons of social cohesion and identity development if the current legitimation crisis is to be attenuated.

19. Secretary of State for Education and Science and Secretary of State for Wales (1977) <u>Education in Schools: A Consultative Document</u>, London: Her Majesty's Stationery Office, p. 6.

20. Op. cit., p. 7.

21. Department of Education and Science (1980) <u>A View of the Curriculum</u> (HMI Series: Matters for Discussion 11) London: Her Majesty's Stationery Office.

22. Department of Education and Science (1980), op. cit., p. 2.

23. Ibid., p. 5.

24. Ibid., p. 7.

25. Ibid., pp. 10-11.

26. Schools Council (1981) <u>The Practical Curriculum</u>, London: Methuen Educational, Schools Council Working Paper 70.

27. Department of Education and Science, Welsh Office, (1980) <u>A Framework for the School Curriculum</u>, London: DES, p. 3, para. 9, iv and v.

28. Department of Education and Science, Welsh Office, (1981) <u>The School Curriculum</u>, London: HMSO, p. 3, para, 11, and loc. cit., p. 6, para. 21.

29. Australia, Curriculum Development Centre (1980) <u>Core Curriculum for Australian Schools</u>, Canberra: CDC.

30. Ibid., p. 15.

31. Ibid., p. 16.

32. In spite of current 'uneasiness' in the United States about multicultural education and its replacement in some cases by intergroup and interpersonal education seen less controversially, a number of State Departments have continued to produce materials and curricula addressing multicultural education. One curricular strategy used by the Illinois Chicago Project for Interethnic Dimensions in Education is to explore the processes of entry by several ethnic groups into the United States as a means of providing both understanding and empathy. See State Board of Education, Illinois Office of Education (1977) <u>Entry into the United</u>

States, Illinois, July, and for details of policies and practices for the whole school in the field of multicultural education, see Illinois State Board of Education, (1980) Planning for Ethnic Education: A Handbook for Planned Change, Illinois, January.

33. It is important to emphasize that it is not claimed that the ideology of multiculturalism is the only imperative to which the core curriculum will need to be attentive. A more extensive exposition of the implicit of an 'interdependent' ideology such as multiculturalism is contained in Lynch, J. (1979) Education for Community: A Cross-Cultural Society in Education, London: Macmillan, pp. 53-69, and particularly pp. 66-68.

34. This point is made in a recent American document. See California State Department of Education (1979) Planning for Multicultural Education as a Part of School Improvement, Sacramento: Office of Intergroup Relations, pp. 9-10.

35. One example of such an approach is Illinois State Board of Education, A Guide for Evaluating and Selecting Multicultural Instructional Materials, Illinois, n.d.

36. This is the argument of a number of American advocates of multicultural education. See, for instance, Banks, J. (1977) Multi-ethnic Education: Practices and Promises, Bloomington, Indiana: The Phi Delta Kappa Educational Foundation.

37. A number of American publications have sought to make a contribution to the derivation of multicultural education from cultural diversity. See, for example, Gold, M.J. et al. (1977) In Praise of Diversity: A Resource Book, Washington, D.C., Teacher Corps: Association of Teacher Educators; Grant, C.A. (ed.) (1977) Multicultural Education: Commitments, Issues and Applications, Washington, D.C.: Association for Supervision and Curriculum Department; Morris, L. et al. (eds.) (1978) Extracting Learning Styles from Social/Cultural Diversity, South West Teacher Core Network.

38. Department of Education and Science and Welsh Office (1977) A New Partnership for Our Schools (The Taylor Report), London: HMSO. Less than 20% of LEA responses to Circular 14/77 made reference to steps to involve parents in helping schools promote racial understanding. See Department of Education and Science, Welsh Office, (1979) Local Authority Arrangements for the School Curriculum, London: HMSO, p. 67.

39. An interesting, if modest, document produced by the New South Wales Department of Education, identifies a number of school management practices which may foster the development of multi-cultural education. See New South Wales, Department of Education (1979) "Multicultural Education Policy Statement", Sydney: NSW, Department of Education, pp. 2-3.

40. In any case, there is an increasingly strong current of opinion which identifies school-based curriculum development as being the most effective and realistic mode of curriculum development. This is perfectly consistent with the idea of objectives as value explicit procedural principles rather than terminal goals found in much of the contemporary curriculum development literature. See, for instance, Stenhouse, L., "Some Limitations on the Use of Objectives in Curriculum Research and Planning", <u>Paedagogica Europaea</u> (1970), 6, pp. 73-83.

41. A good model for this might be the Schools Council History, Geography, Social Science Project.

42. See Venning, P., "Overloading the System", <u>Times Educational Supplement</u> (1980) 31st October, p. 10.

43. I am aware that I have cut a number of corners in this paper in the interests of brevity. For instance, I have 'skipped' discussion of the 'categorical imperative' of Western multicultural society, to aim for "respect for persons". I have, however, presented complementary arguments in a later publication. See Lynch, J., <u>The Multicultural Curriculum</u>, London: Batsford, 1983 forthcoming, especially Chapter One.

Chapter Nine

CHILDREN'S BOOKS AND ETHNIC MINORITIES

Gajendra K. Verma
and Kanka Mallick

INTRODUCTION

With post-war migration from the former Commonwealth Countries in the Caribbean, Africa, India, Pakistan and Bangladesh, Britain has become a multi-ethnic, multicultural society. Because the large majority of migrants were young, there is an increasing number of children of West Indian and Asian parents in British schools. As early as 1970 a survey of 146 local authorities in England and Wales (Townsend, 1971) found that there were 263,710 such children in British schools. Of this number, 29 percent came from, or had parents from, the Indian subcontinent.

Given this situation, there is a greater need than before to ensure that children from non-English speaking groups become fluent in the language of their 'host' country. There are, however, serious gaps in the provision of suitable reading materials for ethnic minority children, and in addition a paucity of books (in English) dealing with the countries of origin of many minority groups - their cultural, social, religious and historical heritages. The provision of such material serves two purposes. First, they bring to ethnic minority children a sense of pride and a knowledge of the land of their ancestors. Second, books which portray the antiquity and the richness of other civilisations and cultures, may serve the host nation in promoting multi-racial understanding and tolerance.

Essentially, in multi-ethnic classrooms, children should learn not only to be secure in and magnanimously proud of their cultural heritage, but should also learn to know and respect the cultural heritage of their fellow-pupils. There is a need therefore, for appropriate reading and reference materials which will enable children to grasp the idea that the world is not homogenous and that different people have different ways of doing essentially the same things, as well as differing values and religious systems. If we ignore the literature from other cultures we are depriving all our pupils of a great deal of potential enjoyment and enrichment.

The present research has been concerned with identifying the gap between the ideal of 'multi-cultural' education (to which most of those involved in education would pay at least lip service) and the reality of actual provision and practice in the classroom. In terms of textbooks and general materials, we are conscious of under-representation of minority ethnic groups and some tendencies towards stereotypic presentation where such groups are represented in written materials. Our observation is in line with most research findings in this area - that minority groups are misrepresented in textbooks by failure to note their positive contributions and qualities, and by leaving out discussion of the present-day situation of minorities.

In considering the contribution of books to curriculum development, one must recognise that a barrier to systematic innovation in any sector of the educational market is the structure of the educational system itself; the limitation of central direction (which many educators consider a blessing) and the autonomy maintained by individual headmasters and classroom teachers renders the task of producing innovative materials in a competitive market situation extremely problematic (Hodges, 1979). In the instance of even specialised language provision where the needs of ethnic minorities are widely recognised, it may be difficult to obtain a second printing of a basic textbook in relatively wide use. The issue of 'multi-cultural' materials is in marketing terms, complex and controversial. For example, whilst coming down firmly in favour of 'multi-cultural' education throughout Britain, the 1972-73 Select Committee on Race Relations and Immigration still found it difficult to accommodate the view that a serious look should be taken at biased teaching materials:

> Such books exist but we think it wise to keep a sense of proportion. Some of our witnesses listed unsuitable works of fiction for the young. Even if they do contain racial

innuendos we doubt whether many of them are
recommended reading in schools. Education
authorities cannot be held responsible for what
is in the public libraries. (On Education, p.
27, D.E.S.)

Part of our research has been concerned with
testing the veracity of such a statement. Simply
the fact that it can be made, however, is also of
importance. Our survey of Middle Schools in two
education authority shows that there are signs of a
resistance to the 'multi-cultural/antiracialist'
approach amongst members of the teaching profession.
It is also clear, however, from the present study
that teachers in multi-cultural situations are
anxious to use appropriate materials, and would like
to see that more materials are available.

SURVEY OF MIDDLE SCHOOLS

One of the dimensions of this research was a survey
of headteachers of middle schools (with pupils aged
10 to 14) in five selected Education Authorities
throughout Britain in order to discover the provision and need for books (both fiction and non-fiction) to meet the specific requirements of ethnic
minority pupils in schools. The postal questionnaire was designed specifically:

(a) to ascertain whether teachers feel the
need for this type of book in their teaching situation;

(b) to discover whether teachers can easily
locate the source of such material;

(c) to identify the areas where increased
provision should be made to meet the future needs of
the pupils.

As happens with most surveys, not all Local
Education Authorities approached were willing to
participate in the research. In fact, of the five
authorities contacted only two agreed to co-operate
in the study. It would appear from replies from
some Directors of Education that there is even some
resistance building up amongst advisers and educators to any emphasis on research into aspects of
multi-cultural education. One of the five authorities refusing to take part in the study wrote:

>...the staff here, these days, are extremely hard-pressed, as are teachers, and I am not prepared to ask them to undertake any additional work whatsoever. But even more than this, you may like to know that this Authority has been approached by five different national bodies in the last few months to provide facilities for research into various aspects of multi-cultural education. At least three of these projects covered much the same ground, so that I was bound to wonder whether our left hand knows what our right hand is doing, and whether educationists these days are interested in other matters apart from multi-cultural education...

The other two authorities refused to co-operate because they felt that all those connected with education were under great pressure and the completion of the questionnaire would add further burdens to them. In the two authorities which participated in the survey, forty-eight schools provided information. These schools, with a roll of 31,671 pupils had 4,908 pupils of ethnic minorities, representing nearly 16 percent of the school population in these two authorities.

Eighty-five percent of the schools felt that it was important to provide books (of both fiction and nonfiction) to meet the needs of ethnic minorities. Fiftyfour percent of the schools provided books 'specifically for ethnic minority children'.

A minority of schools - 44 percent - thought that textbooks which gave more attention to the perspective of colonised peoples on their role in history and current affairs would be helpful to ethnic minority children. This implies that many white teachers would consider an emphasis on the colonial aspect of the history of ethnic minority children to be undesirable, for a variety of reasons.

A considerable majority of schools in both areas - 83 percent - were of the opinion that literature which draws attention to the history, culture, religion and folk heritage of ethnic minority children would be very helpful. Similarly, a substantial majority of the sample (73 percent) favoured the inclusion of literature which refers to the significant role that ethnic minorities play in the contemporary everyday life in Britain. On the other hand, there was little support (33 percent) for literature which portrays ethnic minority children as being identical to English boys and girls. There was considerable support (78 percent) for literature which contains general information about ethnic minorities, but teachers seemed unwilling to accept books which depicted the oppression and exploitation of slavery and colonialism, and the extensions of that oppression into modern British society.

Analyses of the data from forty-eight schools showed considerable support amongst teachers for literature which draws attention, however, to the concept of a multicultural, multi-ethnic society. A small proportion of schools (16 percent) felt that they were well-informed concerning the availability of such materials, and 87 percent (the figure for both LEAs) of schools felt that it would be helpful to have lists of publishers and/or their catalogues showing the range of such books. Eighty percent of the schools indicated that they would be prepared to allocate some of their capitation allowances on books (of both fiction and non-fiction types) for ethnic minorities _if_ they considered them suitable.

It must be mentioned that if such books became increasingly available it would still be essential that teachers should be trained to identify those books which are unsuitable for use in a multi-cultural context. If carefully prepared books are increasingly available for a multi-cultural market, much of the impact accruing from this changed situation will be negated if children are still exposed to materials which are guilty of tokenism (where the arbitrary, solitary and standardised black face or character are included), stereotyping (with the attribution of supposed characteristics of a group to all its individual members, and with the often vicarious reinforcement of prejudice), distortion (where, for example, the impression may be given that all black people live in primitive conditions) and emotive, derogatory or derisive language used in connection with minority groups. The research conducted by Brittan (1976) showed that a high proportion of the teaching force perceived ethnic minority pupils in stereotyped and biased terms. In the event of such a trend being perceived by the publishing industry, it is likely to be difficult to obtain publication of multi-cultural material.

If teachers are to develop the skills to vet the reading materials available for use in a multi-cultural situation, they not only need to be aware of their own prejudices but also need to acquire the skills to identify those books which are racially and culturally biased, and therefore unsuitable for use. Although in-service courses may help to meet these needs it is obvious that neither the resources nor the time is available to adopt such measures on a national scale. It would seem essential therefore that valid and reliable checklists for identifying suitable literature and textbooks need to be available. It would be naive to assume, especially in the present economic situation, that teachers are going to remove texts from their classroom because they have derogatory or racialist implications.

In view of the comments made by schools there seemed to be considerable support for books which were not only relevant to ethnic minority groups but would also be valuable in providing indigenous white children with a healthy understanding about a multi-cultural society. From a practical point of view there would be greater likelihood of publishers producing suitable materials if they could be assured of a viable market. They would also like to have some indication that headteachers are likely to expend increasingly limited resources on purchasing books which have a wider appeal, i.e. for all children in the multi-cultural context rather than children of any particular ethnic background. The latter observation is more relevant in the light of a recent British report which draws attention to the reluctance of many schools to allocate sufficient funds to the purchase of books. These points are supported by the evidence obtained in this research which is outlined in the following section.

SURVEY OF EDUCATIONAL PUBLISHERS

In order to gain some idea of the current state of the market a survey of 22 publishers of children's books and educational material, their response to current market trends and their attitude to 'multi-cultural' material was conducted by use of a postal questionnaire.

Four of the publishers contacted indicated that they were no longer educational publishers, and four declined to answer the questionnaire but expressed their willingness to discuss the issues raised.

Replies from eight publishers formed the basis for ascertaining current market trends and the extent of their interest and expertise in the field of multi-cultural education. Sixty-eight percent of their publications over the past five years have by their accounts, been appropriate for children up to the age of thirteen years, and of these publications 22 percent have been of the formal textbook type, with 78 percent being classified as literature. As mentioned in the section on the schools survey, publishers seem sensitive to the needs of the schools, and are willing to cater for the increasing demand for different types of literature. Most of the production by publishers appears (from the response given by 84 percent) to be of new materials and not of re-runs. There was a clear indication from the publishers' response that the overall number of childrens' books sold in Britain is increasing. However, the greatest upsurge according to them, seems to be for picture books with a decline in demand for fiction and hardbacks. Most of the publishers felt that overall demand would remain steady, but that any growth with reading books would be in the 5-8 year old age range. It was also evident from the questionnaire data that there has been an increasing demand for pre-school children's books, especially of the colour picture book type. Although quota cut-backs and the closing or cutback in Nursery schools was anticipated as a factor in restricted demand, they thought that continued lack of reading skills would help maintain the increase in demand for coloured picture books!

The fact that Britain now has an expanding ethnic minority population implies that there would be an increasing demand for books depicting children of different ethnic origins within British society. It was recognised by most publishers that there is a lack of apparently suitable material in this direction, especially from good writers of appropriate ethnic backgrounds. Publishers thought that demand was still limited and localised. Some publishers had mentioned that they had to rely on Black American authors to write materials for ethnic minority needs because of the dearth of writers in this country. Responses to the questionnaire clearly indicated that most publishers were cautious about any anticipated increase in the demand for books as a result of an increasing ethnic minority school population.

Publishers were also asked to comment on the social and political desirability of having specialist literature appropriate to children of ethnic minority groups living in Britain's inner city areas. Opinions of the publishers varied on this crucial issue. Some felt it was socially and politically desirable to have such materials but because of the relatively small numbers involved, they did not think it economically viable unless the materials are geared for the international market. Others stressed the inadvisability of having specialist literature designed for ethnic minority groups in inner city areas, but recognised the desirability of having books of a good literary standard portraying ethnic minority children in different situations and settings of contemporary British society. This kind of material, according to them, would appeal to children of all races, religions and cultures.

Comments by publishers seem to suggest that there is a need for more systematic research into the means and principles of generating the production of materials appropriate for ethnic minority groups as such, and also for the production of literature appropriate for multicultural education. If materials of the former category are to be produced by commercial publishers it may be necessary for some form of indirect subsidy or guarantees concerning sales to be provided, possibly along the lines of support provided by the Welsh Education Books Council in respect of Welsh language publications. It would be appropriate to involve members of the ethnic minorities in defining the appropriate boundaries of the literature and in producing potential material for publication.

While the questionnaire placed the emphasis on the production of textbooks and literature it is obvious that there is scope for further research into the production of the worksheet booklet resource package which may be acceptable by many publishers as a viable means of catering for a specialised need. There are some Teachers' Centres (Birmingham, Bradford, Huddersfield) who are already engaged in producing materials suitable as teaching kits.

If ways could be found of concentrating the work to be produced by various Teachers' Centres under one agency, then it is most likely that the output could be substantial, of a high enough standard and therefore more commercially viable. Support similar to that given by the Schools Council in respect of the production of second language materials could be extremely useful in generating specialist literature for ethnic minority children and literature depicting ethnic minority children in different environments of contemporary British society.

CLASSROOM MATERIAL AND ETHNIC MINORITIES

The importance of racially or culturally biased material in influencing the affective and cognitive domains of both 'immigrant' and 'indigenous' pupils has received variable attention in Britain. Some studies of the 'problems of immigrant school children' are concerned only with the adaptation of the immigrant to the 'British way of life' (Scott, 1971), and with assisting formal learning difficulties. A survey by Her Majesty's Inspectors (D.E.S., 1972) of 54 Secondary Schools in sixteen Boroughs, all with a high proportion of ethnic minority pupils showed that there was little evidence of curriculum modification to take account of minority pupils. Others fully recognise the problematic nature of much educational material; but are more concerned with the content analysis of the material rather than measuring it's effect (Dixon, 1977; Hannam, 1978). Some work has attempted to analyse the impact of racism in culture and mass media on children (Milner, 1975; Verma and Bagley, 1979; Bagley and Verma, 1979; Bagley, Verma, Mallick and Young, 1979) but there has been little detailed research at the level of the school and the classroom. An evaluation of curriculum innovation emphasised the need for in-service training programmes to help teachers to examine the curriculum of their subject areas in order to avoid cultural, religious or historical bias in presentation (Verma, 1977).

The literature in this area seems to suggest that there are three principal elements in the presentation of material in the classroom which may generate negative forms of learning in terms of 'multi-cultural education':

a) The attitude of the teacher to his or her students, and their backgrounds.
b) The text or material, which in itself may carry positive or negative images of ethnic minority groups.
c) The students, who may fail altogether to appreciate the racism of a particular piece, or may interpret the negative stereotype in terms of his or her own characteristics, where no adverse aspects are perceived in the material by the teacher.

To elaborate on these points: material which attempts to inform all students on, for example, the cultural background of 'Asian immigrants', may result in unfavourable stereotyping of these very groups, whilst explicitly racist material <u>could</u> be used by some teachers to expose the ludicrous nature of many racial myths, and/or the role of literature in producing contemporary racism. However, it may be possible that such an interpretation of the material would be <u>rejected</u> by students who have internalised racist ideology. The difficulties and pitfalls in teaching about race relations are illustrated in the writings of Stenhouse (1975); Jenkins et al. (1979); Bagley and Verma (1982).

CASE STUDY RESEARCH IN SCHOOLS

The study was undertaken with the full cooperation of the headmasters of the two middle schools in Bradford. The first, School A, was an inner city school, and the second, School B, was a suburban school in the Bradford commuter belt. Thus, the two environments were different.

Two classes selected for the purposes of research contained pupils of 11-12 age range. The children of School A were of mixed ability, and those of School B had less wide-ranging abilities. School A had only 46 percent of its pupils from European ethnic backgrounds; the majority of the remainder were Muslim children with parents from Pakistan. In contrast, very few children in School B came from other than the English ethnic group.

On the basis of previous research and discussions with teachers it was decided to restrict the research to non-fictional textbooks in the area of geography. Two research workers attended and analysed a geography lesson as participant observers. At the end of teaching, they directed a group discussion about the lesson and the pupils' images of the Third World in general. One of the research workers acted as interviewer while the other took notes of pupils' responses. A third observer was also introduced at the suburban school in order to assess how this particular lesson and discussion were conducted. The pupils in the class were unaware of the purpose of the study.

In School A, the geography lesson was structured about the people of the Nile Valley, and in School B it was concerned with the Boro of the Amazon Basin. However, both the schools used the same books as a basic text, and the general syllabus was almost identical. This meant that pupils in the two schools could be directed to discuss about their images of the Third World in general and the two areas mentioned above in particular.

The following specific questions were raised about the materials used in teaching the geography lesson:

    a. The date of the text's publication;
    b. Suitability for a multi-cultural, multi-racial society;
    c. The sensitivity of approach;
    d. The images of the people who were portrayed in the text.

The discussion with the children at the end of teaching was directed to include the images that they had of:

    (a) The Third World Countries themselves;
    (b) The inhabitants of those countries;
    (c) Their economy
    (d) Their lifestyle.

Other questions encouraged the children to make contrasts and comparisons between their images of the Third World and Britain. The final questions were posed to assess the children's general impressions of Third World countries and their reactions to those countries and Britain. All the questions were presented to the group in a manner which eleven and twelve year olds would be able to relate.

The study took place in the presence of the children's usual teacher in order that the situation was not too threatening and because the study was concerned with the interaction of pupils with material with teacher. However, there were certain problems with this. It was suggested by the observer that some of the more reticent pupils might have been more vocal if their teacher had not been present, but it proved difficult to obtain an interview in the classroom without the teacher. On the other hand there was a certain amount of attention seeking on the part of some of the pupils. The independent observer agreed that the interviewer did encourage most of the pupils to respond and that she did manage to obtain an idea of the imagery of individual members of the class as well as a group opinion. She also attempted to respond to individuals if there was obvious disagreement to the general flow of the discussion.

Table 1.1: Pupils in the Study

Ethnic Group	School A Boys	School A Girls	School B Boys	School B Girls
South Asian	8	8	0	0
West Indian	2	0	0	0
European	5	3	11	11

The interviewers were West Indian females. The fact that the experimenters were black may have influenced responses in a particular direction, but to what degree is unclear. The pupils expected the interviewers to share their image of the Third World, although some of the pupils did work out the aim of the experiment and gradually gave more 'acceptable' responses. This was particularly true of the inner city school where the teacher, disturbed by the biased comments which he had not expected, gave the children cues towards expected responses.

Spontaneous Comments on Economic Activity

School A: "They don't need money, people come from abroad and give them money". Despite the film on irrigation in the Nile Basin, one child believed that "Africans only grow things that survive without water". Some pupils showed a distinct 'Oxfam mentality', but others, in particular the South Asian pupils, emphasised contrasting types of employment in Britain, so their images of Europe included jobs and 'mills and factories'. One pupil had elements of a naive comprehension of 'exploitation' in Europe. He told the experimenters "They work for a living, we work for other people who give us money to buy what we want".

School B: "We use tractors and they use sticks". "They are like animals, they go hunting". The Third World was seen as 'primitive, with

Europeans at the top of a hierarchical scale and the Third World people very low in relation to Europe. They were seen as one step above the animals. International exchange between the two worlds was seen as a large scale bartering system. One child commented: "We give them motor cars. They give us bananas".

Lifestyle

School A: "In Cairo they have houses and grass huts". One South Asian girl did not identify with the British lifestyle despite the fact that she was born in Britain. She indicated her anomalous status when she said: "They (i.e. the British) live in a better modern way". Cairo, as a town which the pupils knew about, acted as a mediator in this sphere. Thus Cairo was described as "not as good as Britain, but better than (rural) Africa".

School B: "They never argue". "They can't read or write, they have no need to". The pupils were convinced that the European lifestyle was superior to that of the Third World. They attributed a great deal of importance to the European conception of education and ability and assumed that Third World people are 'simple' in all senses of that word.

Eurocentrism

School A: "I wouldn't like to live in those places. There are bugs, heat and disease. People like us aren't used to it, they are". The pupil's comments indicated hostility and contempt of Third World countries. They were aware of negative images but not the positive images of the Third World countries that they studied. The Asian and West Indian pupils seemed embarrassed to openly reject this Eurocentric approach to the Third World.

School B: "They live far away from Europe". The pupils tended to be ethnocentric. They categorised other people in relation to Europe. They assumed that Britain was superior in all respects, and that Third World people were beneficiaries of all things European. Although the children understood that raw food and materials are found in Third World countries, they did not see Europe as recipients of anything worthwhile from the Third World. They rejected the idea that Third World people could be inventors, assuming that knowledge and intelligence are European prerogative.

Stereotypes

School A: "You <u>can</u> tell them apart. People in Cairo wear better clothes". The pupils generally had no clear idea of members of the Third World as other than an undifferentiated group described in terms of general stereotypes. The pupils' knowledge of Cairo helped only a little. There was disagreement about the idea of the identical image of Third World people. Some pupils claimed that people in Cairo were individuals as they wore European clothes, which they described as 'better' than those worn in rural areas. Clothes distinguished them from other Africans and from each other.

School B: "They might eat us. They've never seen anything like us. They might think we're animals". The childrens' image of the Third World was of people identical in character and appearance. They had no conception of them as individuals. They believe that black people in the Third World were by and large hostile. They had an odd idea of their appearance which they assumed to be dirty, and had a distorted idea of the people's proximity to wild animals in their forest setting.

Analysis of the textbook

Despite its recent publication date the geography textbook used in both schools noticeably failed to understand or anticipate the backgrounds of all the recipients of its message. Its readership comprises young children of differing ethnic origins, yet the textbook does not really consider their interests. Its approach could in effect damage the developing self-esteem of ethnic minority children which, in turn, may affect their overall educational attainment.

IMAGES OF THE THIRD WORLD IN TEXTBOOK, LESSON PLAN AND PUPILS' COMMENTS

School A

Economy:
Third World: No Jobs
Europe: Employment (jobs, mills, factories)
Third World: Technology

Europe: Machines (houses, fridges) luxuries (cigarettes tinned food)
Pupil Comments: "In the Third World you go out and get food, in civilised countries, you go to the shops".

Lifestyle:
Third World: rags, or naked people. No clothes, grass huts
Europe: Clothing, sophisticated
Pupil Comments: "They get water from the river, ours comes from taps". "There are storms every day". One Asian girl said: "They (i.e. the British)
live in a better, modern way". Cairo acts as a mediator in this sphere: "Urban Cairo is <u>not as good as Europe</u> but better than those in England". "In Cairo they have houses and grass huts".

Eurocentrism:
Third World: Unattractive, oppressive (Mosquitos, heat disease)
Europe: Attractive
Pupil Comments: "They are isolated from the world".

Stereotyping:
Third World: dark skinned, fuzzy-haired, identical, live among wild animals
Europe: Individuals
Pupil Comments: "They are all dark skinned with fuzzy hair. You can't tell them apart".

School B

Economy:
Third World: Agriculture: sticks
   Trade: bananas
   Production: primitive, subsistence non-industrial, labour intensive
Europe: Agriculture: machinery
   Trade: motor cars
   Production: industrial, capital intensive service industry (shops, banks, etc.)
Pupil Comments: "We use tractors and they use sticks. They are like animals, they go hunting".

177

Communication:
Third World: Non-literate, i.e. skills and knowledge transmitted by parents. Small scale communication network; isolated (i.e. from Europe)
Pupil Comments: "They can't read or write, they have no need to".

Education:
Third World: No need to read or write.
Europe: Academic skill
Pupil Comments: "They would learn to read and write if they came to Europe. We would not learn anything if we went there except perhaps how to hunt animals".

Eurocentrism:
Third World: Inferior; recipients of goods; raw materials; beneficiaries of skills; recipients of superior knowledge
Europe: Superior; wealthier; material goods; inventors, initiators; superior knowledge
Pupil Comments: "If we went there we wouldn't learn anything but they would learn how to make things if they came here, how to make spades instead of sticks. They don't have factories they wouldn't know how to do it".

Stereotyping:
Third World: Black, oil (sic) skins; fuzzy hair (uncut hair and beards); animal skins as clothing (aprons around the waist); animals
Europe: White individuals; wear clothes
Pupil Comments: "They are dark-skinned - not like us - more like Pakistanis".

CONCLUSIONS

On the basis of the comments made by pupils in these two schools it appears that one of the most important sources of bias is the artists' impressions in illustrations. The texts which employed photographs are less likely to suffer from the effects of artistic license. The set text also assumed that there are 'national characteristics' which people can judge. Thus, school pupils are often told to categorise, draw contrasts between peoples and to judge others stereotypically.
The data obtained from the classroom research seemed to suggest that people from the Third World are perceived as weird and exotic. Their pattern of

similarities to Europeans are mostly ignored and the and the differences highlighted. For example, it is unusual to find black people in a manufactured world, such as urban Africa or white people in primitive surroundings such as poor areas of rural England.

Children in this study were asked to draw comparisons between themselves and the Boro in the text. Their responses clearly indicated that they have gained the impression that the individual European has a special role to play in Boro development, and what is more, that the European is responsible for the Boro.

The lesson plan in the classroom suggested that the description of the Boro gave no impression of individual differences. They were described as a group, rather than as individuals. In drawing comparisons with Europe with a view to holdig pupils' attention, teachers may enforce a Eurocentric view implying inferiority rather than simply differences. The approaches of the teachers, and the pupil responses did not differ markedly between the two schools: multiethnicity in one school seemed to have had little positive influence on curriculum organisation in this school, a generalisation we would extend to curriculum development in most so-called multicultural schools: the ethnocentric values of the dominant, while majority group continue to be represented in the explicit and implicit ideologies of many textbooks, and of many teachers, whether or not they are teaching in multi-ethnic settings.

INTERVIEWS WITH PUPILS AND PARENTS

In a further study a number of exploratory interviews were conducted with parents and children of ethnic minorities to determine their attitudes to reading and reading habits. While time did not allow for more than a small group of children to be interviewed at depth, the analysis of interview data suggested that the books read by ethnic minority children were of the English classic type, popular English children's writers (e.g. Enid Blyton) and adventure stories. None of the children interviewed mentioned that they read books depicting ethnic minority children in a contemporary British setting or books which drew upon the cultural background of ethnic minority groups. It is also interesting to note from children's responses that very few books were bought, and most children used public library facilities. This implies that there is poverty of materials in libraries relevant to multi-racial society.

AN OVERVIEW

There was evidence of a lack of literature giving proper representation of ethnic minority groups, and of some tendencies towards stereotypic presentation where such groups were represented in written materials. At a time when schools have a decreasing spending power in relation to books, it seems essential that teachers be able to make informed choices with regard to the materials which are suitable for and conducive to satisfactory multi-racial education.

A survey of publishers confirmed that there is a shortage of writers with an ethnic background of sympathy for children's literature. However, resources should be provided to enable the few individuals (authors) to produce innovative materials to cover the identified gaps.

There is a considerable fund of expertise in Teachers' Centres and library services in areas of immigrant settlements, and these should be exploited more successfully.

From our case study of two schools, we conclude that people from the Third World are perceived as members of an undeveloped continent who are primitives, battling unsuccessfully against their environment. In contrast, Europeans and white people in general tend to live in manufactured surroundings where they can employ machines, advanced technology and skills. These perceptions and images are created through literature and textbooks which have been found to embody 'stereotyping', 'ethnocentrism', and 'tokenism'.

The process of transmission of images and perception from book to child is mediated through the presence of the teacher who interprets the material to the child in various ways. The aspect of the study concerned with classroom research confirmed this.

In general, we conclude that books as resource materials in classrooms and school libraries, are crucially important elements in the day to day working of the school, and in the messages and codes which it transmits to pupils. Books are crucial resources too in curriculum responses to the challenge of multiculturalism in British schools. Teachers are crucially important too in interpreting textbooks for pupils. Unfortunately, the evidence to date suggests that only a minority of teachers approach this task in an unbiased or unprejudiced way (Verma and Bagley, 1982). The 'culture of racism' still has a powerful influence in Britain, and informs the thinking, feeling, perception and action of a majority of the population, including professionals such as teachers (Bagley and Verma, 1979).

The response of publishers to the need for new textbooks in the multicultural area has, understandably, followed the demands of teachers and education authorities, who make recommendations about purchasing and using appropriate materials. While some publishers have pioneered with imaginative new materials most have had little alternative to following market demand.

Textbooks and children's fiction in Britain can be classified in three types. First of all are traditional materials, ignoring or denigrating people who are not white, or not European. The modern geography textbook used in the case study described above is a case in point.

Secondly, are books reflecting a multicultural view, stressing important differences between people and stressing sometimes the formal equality of different peoples or cultures, but ignoring the political realities of economic and racial exploitation. Mullard (1981) has vigorously exposed this approach as one which is implicitly racist: ignoring racist realities simply gives a free field for the not-so-hidden curriculum.

Thirdly, there are materials, still few in number, for the 'multicultural' classroom which do attempt to give an account of history and social structure which shows how Europeans and their supposedly Christian culture enslaved and exploited peoples of the Third World, and have created second-class citizenship not only for the children of migrants from Asia, Africa and the Caribbean, but also for white working class children of inner-city Britain as well. A potentially powerful type of curriculum innovation we have in mind is the "Geography and the Young School Leaver" development in some British schools. This new curriculum development and its published materials attempts to analyse and expose the power bases of urban Britain, and the alienation and exploitation of working people of all races.

Such an approach is, of course, controversial, and has many enemies. The matter is avowedly political, and the struggle to achieve a 'just' curriculum based on adequate books and other materials in the classroom will be a long one.

ACKNOWLEDGEMENT

We would like to record our sense of debt to: the headteachers, teachers and pupils who cooperated in these studies; and to our colleagues, Olivia Foster-Carter, Vanessa Heslop, Ian Pickard, Peter Sanderson and Harry Jones for assistance in data collection.

REFERENCES

Bagley, C., Verma, G.K., Mallick, K. and Young, L., Personality, Self-Esteem and Prejudice, Saxon House, Farnborough, 1979.
Bagley, C. and Verma, G.K., Multicultural Childhood, Gower, Aldershot, 1982.
Brittan, E., 'Multi-Racial Education II - Teacher Opinion on Aspects of School Life', Educational Research, vol. 18, pp. 182-191, 1976
Department of Education and Science, The Continuing Needs of Immigrants, Education Survey, 14, H.M.S.O., London, 1972.
Dixon, R., Catching Them Young, Pluto Press, London, 1977.
Hannam, C., 'History and Prejudice', Teaching History, October 22, 1978.
Hodges, M., 'Constraints in Experimental History Publishing', Teaching History, June 24, 1979.
Jenkins, D., Kemmis, S., MacDonald, B. and Verma, G., 'Racism and Educational Evaluation', in Verma, G. and Bagley, C. (eds), Race, Education and Identity, MacMillan, London, 1979.
Milner, D., Children and Race, Penguin, Harmondsworth, 1975.
Mullard, C., 'Black Kids in White Schools: Multi-racial Education in Britain', Plural Societies, vol. 12, p. 1. 1981.
Proctor, C., Racist Textbooks, National Union of Students, London, 1975.
Scott, R., A Wedding Man is Nicer Than Cats, Miss, David and Charles, Exeter, 1971.
Stenhouse, L., 'Problems of Research in Teaching About Race Relations', in Verma, G.K. and

Bagley, C. (eds), <u>Race and Education Across Cultures</u>, Heinemann, London, 1975.

Townsend, H., <u>The Education of Immigrant Children</u>, National Foundation for Educational Research, Windsor, 1971.

Verma, G.K., 'Some Effects of Curriculum Innovation on the Racial Attitudes of Adolescents', <u>International Journal of Intercultural Relations</u>, vol. 3, pp. 1-11.

Verma, G.K. and Bagley, C., 'Teaching Styles and Race Relations: Some Effects on White Teenagers', <u>The New Era</u>, vol. 59, pp. 53-57, 1978.

Verma, G.K. and Bagley, C., 'Issues in Multicultural Education', in Bagley, C. and Verma, G.K. (eds), <u>Self-Concept, Achievement and Multicultural Education</u>, MacMillan, London, 1982.

Verma, G.K. and Bagley, C., 'Measured Changes in Racial Attitudes Following the Use of Three Teaching Methods', in Verma, G.K. and Bagley, C. (eds), <u>Race, Education and Identity</u>, MacMillan, London, 1979.

Chapter Ten

SECOND LANGUAGES IN THE PRIMARY SCHOOL: THE AUSTRALIAN EXPERIENCE

Barbara McLean

GENERAL BACKGROUND

Historical Context of Immigration

Australia is a nation of immigrants. It was not until the 1891 Census that a majority of the population of 3 1/4 million were found to have been born in the country. At that time 90% of the population was of British background, 3% German, 3% Chinese and other non European groups, with the remaining 4% coming from a wide variety of countries.

After World War II, the Government actively continued its policy of increasing population through immigration. From 1948-51 Australia accepted 170,000 refugees as well as other unassisted migrants from countries such as Greece, Italy and Holland. The majority of immigrants still came from Britain however. In the period 1951-1961, Southern European immigration exceeded that from Britain and net migration averaged about 78,000 persons per year.

By 1980, twenty percent of Australia's population was born overseas and over half of these came from non-English speaking countries. They and their children born in Australia numbered more than 2.5 million in a population of 15 million. More than one-third of overseas born people regularly use a language other than English and over 500,000 are estimated to suffer a severe disadvantage because of their lack of English (Australian Council on Population & Ethnic Affairs, 1982:1).

In 1978, the major non-English speaking countries of origin of immigrants and their children were Italy (10.19 %), Greece (5.46%), Yugoslavia (5.26%), Germany (3.94%), Netherlands (3.30%), Poland (2.5%), Lebanon & Syria (1.80%), China, Singapore & Hong Kong (1.55%), South America (1.47%), and India (1.37%). At that time, the various South East Asian countries contributed 2.28% to the population, though with the refugee intake (15,000 p.a.) which has included many Vietnamese and Kampuchians, this percentage has since increased.

The Child Migrant Education Program

The first formal recognition of the special needs of children from non-English speaking background was the entry of the Commonwealth Government into the area of education, traditionally a matter of individual responsibility by each of the States. An announcement was made by the Minister for Immigration that funds were to be provided to cover the salary of specialist teachers in English as a Second Language (ESL), training courses for these teachers and the provision of suitable learning and teaching materials.

The main reason for establishing this program was recognition of the fact that it was difficult for children to 'pick up' adequate English without formal instruction, and that general educational attainment suffered if there was a poor command of English.

The teaching of ESL did not prove to be the panacea some thought it would be. There were never enough resources to cater for all those who could have benefited from such a program, and it must be said in hindsight, that many of the programs, in terms of methodology and materials, were inadequate.

Multiculturalism and Schools

In the early 1970's more recognition was given to the claim that lack of recognition and in some cases the actual devaluation of the cultural core values of children, together with the loss of one's home language could have a serious effect on the self esteem of the child and in turn, affect achievement at school.

Typical of the statement to be found was:

> It follows that the multicultural reality of Australian society needs to be reflected in school curricula - languages, social studies, history, literature, the arts and crafts - in staffing and in school organization. While these changes are particularly important to undergird the self-esteem of migrant children they also have application for all Australian

children growing up in a society which could be greatly enriched through a wider sharing in the cultural heritages now present in it.
(Schools Commission, 1975:91)

This recognition came at a time of increased interest in educational change and innovation supported by a substantial injection of funds into the system. The Schools Commission was established by the Commonwealth in 1973 to enquire into and report upon any aspect of primary or secondary schooling, to ascertain needs, and to recommend what Australian Government funds should be made available to schools and school systems throughout the country in order to ensure acceptable standards. The aim was to improve the quality of schooling and promote increased and equal educational opportunities. Two of the programs set up by the Schools Commission were the Disadvantaged Schools Program (to provide extra resources to identified 'needy' schools in response to submissions of proposals from these schools to improve their effectiveness) and the Special Projects Program (to foster change and encourage innovation). Both programs were used by schools to initiate and support, among other things, multicultural and LOTE programs.

INITIATIVES IN THE PRIMARY SCHOOL

It must be recognized that to introduce the teaching of languages other than English into the primary school involves quite major changes within the education systems. This is because the Primary teacher has traditionally been a generalist classroom teacher, and little, if any, provision has been made for specialist teachers.

Another important consideration in the successful introduction of languages into the primary curriculum is the climate of opinion regarding such an innovation. Are classroom teachers, and the community in general, convinced of the desirability and the advantages to be gained from introducing languages other than English? Is there sufficient knowledge available about appropriate teaching methodologies, and are there the curriculum resources to back it up? And thirdly, are there successful models which can be referred to? Positive responses to these questions would tend to suggest a favourable climate for the introduction of a LOTE program.

For most of the 1970's, the answer to these questions in Australia overall would have had to be in the negative. There was without doubt, a vocal lobby group which was pressing for the introduction of languages other than English, particularly those languages spoken in the homes of many of the children. This lobby could be seen as part of a broader 'ethnic rights' movement in which different ethnic community organizations and other concerned people such as social workers and academics, played an important role.

New South Wales
In N.S.W. by the end of 1977, 34 'language programs' were operating in State run infants and primary schools. A brief analysis of these is set out in the table below.

From the table, it is significant to note that the majority of these programs were operating in the context of multicultural and intercultural awareness, and only in nine cases was language itself the specific focus of attention of the program - either as language maintenance and development for children from non-English speaking backgrounds, or as a second language experience for other children. The majority of these programs were available for small groups within the school and in general did not have a great deal of time devoted to them. One of the most notable exceptions was an inner city public school which ran classes in Turkish, Greek, Serbo-Croatian and Macedonian for 5 x 30 minutes a week for the whole upper primary school.

South Australia
In South Australia, the first language programs introduced in response to the multicultural nature of the schools tended to follow the same pattern as the earlier French and German classes, that is, mostly taught by a few enthusiastic individuals working in isolation. There was no monetary support and no curriculum guidance. The most common approach was for a class teacher to work with his or her own class, or to perhaps swap periods with another teacher.

In one school where there was a high concentration of students from different ethnic backgrounds, the language programme evolved over time. In 1970

Table 1.1: Community Language Programs in N.S.W. State Primary Schools

Number of Schools		
Primary only	27	
Infants only	4	
Primary and Infants	3	34
Number of Schools by Languages		
Arabic	2	
Greek	7	
Italian	11	
Laotian	1	
Macedonian	1	
Spanish	4	
Turkish	1	
Two or more languages	7	34

Approximate Number of Students Involved	No. Programs	No. Students
Native speakers of the language only	10	304
Non-native speakers only	1	20
Mixed native and non-native speakers	23	2081
	34	2405

Origin of Teachers		
E.S.L. Teachers	16	
Other teachers	8	
Teachers' aides	2	
Community members - paid	7	
- unpaid	4	
High school students	2	
Organization of Programs		
In school hours - normal classes	20	
- special groups	13	
In and after school hours	1	34
Type of Language Program		
Incidental use	0	
Support for E.S.L. education	6	
Ethnic studies	1	
Multicultural and inter-cultural experience (often a quasi-ethnic studies program)	18	
Community Language education	9	
Bilingual education	0	34

Source: Child Migrant Education Newsletter, 6:3:11

and 1972 informal arrangements had existed whereby bilingual class teachers introduced some Greek or Italian into their lessons. This led on to a formal systematic program across the school in 1975. Children of Italian, Greek and Serbo-Croatian background were taught bilingually for half an hour daily in a withdrawal situation. Other languages - for example French, were also available, but not taught bilingually. In 1977, further language and culture exposure courses were developed for all students in Years 6 and 7. In this school, as with others in a similar situation, the languages which could be offered depended upon the language skills of the regular class teachers and sometimes the availability of ethnic aides (unqualified persons who were employed to help with administrative tasks, translations, and general classroom activities).

In 1975, the Italian community, with the support of other interested groups, petitioned the Minister for Education that children be given the opportunity to be taught Italian language and culture as part of the school curriculum, and that a specialized language training program for teachers be established. As a result, two teachers were seconded to undertake a feasibility study and develop courses in Italian. In 1976, Italian was introduced as a bilingual program in two pilot schools and as a second language in another. All the schools had a high proportion of children from an Italian background. In November 1975, following upon the Italian Project Team's Feasibility Study, the State Premier also announced a special grant of $69,000 to establish immediately a teacher training course in Italian at the Adelaide College of Advanced Education. This was a special six months course aimed at upgrading the language skills of teachers in the system and providing them with some teaching methodology. It was followed in 1977 by the introduction of a formal three year study program in both Italian and Greek available to students in the Diploma of Teaching and Bachelor of Education (Secondary) and in 1980 a three year Graduate Diploma in Community Languages - again only in Italian and Greek, was initiated. Although not all students in the Diploma would necessarily be entering the teaching profession, there was at least a formal path established whereby prospective teachers could develop language and methodology skills.

From the six or so Italian programs operating in State primary schools in 1976, the number had increased by 1981 to 32. In the South Australian Catholic Education system there were a further 28 primary schools teaching Italian, and it was estimated that across the State about 8,000 children were involved in this one language alone. A new Italian curriculum based on functional notional principles was also being developed and trialed in schools. In this curriculum, an emphasis was placed on reading material suitable to the language level skills of children born in Australia and relevant to their needs. As with all the other language groups, it had been found that importing material from the country of origin was not satisfactory as the level of language was usually far too high for students in Australia, most of whom had not had a chance to develop formal language skills in their home language.

Further Development

The growth in the number of schools offering languages other than English at the primary school level across Australia can be attributed to two factors - increased awareness often associated with pressure from various lobby groups, and Federal Government acceptance of the recommendations of the 1978 Galbally Report. This was the report of a committee set up to review the Post-Arrival Programs and Services for Migrants. The philosophy underlying the Report was clearly premised on the desire to promote a multicultural society. In the section relating to education, it was noted that there was still considerable apathy if not obstruction among some educators to the development of multicultural education. Schools and school systems should be encouraged therefore to develop more rapidly "various initiatives aimed at improving the understanding of the different histories, cultures, languages and attitudes of those who make up our society" (Galbally, 1978:106). Unlike numerous similar recommendations coming from other groups, the Galbally committee identified the means to implement such a proposal - money, and the establishment of State committees to oversee the allocation of funds. For the triennium 1979-81, an additional $5m. was to be allocated specifically for the promotion of multicultural education, and it was recommended that a large part of these funds should be applied to initiatives in schools such as pilot projects in the teaching of community languages and

cultures, and bilingual approaches to education
(Galbally, 1978:108).

New South Wales
Apart from the existence of Galbally money, schools in N.S.W. were particularly encouraged to introduce language programs as a result of a formal policy on Multicultural Education announced by the State Minister of Education in November 1979. The policy stated that multicultural perspectives and education for intercultural understanding should be fundamental to the practice of all schools and for all students and that other aspects of multicultural education could be developed for specific groups of students according to interests and needs. The other aspects referred to were:

(a) Ethnic Studies. These involve in-depth studies of one or more specific Australian ethnic groups. They may be parts of subjects and programs, both existing and new.

(b) English as a Second Language Education. For students from non-English speaking backgrounds, this aspect is concerned with the acquisition and development of English, the national language; and

(c) Culture-through-language Education. Experiences of one's own culture and language, and those of other people, can contribute to a sense of personal worth and to intercultural understanding. In primary education, the cultures and languages of the community may be studied as part of the curriculum developed by the school. In secondary education, language studies are available as courses approved by the Secondary Schools Board and the Board of Senior School Studies.

Culture-through language education was detailed as follows:
> Culture-through-language education in primary schools comprises both community and foreign culture-through-language programs. The activities and materials in these programs should, as far as possible, be appropriate to the age of the students. Culture-through-language programs will find their place mainly in the existing language and social studies programmes, and will be offered in either K-2, 3-6 or K-6 sequences. These will be taken by

generalist classroom teachers with appropriate language skills.
(NSW Department of Education, 1979:3)

Community language programs were to be given precedence over foreign language programs, "community language" being defined as those programs where the majority of the children were native speakers of the language or where it was the language spoken by a significant number of people within the school's local community. Using this definition, Italian would only be viewed as a community language within certain suburbs or areas.

It is important to note that the prerequisite for introducing a language program were identified as being:

1. a need had to be established
2. a qualified teacher had to be available

and

3. there had to be a position within the normal staffing establishment of the school for the teacher to move into.

Further, the teacher with language skills was to be appointed as a general classroom teacher which meant working full time with the one class, teaching all subjects. This did not allow for much opportunity to develop a language program across grade and year level.

South Australia

In South Australia, although there were no official specialist language teaching positions in the primary schools, the situation was in fact much more flexible. This was because since 1977 primary teachers had been awarded 6 percent non-contact time (increased to 8 percent in 1978). To service this 'lost' class time, additional teachers had to be appointed to schools, and in some cases, this involved teachers with special language skills. A language program could then be set up across classes, with the class teacher being freed to take up the 'non-contact' allowance while the language lessons were in progress.

Another administrative change also facilitated the implementation of language programs. From 1977, the formula for school staffing became a base allocation determined by the size of the school which could then be supplemented by extra staff depending on the documented special needs of the school. There was, of course, a limit on the number of such positions available and schools had to compete with each other, arguing for remedial teachers, physical education teachers, music teachers, craft teachers or specialist language teachers, depending on their priorities. There is a danger that a disproportionate amount of the funds available for negotiable staff may be used for language teachers, leaving little in the kitty for other needs. When language programs are astarted with the use of negotiable staff there is also the danger that there will be no continuity as the school may not be successful in its application the following year. Nonetheless, the combination of a 'noncontact' allowance and the availability of negotiable staff has encouraged a variety of organizational patterns to implement language programs in different schools and these seem to be working very well.

Victoria
Like South Australia, Victoria also has specialist teachers for subjects such as library, music, physical education and art and craft, but these are allocated by the Department according to the number of students in the school. Language has not been listed as a specialist subject. The extra teachers in the school do however allow the possibility of re-arrangement of timetables such that language programs may be facilitated. This is further helped by the State Department of Education policy relating to the encouragement of support staff in schools.

In 1974, legislation had been passed which would permit School Councils, on the recommendation of principals and staff, to employ teacher aides. By this legislation the way was cleared for a great increase in ancillary staff, the supply of which had previously been controlled by the Department of Education.

In 1979, the Department responded to the needs of high migrant density schools and funded 100 additional positions for ethnic aides, these to be appointed over 3 years. This was the first time Ethnic Teacher Aide was acknowledged as a particular category of Aide. In addition, a considerable degree of centralization of control over recruitment and selection, terms of employment, appointment, qualifications, training and duties of aides was laid down.

Further to this policy of adding support staff to schools was the establishment of positions for Special Assistance Resource Teachers. The aim was to place one of these in each school where they could be used for remedial teaching, helping with the development of programs, working with special groups and so on.

The exception to the lack of provision of specialist language teachers is the Greek bilingual pilot project which began in four schools in the Richmond-Collingwood area in 1981. The teachers were appointed by the Department of Education additional to base staffing. The funds for their salaries however come from the Project grant. In addition, a Greek ethnic aide was appointed to each school. Students entering school in the Preparatory grade move either into classes which are essentially for Greek speaking children with instruction in that language, or into parallel classes where instruction is in English but Greek is also taught. As the children progress through the school, Greek will continue to be offered for language maintenance and development purposes, but instruction in the language will be phased out by Grade 3.

THREE CASE STUDIES

Relating decisions taken at a macro level does not always provide an insight into the actual implementation of these at the work face. Three brief case studies are therefore reported to try to remedy this deficiency. It should be pointed out that the schools described are not chosen as model programs, nor should they be seen as representative of the many initiatives which have been taken. However, they each illustrate a number of points from which certain conclusions relating to the implementation of language programs in the primary school can be drawn.

School A - N.S.W.

Background: School A was a very large primary school of over 1,000 students, 68 percent of whom were of a non-English speaking background. In 1980, 24% of the students were from a South-East Asian background and this had increased to 33% by 1981. The next largest language group was Spanish (12%) followed by Serbian (10%). Most of the parents worked in factories as process workers or were unemployed.

Introduction of Spanish: At the beginning of the 1981 school year, the Principal was approached by the Department of Education in regard to having having one of the newly appointed specialist language teachers attached to her school. Having been interested in promoting multicultural education for a long time, and in fact having encouraged individual teachers over the years to teach language to their own classes, she agreed. She asked for a Spanish teacher rather than a Vietnamese/Chinese teacher because she was concerned that the Vietnamese/Chinese speakers were recently arrived, needed more time to settle and to learn English, and were too numerous for only one language teacher. The Spanish speaking children on the other hand had been in the country longer and there was greater danger that their language skills would atrophy.

Student Opinion: When asked why they thought it was a good idea to learn another language most of the Year 3 students from the non-native speaking class replied that it would be helpful for travelling and for talking with people. One rather imaginative response was "If you become a secret agent you might need to go to another country to speak to a man who speaks Spanish"! Not surprisingly, the Spanish speaking children almost unanimously emphasised the desirability of improving skills in Spanish "to write letters, so you can read Spanish. So we can talk in two languages, so when our mothers and fathers talk to you, you can understand them better".

Students in the top Year 5 class were also asked their opinion. None were studying Spanish though 20 of the 26 had learnt either some Italian or German when they were in the second or third grade. All but three said they had liked this early language experience. Six indcated they would have liked to start Spanish at the start of the year but had decided not to for some reason, and nine thought they might like to learn it the next year.

Of the nine children who could already speak another language, three did not think it was a good idea to learn another language at school - for them at least. One child wrote: "I would not like to learn another language because it would be too much to handle". Another wrote:

I would not like to learn another language
because you learn another language for about

half an hour and then you go back to normal Australian classes and the next time you go to the other language class you forget everything and get into trouble.

On the more positive side, the other six children thought having another language would help them communicate with friends and help them to get a job more easily.

Of the seventeen children who could not speak another language, two did not want to learn another one because "people might think you come from another country". Another thought it wasted time, while one child seemed to think learning another language was disloyal - "I like Australia the best". Most of the other children thought it would be a good idea - making communication with friends, travelling, or getting a job much easier. Two saw it as being useful for watching television shows in the different languages (4).

From these kind of responses, it could not be said that there is an unfavourable attitude to languages in general, although some hardened opinions (often one might suggest stemming from parents) reflect some serious misconceptions about language and language learning. The concerns expressed by these children are important to recognise however as they need to be addressed if motivation, an important ingredient in language learning, is to work _for_ a language program, and not against it.

Because the program is optional, it was not surprising that the parents of the children involved were very supportive of the language classes. Being optional posed some difficulties for the teacher however. Occcasionally other class teachers placed less importance on Spanish than other subjects as in the case where a student missed several Spanish lessons because he had to stay behind to finish his other class work. The result was that he then got behind in Spanish. At other times students can disrupt the class by saying 'they don't like it', 'they're not learning anything', and 'they're not going to come any more'. Even when they don't really mean what they are saying, such statements can have a negative effect on other students. There can also be difficulties following on from children wanting to enter or leave the program at different points of time. Nonetheless, given the size of the school, language classes will have to remain optional if a further 8-9 teachers are not employed! The one teacher cannot physically cope with many more children than she is already teaching. It must also be recognised that teaching language full time with no breaks is a very exhausting business.

School B - Victoria

Background: This school also had a high proportion of children from a non-English speaking background - 81 percent of the 405 students in fact. The major ethnic groups were Italian (25 percent), Greek (23 percent), Turkish (14 percent) and Lebanese (8 percent). At least 15 other countries were represented.

The school had been classified as one of the schools eligible to apply for special grants from the Disadvantaged Schools Programs of the Schools Commission and through this funding, was employing three bilingual teacher aides. Initially their main function had been to establish and maintain lines of communication with parents and to help teachers in the classroom, but their presence in the school was a significant factor in the establishment of a language program.

Introduction of Languages: In Victoria, there is a considerable degree of community involvement in schools through the elected School Councils. At this school, a number of the parents on the Council had been born overseas or had close contacts with such people, and they wanted language introduced into the curriculum of the school. The initial reaction of the staff to this request was "How dare they sit back and tell us what they want". Opposition to the teaching of languages was based on beliefs that:

> they felt that children should be learning English/ Australian culture if they were living in Australia;

> there were not enough language teachers;

> there were no suitable books, aids or materials to teach languages at the primary school level;

> that the teaching of English would be neglected;

the timetable would be difficult to organize as other specialist teachers/sport had to be catered for also.

By the end of the year, however, a grudging commitment had been given to the idea that an experimental language program should take place. It could be argued that the general rhetoric relating to the promotion of a multicultural society and the perceived importance of languages to this, was having an effect.

The following year, 1979, the position of Child Migrant Education Co-ordinator (responsible for teaching in and organising the ESL programs at the school) was filled by a lady who was vitally interested in the broader language issue. An ethnic story telling program was started for the Year 3 children with the teacher aides, or community people coming into the classes to tell the stories. In the meantime, a few words in the different languages were being introduced in other lessons. No one was really aware that language teaching had already begun in a very small and informal way.

At the end of 1979, following a number of staff meetings and a special inservice day, it was decided to send a note to parents asking what languages they would like to see taught at the school. The initial response was very low and a follow-up questionnaire needed to be sent.

A Multilingual Program: Further meetings took place between staff and parents, and on the basis of the survey of parents, the school decided to go ahead with a pilot language program for Grade 4 students in 1980. Four languages were to be offered - Italian, Greek, Turkish and German. Grade 4 was chosen as a suitable starting point because this particular group of children had already been having a very informal introduction to language through the ethnic story-telling program when in Grade 3, another school which had been visited had successfully started at this level, and because it allowed for extension of the program into Grades 5 and 6 in the following years. The languages selected were based on the three major ethnic groups at the school and availability of staff. The majority of students chose to study Italian and this group was taught by a parent (ex high school language teacher and member of the School Council), an Italian staff member and the Italian teacher aide. The Turkish and Greek groups were taken by the teacher aides and German by a Grade 4 class teacher.

Organization: Lessons were originally time-tabled for two half hour sessions per week, but these were extended to 45 minutes later in the year. Each session was block timetabled so that all language lessons occurred at the same time. Lebanese/Arabic was also introduced in the third term when funds and a resource person for this area became available (shared with another school in the area). A more bilingual approach in the infants school - with the teacher aides working with the class teachers, was also begun informally.

The language program was optional but, because of parental interest and support and the wide range of languages, only 6 or 7 students chose not to participate, and most of these later requested permission to join a class.

The language program for 1981 was extended to cover both the new Fourth Grade and the continuing group into Fifth Grade. It was no longer optional, but with the range of languages available this did not seem to pose any problem. Not all children were studying their home language. Many Turkish students had elected to learn German and quite a number, if not most of the Greek speaking children, had chosen to study Italian. The children from Italian background, perhaps not so familiar with their own language tended to stay with Italian.

Once students had made their choice of language they were expected to continue with this throughout. Parents were sent a letter at the end of the school year letting them know of the options, but since only half returned the form, the children ended up making the choice themselves. Often they had little experience on which to base this choice. One little Anglo-Australian boy, for example, chose to do Turkish - not because he lived near Turks or had any Turkish friends but because he liked the teacher's husband whom he had met at a school function! On occasion, where parents and children had not seen eye to eye with regard to the language chosen, it was the opinion of the teachers that the children usually won the day.

The children have had a say in another way too. In 1981, there was a composite Grade 5/6 class. Those in Grade 5 were going out to language classes but the Grade 6 children were remaining to do other work. These children wanted to know why they couldn't do language too. In response, the Deputy Principal volunteered to take some of them for Italian and the class teachers brushed up on their basic French. They could however only be accommodated for one 45 minute language period per week. The children were most enthusiastic and one teacher became 'supermotivated' to learn more French. The general language program was further extended to all Grade 3 children in June.

Continuity: At the end of 1981, the school was facing a crisis. The language program had become an integral part of the school with 15 of the 18 teachers fully supporting the program. Students in Grades 5 and 6 were very much in favour of continuing to learn a language (87 percent). Only 14 of the 182 students had said they did not want to continue, basically because it was 'too hard', 'boring', or 'I don't want to'. Yet the presence of the teacher aides was fundamental to the availability of the variety of languages offered. It was their future that was in doubt. The school had been told its grant eligibility for the following year had been lowered so that it was highly unlikely funds would be available to pay the aides. In addition, the position of CME Co-ordinator had been taken away, and if this member of staff were to stay at the school, it would be in the role of a general classroom teacher, without the time allocated to plan and co-ordinate the language program.

The school was mounting a campaign for support for the LOTE program which involved letters to people in the educational hierarchy and the Government, arranging inspection visits, documenting activities, making submissions - in general making themselves very visible. This involved a great deal of time and energy - time that could well be devoted to other things. What those involved in the program desperately wanted was a guarantee of conti- nuity to allow them to get down to the business of teaching.

School C - South Australia

Background: This school is situated in a growing middle class suburb. Approximately 40% of the 450 students at the school had at least one parent born in Italy. The majority of the remaining students were of Anglo-Celtic background. Nearly all the children were born in Australia and competence in English was not a problem.

Introduction of a Language Program: A new principal was appointed to the school in 1975. He was young, dynamic, and keen to bring the school closer to the community. The introduction of Italian language and culture studies was one possibility. Quite fortuitously, two teachers who were completing the special, once only, one semester course on Italian language teaching at the Adelaide College of Advanced Education held in 1976, visited the school with a view to seeking employment there and setting up an Italian program. The matter was discussed with the staff, the school council and parents, and the result was the introduction of 2 x 30 minute Italian studies lessons per week for all classes starting in the mid year when the teachers became available. It was left to individual class teachers to decide whether their class should have specific language lessons or to focus on culture with some incidental language brought in.

Organization: This first year was basically trial and error. The two teachers of Italian shared a Year 3 class and the Italian lessons. They were given about $200 to set up the language program and the resources to accompany it. A tremendous amount of time was spent making teaching aids, which proved to be very exhausting especially on top of trying to build a workable program. There was very little in the way of prepared materials of any kind, and trying to work in with general classroom themes being taught by the class teacher was almost impossible - level of language, amount of time available and continuity (reinforcement and development) being some of the difficulties. Whole classes were taught, which meant working with a wide variety of levels, interest and ability. Nor could it be assumed that children who spoke dialect fluently were very capable in respect of standard Italian. In contrast, children of no or little Italian language background who learnt words and phrases very quickly, themselves experienced difficulties due to lack of background cultural understanding. Grouping children was difficult within classes as the teachers did not have access to facilities such as listening posts - these already being used elsewhere and not, in any case, easy to cart from room to room every 30 minutes. This would have been necessary as there was at this time no language room as such. Everything had to be taken to a class - too bad if the teacher forgot something or if something unanticipated came up. As one teacher said, it was frustrating to have a child ask a question, know you had just the right thing to show him - but not to have it with you.

At the end of the year a survey showed about 90 percent of parents supported continuation of the program. Staffing proved something of a difficulty though, with one teacher going on leave and the other being seconded to another job. The replacement arrangements were not totally satisfactory, but the program survived into the following year when the teacher on leave returned and took over all the language teaching.

Integration into Other Subjects: Integration of Italian into the total school program was not always easy. Since the Italian lessons were being used by teachers as part of their non-contact allotment, follow-up activities in class and teacher understanding of what was going on in the language classes was difficult. This became even more difficult with the acquisition of a portable to serve as a specialist language classroom. When this arrived halfway through 1978, it had been met with great joy and much relief by the language teacher. To her it meant a home room, resources at fingertips, and potential to develop an Italian atmosphere. But once isolated into one's own little room, it became more difficult to see what was going on in the other classrooms and hence to tie in language activities with class themes. The reverse situation also held. Work which the children had done in Italian lessons remained in the Italian room and did not get hung up in the classroom, again isolating Italian from the rest of the curriculum. It was more difficult to steal an extra few minutes to finish work, as the children had to pack up and return to other classes. Several teachers recognised the problem and were happy to allow Italian games, books or tapes which had been prepared by the teacher to be used in their classroom whenever (if ever) there was spare time, and it was all very ad hoc, and again put additional pressure on the Italian teacher.

The school was however, very fortunate in having several members of staff who knew the languages being taught and were familiar with the culture. After an Italian lesson dealing with wine making, one class teacher was able to talk about how he too had been making wine. Another teacher tried to follow up cultural items but chose to read Italian stories in English to her class because some were learning German and would not understand.

<u>Parental Support</u>: As with the other schools, there was a considerable degree of parental support. Some examples of responses given on a school questionnaire sent to parents are representative. While there were a few negative comments such as "Italian wasn't an important language", and "it would be better to learn English properly" were to be found, the majority felt that learning a language was a good thing in itself.

> It is good for the children to have a second language, particularly one spoken so widely in our community.

and

> I believe it is necessary for children to be introduced to a second language otherwise they think that English is the only language that matters. I wouldn't mind if they were taught Italian, German or Japanese.

That learning another language contributes to better understanding was seen in the following comments:

> (It) Helps my children to understand how difficult it can be learning English.

> (It) Promotes understanding of Italians.

> I think it is valuable to know of another culture. It stops prejudices.

Especially for those of Italian background, language study was seen to be very relevant in terms of identity:

> We are Italian, but our children seem to prefer to speak in English at home. The more exposure they have to the language the more likely they are to remember it, which we think is very important. Also, a study of the language helps the child to realize that this part of his heritage is important.

Specific advantages parents saw their children to have as a result of being involved in the program included - broadening horizons (26 comments), improved command of the language (11 comments), would provide better qualifications for job hunting (8 comments), would be helpful for Italian studies at high school (6 comments).

A comment by a parent who had originally come from Fiji is worth quoting in full.

> If I spoke Hindi and Fijian better, I would teach them myself. Grandma and Grandad speak on the phone from Fiji in Hindi. I speak to them in Hindi, the children speak in English. I translate what Grandma says in Hindi, and my brother in Fiji can translate from English, what the children say to her. I would like therefore if they learned Hindi at school.
>
> I accept the fact that Italian is the most common language in this community and so is taught at school. I like them doing Italian because they'll use it. There are lots of Italians' in Adelaide. My daughter wants to do pharmacy - she'll use it over the counter. It may assist in learning Latin also.
>
> You're accepted into the community if you speak their language. My neighbour's child (Italian) comes here to help in English, and my child goes there for some Italian words. A chain reaction effect occurs when one family asks an Italian family for a translation. They ring up someone else and so on. This is must in doing homework. Sometimes they're late for the homework, but at least they have the answer and we put it in the book. The children never forget that concept or word because they had to go and find out.
>
> If I had to choose between Italian and Hindi, I would choose Italian - it's the community language.
>
> When my daughter first went to primary school, she got teased and called an aboriginal. I went and took a couple of lessons about Fiji - at the teacher's suggestion - to help increase awareness of other cultures. The teacher followed it up with more lessons. Now that my son is learning a language and his mates are

too, he doesn't get teased about being different. If they can understand and speak a bit of another language (hear themselves) they accept foreign language speakers more.

Another parent of Greek background said he was happy for his daughter to learn Italian. She already knew Greek and it was good to have another language. Italian was spoken in the community, so that was a good reason to learn it. Besides, his daughter had Italian friends, and it was good to be able to speak with them in Italian.

ISSUES

In introducing second languages into the curriculum it is clear that numbers of issues have to be faced.

One point relates to system support - that is the adequate provision of teachers, resources and the possibility of continuity of a program. In the majority of cases in the three States referred to in this paper, these issues were still unresolved. Some further comments relating to these points will be dealt with later in this section.

Issues relating to attitudinal factors and desired goals

The extent to which staff of the school, the parents and the children believe in the validity of teaching second languages in the primary school is fundamental to the success of any program. Considerable effort needs to be taken to ensure such commitment.

Just as important is the need for the aims of the language program to be thought through, so that people have a realistic idea of what can be achieved in the time available. As a general comment, it would seem that the majority of teachers have a vague idea that learning another language contributes to more positive feelings towards other groups and provides an added insight into the culture of the group. It is certainly true that language and culture are inextricably linked, but one does have to ask to what extent the language skills which can be gained in the classroom will be adequate to make a significant contribution to such understanding. While this should remain an important goal of language classes, the primary focus must be on the development of language skills. This does not however mean teaching formal grammar through repetition and drills, but aims at developing communicative competence in culturally relevant situations. The importance of children feeling a sense of achievement and developing communication skills that are perceived to be useful is attested to by much of the research literature (Burstall et al., 1974; Cohen, 1976; Gardner, 1979). For all these reasons it is important that the aims be carefully thought through.

Clarity in perception of goals also facilitates evaluation, a vital process in the development of a healthy program. Too often, evaluation is viewed as an end product, something to think about once a program has been firmly established. Instead it should be an integral part of an ongoing program. Evaluation can take many forms - measures of students' competence and attitudes, as well as consideration of the philosophical rationale for having the program, the types of content and ways of organizing the program. Such discussions take time and it would seem advisable to set aside a special staff conference day rather than trying to tack on a brief discussion to already lengthy meetings dealing with other matters. The general impression gained from observing a number of language programs in Australian schools is that there is room for much improvement in this area.

Issues Relating to Organisation

Time Allocation: One important decision concerns the amount of time given to language study. The range within schools in the three states referred to in this paper is from 1/2 hour to 2 1/2 hours per week. Countries such as Sweden allocate 2-4 hours per week, depending on the age of the children. The idea of a 2-2 1/2 hours as being a useful amount of time to devote to language study seems to have some basis in the belief that daily exposure is important. Given class periods of a minimum of 20 to 30 minutes, one arrives at the above figure. The effectiveness of different time arrangements, however, is a matter for further research. Those schools which have given less time to language study appear to have been influenced by perceptions of the amount of time that they felt could safely be stolen from other areas, plus possibly an implicit belief that too much language might be a burden on the child - a patently false assumption in the light of the Canadian Immersion language programmes. In other words, the amount of time devoted to a programme may give some idea of the real level of commitment and belief in the programme which is felt by the school administration and staff.

Timetabling: Timetabling considerations are obviously affected by factors such as the amount of time allocated per week, availability of staff, policies relating to the grouping of students, and whether the programme is optional. Comments by teachers would seem to indicate that the practice of withdrawing students from other classes in order to have language lessons was not looked upon with any degree of favour. The exception was if half a class was withdrawn at a time, as this made it more feasible for the lesson to be repeated with the second group. Where all children were involved in a language programme, block timetabling seemed to offer many possibilities, as this allowed for grouping of children.

Heterogenous grouping versus streamed classes: Whilst it is a certain fact that second languages can be satisfactorily learnt by children of all abilities, the task of the language teacher is often made simpler when students are grouped according to achievement or, in some cases, ethnic background. The danger of such an organisational procedure is that the emphasis in lessons can come to be placed on academic achievement rather than on communicative competence and interaction between students. The advantage seems to lie in being able to pace material to the needs of the students so that they all feel a sense of accomplishment. It would seem that in practical terms, the question of whether to stream or not is tied up with issues of class size - the larger the class, the greater advantages to be obtained from streaming.

Class size: On commonsense grounds alone, the smaller the class the more opportunity the child has for individual attention and practice. Attention is easier to maintain and there are fewer discipline problems. Teachers liked the small groups. This is not to say language cannot be taught in large groups - just that it is more difficult and perhaps less cost efficient. It is usually necessary to modify the level of expectation as to what can be achieved, and it takes more skill to cater for the different levels and maintain motivation.

How many languages?: The availability of more than one language gives flexibility to the organization of a programme, and allows choice. This was demonstrated in one school at least, to affect students' attitudes in a positive direction. However, one difficulty which arises from making available a large number of languages is the resource issue - both in terms of staff and materials. Almost inevitably classes tend to be smaller, and so more teachers are needed. With very small classes there may be problems of continuity if some students leave and further reduce the size of the group. A range of materials and teaching aids needs to be provided for all levels and this can be expensive. As well, room accommodation may become a problem.

Which language/languages?: One of the commonly given reasons for including a particular language is that it is the home language of many of the children. This argument needs to be examined with great care. It cannot be assumed that because children come from a certain ethnic background, they automatically want to study their own language. When the opportunity is provided, many often choose to study a third language, believing that they already have a grounding in their own language. Indeed, where language classes are provided to develop the skills of native speakers, different approaches are needed from those used with non-native speakers. This distinction is not always borne in mind.

If languages other than English are to be an important part of the curriculum, they must be available to all children and not a selected few. This does not mean that if there are children from 14 different language backgrounds in the school that 14 languages would need to be included in the programme on the grounds of fairness. Nor does it mean that a language other than any of those spoken by the school population should be chosen. The essential criteria for choosing which languages are that there should be some agreement, that there be a choice if at all possible, and that whichever language is studied, the aim should be one of communication. Apart from that, there is no intrinsic merit in one language over another.

Relationship with ethnic schools: Since 1981, the Commonwealth government has given a grant of $30 per head to ethnic schools - that is, those after hours schools run by the different ethnic communities as non-profit concerns and whose primary purpose is the teaching of language and culture - not religion or politics. Some State governments also provide some assistance. One of the effects of this formal recognition of the role these schools play has been to encourage their development and the quality of teaching they are able to provide. It also raises the question of whether there is a need to develop further language and culture programmes in the regular day schools. That there is such a need receives a wide degree of support. In the first place it must be remembered that ethnic schools are not language schools alone. They exist to serve a wider purpose within their particular community. Whilst access to these schools may be open to all students, it is unrealistic to expect them to adjust their aims to suit these students. Secondly, relying on voluntary groups is seen as an abrogation of the rights of children to receive language instruction as part of their formal schooling. It would be shortsighted for government to view ethnic schools as a cheap alternative to implementing LOTE programs in regular day schools. Their roles are complementary rather than a duplication.

Continuity into high school: The issue of continuity of a programme within a school has already been mentioned. There is also the question of continuity across schools, particularly from primary school to high school. This is probably one of the most important and least well articulated aspect of language provision. Some high schools do not have continuation classes for all the languages taught in the primary schools which it services, often because the resources are not available or the number of interested students do not warrant this provision. In such cases, the student might be able to take advantage of other avenues, e.g., correspondence classes, Saturday language schools (special classes taught by Department teachers, preparing students for the external examinations, and drawing students from a wide area. The language studied at these schools is counted as part of the regular school programme of the student), ethnic schools, or vouchers for intensive language study at various centres.

The most serious problem from the point of view of the high school, however, is when a language is offered but no special provision is made for students who have already had some experience of the language. If children who have already learned some language just have to mark time while the others catch up, not only will much of the time spent in primary school be wasted, but boredom can lead to reduced motivation and also behaviour problems, with the result that the children drop the subject as soon as they are able.

A second issue which must be faced by high schools is that the teaching of language has traditionally been exam oriented, and thus some of the skills developed in primary school may not always be sufficiently capitalized upon. Teachers looking at language study from one perspective, may find it too easy to say that the children have been insufficiently prepared and that it is necessary for them to begin at the beginning again.

The dangers inherent in making the transition to secondary school in the absence of adequate provision and close liaison with the primary schools cannot be stressed too much. Means of easing this transition is an important priority for future research.

Teachers: Teachers are the backbone of any language programme. An adequate supply of qualified staff, fluent in the many language schools are increasingly interested in teaching, is essential if LOTE programs are to be more widely implemented. One encouraging move in this direction has been the decision of the Commonwealth government to accept the recommendation of the Tertiary Education Commission to provide recurrent grants for establishing language courses in universities and Colleges of Advanced Education to overcome the under-representation of certain community languages already taught and the lack of representation of others. At the end of 1981 approval was given to introduce 12 new courses covering Polish, Vietnamese, Turkish, Maltese, Greek, Italian, Serbian, Croatian, Macedonian, Arabic, Portugese and Pitjantjatjara across a number of tertiary institutions. With the greater availability of a wider range of languages, more students will be encouraged to take these subjects, and the potential supply of teachers will be increased. The next step will be the need to provide language methodology courses for primary teachers in recognition of the different learning styles, teaching methods, curriculum materials and other resources which are appropriate for this age group.

One could go further to argue that all prospective teachers should have some experience of learning a second language, and certainly, a basic knowledge about the structure of language and the language acquisition process for first and second languages. Such knowledge would be particularly important in Infants classes when teachers could develop "listening for meaning' programmes (Hawkins, 1981) which in turn could provide a firm foundation for later language studies.

Apart from pre-service education, in-service courses will be needed - both for the opportunity they provide for teachers to discuss issues, share ideas, develop resources, as well as to be kept informed of the latest research findings. Such opportunities for sharing and developing skills are even more important when specialist language teachers are working on their own in a school.

CONCLUSION

The teaching of languages other than English in primary schools is still in its infancy. There is a great deal more knowledge and experience which needs to be accumulated before many of the complexities become unravelled. Research is needed in particular into curriculum content and approaches for the different age levels and language experience of the children. Research into how much time is desirable, and what is an effective distribution of time, is also needed. More documentation is needed on effective ways of integrating language programmes into the total curriculum, and how the transition from school to school, especially to high school, can be best accomplished.

These are only some of the many issues which need exploring. Provision of staff, training, continuity of staff, and resources are other aspects which must also be resolved if LOTE programmes are to fulfill their potential in Australian schools.

NOTES

1. The provision of compulsory education in Australia is a State responsibility. In recent years, however, the Commonwealth of Australia has played an increasing role in policy decisions through the provision of special purpose funding. Within each State there are three education 'systems' - state schools, Catholic parochial schools and a loosely knit grouping of private or

independent schools. All schools receive some government funding, but the private schools rely heavily on student fees, the Catholic parochial schools to some extent, and the State schools not at all. For the sake of simplicity, the points made in this paper relate to government run schools in three states - New South Wales, Victoria and South Australia.

2. During the 70's, the phrases 'migrant languages', 'ethnic languages' and 'commmunity languages' tended to be used interchangeably. The distinction between these languages (often ill-defined) and other languages seemed to serve little point and the more neutral term 'languages other than English' or LOTE is attaining greater currency.

3. The research on which these case studies are based was funded by the Schools Commission. The aim was to describe the implementation of a number of language programs in order to stimulate interest and discussion of the issues raised.

4. A special broadcasting service was established in 1980 to run the ethnic radio station and the new television channel which would broadcast programs in the different languages, with sub-titles in English. This service was only available in Sydney and Melbourne in 1982, though funds have been set aside to introduce it in other capital cities.

REFERENCES

Australian Council on Population and Ethnic Affairs, Multiculturalism for all Australians: Our Developing Nationhood, Australian Government Publishing Service, Canberra, 1982.

Australian Institute of Multicultural Affairs, Review of Multicultural and Migrant Education, AIMA, Melbourne, 1980.

Burstall, C., Jamieson, M., Cohen, S. and Hargreaves, M., Primary French in the Balance, N.F.E.R. Slough.

Cohen, A., 'The Case for Partial or Total Immersion Education', The Bilingual Child, A. Simoes (ed.), Academic Press, New York, pp. 65-89.

Galbally, F., Migrant Services and Programs: Report of the Review of Post-Arrival Programs and Services for Migrants, Australian Government Publishing Service, Canberra, 1978.

Gardner, R.C., 'Social Psychological Aspects of Second Language Acquisition', Language and

Social Psychology, H. Giles and R. St. Clair (eds.), Blackwell, Oxford, 1979.

Hawkins, E., Modern Languages in the Curriculum, Cambridge University Press, Cambridge, 1981.

Martin, J., The Migrant Presence, George Allen & Unwin, Sydney, 1978.

Mather, J., Report of the Committee on the Teaching of Migrant Languages in Schools, A.G.P.S., Canberra, 1976.

Matthews, P. and Sheen, J., 'Community Language Programs in Infants and Primary Schools: A Review of the Situation in NSW Department of Education Schools, November, 1977', Child Migrant Education Newsletter, vol. 6, no. 3, pp. 3-11.

Merry, D., Zangalis, C. and Zangalis, G., 'Migrant Education Action in Victoria', Ethnic Studies, vol. 2, pp. 59-69.

NSW Department of Education, 'Policy on Multicultural Education', mimeo, 1979.

Schools Commission, Report for the Triennium, 1976-78, 1975.

Schools Commission, Report for the Triennium, 1979-81, 1978.

PART III

MINORITY GROUP CHILDREN IN MULTICULTURAL
CONTEXTS

Chapter Eleven

CULTURAL DIVERSITY, MIGRATION AND COGNITIVE STYLES:
A STUDY OF BRITISH, JAPANESE, JAMAICAN AND INDIAN
CHILDREN (1)

Christopher Bagley

Multicultural education is a system of education which, in an ethnically complex society attempts to meet the cultural, cognitive and self-concept needs of groups and individuals from diverse ethnic backgrounds. In addition, such education aims to promote equality of educational achievement between groups and between individuals, mutuality of respect and tolerance between different ethnic groups, and ultimately equality of status, resource access and economic power between different ethnic groups of society (Bagley & Verma, 1982).

The extreme antithesis of multicultural education has been an educational system in which children of ethnic minorities are removed from their parents, ritually subordinated and then educated in mainstream culture, while the traditional culture and language of that group is denigrated and suppressed. In Canada this culturally imperialist educational style was practised in recent postwar times, and many Native people will tell of the tribulation and mental and physical pain which that system of cultural suppression caused them. This educational system was demoralizing, but it did not destroy Native culture and language, which survives today despite, rather than because of any multicultural educational policy in Canada (Kirkness, 1981).

Among Canada's many ethnic groups are relatively recent immigrants from the Caribbean, the Indian sub-continent, and from elsewhere in Asia, and it is ironic that the cultural aspirations of these groups have received greater sympathy than those of Native people (Campfens, 1980). I stress this because although research described in this paper is derived from fieldwork with West Indian and Asian subjects, I am continually conscious of the profound anomaly of the often remarked but profound degradation - cultural, spiritual and material - of Native people in Canada, which multicultural educational policies have hardly begun to address.

The research reported here considers the influence of culture and socialisation on cognitive style in migrant and non-migrant groups. Cognitive Styles - ways of interpreting, perceiving and ordering the objects and concepts of the external world - are numerous and complex (Kogan, 1977). Our research has concentrated on one aspect of cognitive style, the system developed by Herman Witkin and his colleagues (Witkin, 1967) known as 'psychological differentiation'. Psychological differentiation is characterised by Lloyd (1972) as one of the three major types of intelligence which cross-cultural studies must consider, the other two being psychometric intelligence (see Vernon, 1975) and Piagetian intelligence (see Elkind, 1981).

The idea of cognitive style developed by Witkin has considerable importance for practitioners in education, since such styles influence the learning of social material, the effects of reinforcement, the use of mediators in learning, cue salience, teachers' instructional style, how teachers and students interact, different types of career choice, specialisation in secondary schooling, achievement with specialisations, and sex differences in specialisation and achievement (Witkin et al., 1977 a and b).

Understanding cognitive styles may be particularly important for teachers working in the field of multicultural education (Laosa, 1977), a fact recognised by the British Advisory Committee on Race Relations Research in 1975 which recommended that research should establish whether different ethnic groups had different cognitive styles which would make one approach more appropriate than another. Although the question was naively framed, it is significant that in this as in other vital areas of multicultural education, little relevant research in this area has been carried out.

Psychological differentiation as developed by Witkin, involves among other skills the ability to orient oneself in space in the face of disorienting stimuli, and the ability to perceive complex shapes in a more complex background. This cognitive style - the ability to visually discriminate figures separately from their complex background is known as field independence-dependence. Individuals who lack such ability are seen as field dependent. Various measures have been developed to estimate levels of field dependence, including the individually administered Children's Embedded Figures Test (Witkin et al., 1971) which is used in the present study.

An interesting facet of field dependence-independence is its wide range of correlations in the area of social behaviour and personality. Field dependence is associated with a child's early global conception of his or her body, which is replaced - at different rates and levels under varying social and cultural conditions and types of socialisation - by a more "articulated" body concept, with an impression of the body as having definite limits or boundaries with its parts being discrete and interrelated in a definite structure. Progress toward more articulated experience of the self also shows itself in growing awareness of needs, feelings and attributes which the child identifies as his own and as distinct from those of others (Witkin, 1967).

Reviewing the evidence on field dependence and interpersonal behaviour, Witkin and Goodenough (1977c) concluded, after an examination of some 200 studies, that people with field-dependent or field-independent cognitive styles are markedly different in their interpersonal behaviour, in ways which the original theory of psychological differentiation (Witkin et al., 1962) had predicted. Field-dependent people, adults and children, make greater use of external social cues in their environment while field-independent people function with greater autonomy under such conditions. Field dependent people have an interpersonal orientation - they show strong interest in others, prefer to be physically close to people, are emotionally open, and gravitate toward socially constructed situations. Field-independent people by contrast have an impersonal orientation - they are not very interested in others, show both physical and psychological distancing from people, and prefer non-social situations.

Field-dependent and field-independent people are different in an array of characteristics that make it likely that field-dependent people will get along better with others. Altogether, field-dependent people have a set of social skills that are less evident in fieldindependent people. On the other hand, field-independent people have greater skill in cognitive analysis and structuring. Thus there are particular advantages from being field independent, and advantages from being field dependent - each of the contrasting cognitive styles has components that are adaptive to particular situations. Witkin and Goodenough suggest that what is particularly important is that educators - teachers and others - shall be aware of their own cognitive styles, and those of their individual pupils so that types of learning can be maximized, and subject specialisation and career choice can be most usefully aided. It should be stressed too that there is a dynamic relationship between schooling and field-independence, since some types of schooling do influence pupils in a field-independent direction (Serpell, 1976; Wagner, 1978). It is possible that individuals whose socialisation (encouraging close psychological and social relationships to others) can retain aspects of field-dependent cognitive style, but through schooling in adolescence and beyond also develop field-independent styles (Witkin and Goodenough, 1977b). Such individuals are particularly fortunate, since they can operate effectively in a variety of social and non-social situations.

COGNITIVE STYLES: A MULTI-CULTURAL PERSPECTIVE

A systematic attempt to measure the variation of psychological differentiation across cultures has been made by Witkin and his colleagues in the Netherlands, Italy and Mexico (Witkin et al., 1974). Within each culture, ethnographic data were drawn on to select pairs of villages which emphasised (through socialisation and social control) either much conformity, or little conformity. Witkin's hypothesis (that children in villages with a traditional and authoritarian ethos would be much more field dependent than children in villages with much less emphasis on conformity) was borne out in all three cultures studied, in both younger and older children, on a variety of measures of psychological differentiation including the Children's Embedded Figures Test.

Ramirez, Castenada and Herold (1974) have tested in some detail the hypothesis that Mexican Americans subjected to traditional influences would be more field dependent than acculturated Mexican Americans, and studied 541 Mexican American children and their mothers in three communities in southern California. The three communities emphasised traditional, dualistic and mainstream American values respectively. As expected, children in the traditional community were much more field dependent than those in the modernised community, while those in the dualistic community were in an intermediate position. Mothers of the children completed a questionnaire about methods of socialisation, and as expected mothers of field-dependent children said that they used much more traditional methods of child-rearing. In all communities females scored in a more field-dependent direction than males, and younger children were more field-dependent than older children.

The most ambitious cross-cultural study of cognitive style and psychological differentiation is that of Berry (1976 and 1977) who compared field-dependence in a large sample of subjects in 17 centres around the world (Africa, Australia, New Guinea, and North America). Berry's perspective was an ecological one, and his main thesis was that the main determinant of socialisation practices in pretechnical societies would be the relative emphasis on the one hand on hunting (required individual perceptual and motor skills, and an individualistic style of socialisation) and settled agriculture (in which group co-operation and social conformity were stressed) on the other.

The embedded figures test correlated at a highly significant level in Berry's study, with a combined index of cultural style, socialisation and acculturation in the various pretechnical societies studied, indicating that scores on the embedded figures test can be readily predicted from other information about the culture in which a group of individuals live. As in all previous studies, the greater the emphasis in the culture on socialisation for conformity, the greater the amount of perceptual field-dependence. Commenting on sex differences in field-dependence in his samples, Berry indicates that differences between males and females were by no means universal, and seemed to be confined to cultures (usually pastoral ones) which emphasise role differentiation. The less role differentiation in a culture, the less likely it is that significant sex differences in perceptual tasks such as the embedded figures test will emerge.

Cross-cultural studies of psychological differentiation have been systematically reviewed in detail by Witkin and Berry (1975). The bibliography of their paper, referencing some 180 studies, indicates the great number of studies which have been carried out comparing psychological differentiation across cultures. It is both interesting and significant however that no study is reported which has compared English subjects with subjects in other cultures. Indeed, the British work on cognitive style is very slight, as is work on Caribbean and Japanese subjects.

In Britain, Ghuman (1977) investigated field dependence in a sample of school children aged 11 and 12, and found that field dependence-independence had no significant correlation with Porter and Cattell's Children's Personality Questionnaire. Middle-class children were significantly more field-independent than working-class children, but no significant sex differences emerged.

In a further study with 13-year olds attending a multiracial comprehensive school in a British city, Ghuman (1978) found that although West Indians had the lowest score of all groups (White, Asian and West Indian), on a group measure of field dependence differences were not statistically significant. However, on tests of mathematics West Indian pupils did significantly less well than other pupils, leading to the presumption that West Indian pupils are underachieving academically. Overall, mathematical ability correlated 0.50 with scores on the group embedded figures test (measuring field dependence-independence).

The largest study of British children, in terms of the variables explored, is Machtiger's (1974) investigation of the Children's Embedded Figures Test (Witkin's measure of cognitive style) and a wide range of cognitive and affective measures, in a sample of London infant school children. She found that cognitive style was highly correlated with proficiency in reading, perceptual motor performance, aspects of linguistic proficiencies, and certain indices of psychodynamic functioning, including ego strength and attitudes towards the self. Cognitive style appeared to be a pervasive personality trait, even in children of this age, and was important in understanding learning disabilities.

In conclusion, it is clear from the literature reviewed here and elsewhere (Bagley, 1982) that Witkin's cognitive style is related to differences in culture, ecology, and socialisation. In general females tend to be more field-dependent than males, but this finding is less universal than that relating to type of socialisation. Socialisation is the primary influence on field-dependence, and much depends on how girls are socialised compared with boys. If both sexes are socialised in rather similar ways, differences in field-dependence should not emerge. Educational stimulation may be significant factor in field independence in modernising societies.

Black children seem to be more field-dependent than white children, but whether this is due to the effects of culture, or of social class is not entirely clear. The influence of social class is itself somewhat ambiguous.

In our cross-cultural work with 8 to 11 year olds in England, Japan, Jamaica, America and Gujerat we have explored various hypotheses arising out of this review of cross-cultural aspects of cognitive style as measured by Herman Witkin and his associates. We try and answer the questions: How do socialisation styles in different cultures influence levels of field dependent cognitive style? How has migration to Britain influenced styles of socialisation in Jamaican parents, in ways which influence their children's cognitive style? How are social class and field dependent cognitive styles related? How are self-esteem, group dependence and field dependent cognitive styles related? And how does the extreme group dependence which seems to permeate much of Japanese culture (Bagley, Iwawaki and Young, 1982) influence Japanese cognitive style?

The English Sample (English and Jamaican)
In England we studied 236 children aged 9 to 11 attending four elementary schools in London and Southern England. The areas served by the schools ranged from a depressed, slum area to a wealthy, middle class area. All of the children of Jamaican cultural origin attended schools in working class areas of London.

The English Sample (Japanese)
Forty-two children were tested, 23 boys and 19 girls aged 8 to 11. Subjects were located through contacts with the Japanese community in South London. The parents of these children were diplomats, scholars and business people.

The Japanese Sample
The sample of middle class children consisted of 63 children aged 8 to 10 in the city of Nagoya. The second group of 85 boys and 87 girls aged 8-10 were resident in the industrial city of Hamamatsu. We judged that both these groups were influenced by the

cultural tradition of amae, which epitomizes self-non-self differentiation (Doi, 1973).

The Gujerati Samples - Gujerat, England and Eastern United States

The 72 children, all boys, in Rajkot, a regional capital in Gujerat State, North Western India were aged 10 to 12 years. The U.S. sample, preliminary only, included 16 children of Gujerati parents in Hoboken, New Jersey, Philadelphia, Pa., both areas of Gujerati settlement. In London, England 27 children aged 10-11 of Gujerati parents were obtained in schools in areas of Gujerati settlement in East London.

The Rural Jamaican Sample

This sample was obtained from a large elementary school serving a rural population, many living in extreme poverty. Because of the practice of dividing children by supposed ability, and the sex bias in this process, our final sample consisted of 48 boys and 80 girls aged 10-11, being children in the upper two streams for this age group. In the lowest stream literacy skills were so undeveloped as to make general testing and the application of a reading test inappropriate (see Bagley, 1979 for a critical view of problems of the Jamaican educational system). Culturally, the environment of these children seems to be close to the traditionalism of the rural Panamanian communities studied by Irwin et al., (1976).

INSTRUMENTS AND TESTERS

Our principle aim was to examine cross-cultural variation in psychological differentiation, using Witkin's Children's Embedded Figures Test (Witkin et al., 1971) which is individually administered and involves the ability to visually locate two shapes, a tepee and a Western-style house, in an increasingly complex background of shapes and colours. We sought to explain such ability in terms of parental socialisation styles; group orientation and lack of self-differentiation in particular cultures; sex differences; educational systems and general intellectual development; socioeconomic status; and modernisation and social change involved in the migration experience. We also examined, in subjects in Britain, whether there was any systematic relationship (as Ziller, 1972 had suggested) between field dependency and poorer self-esteem.

Social class was usually measured in three broad categories: I - Professional, managerial, landlords, large farmers; II - Intermediate semi-professionals, clerks, skilled and semi-skilled workers; III - Peasants, labourers, subsistence farmers, and the poorest people, employed or not. These broad social divisions are useful for cross-cultural analyses, but require refinement for comparisons of special groups such as the Gujeratis for whom traditional caste divisions are still important.

The instruments included Miller's questionnaire, for completion by ten-year-olds to describe their parents' socialisation practices. The original instrument devised by Miller (1970) was validated and shortened to a 15-item version using factor analysis (Bagley and Wong, 1982). Coopersmith and Piers-Harris self-esteem measures were used in subjects studied in England (Bagley, Verma and Mallick, 1981). A measure of verbal reasoning (Schonell, 1956) was used for subjects tested in English. All subjects studied in England, Jamaica and the United States were tested in English. All Gujerati children were tested by H.V., who used Gujerati medium and translated instruments into Gujerati in the Indian fieldwork. In Jamaica, L.Y. used Jamaican Creole as a medium of testing for subjects who did not speak 'standard Jamaican' (Craig, 1971). In Japan, instruments were translated into Japanese by S.I. and were administered by his postgraduate students. In England, Japanese, English and Jamaican children were tested by C.B., L.Y. or J.S.-Y.W.

CROSS-CULTURAL VARIATION IN PERCEPTUAL DISEMBEDDING

The main data, in Table 1 reveal wide and significant differences in 'perceptual disembedding' (field dependence-independence) between cultural groups as indicated by scores on the Children's Embedded Figures Test. When age was controlled in an analysis of variance design, differences emerged as highly significant. Despite hypotheses that Japanese children would be highly group dependent and would therefore lack the aspect of self-non-self-differentiation which the CEFT measures

(Bagley, Iwawaki and Young, 1982), results completely disconfirmed this expectation. Japanese children, both in Japan and in England, performed exceptionally well on this test, over a tenth having a maximum score of 25 on the test. The possible reasons we adduced for this were the visual acuity which becoming literate in Japanese symbols involved (slightly lower CEFT scores for the Japanese children in England, somewhat less literate and practised in symbols tended to confirm this); very high achievement motivation of Japanese children (somewhat lower scores for the working class children in Japan supported that view); and the general tendency for Japanese children to score higher than the average Western child on a variety of cognitive and achievement tests (Lynn, 1977).

In every group of children we have studied, boys have slightly higher CEFT scores (as in Witkin's normative American groups) which is in keeping with previous work suggesting that boys are frequently socialised for greater self-differentiation.

The results from the rural Jamaican sample are particularly interesting in this respect. The girls in our sample in Jamaica have particularly low scores on the CEFT, in comparison with boys in Jamaica and compared with all other groups. We have interpreted these low scores in the light of traditional forms of Jamaican socialisation in female-dominated families: girls are retained within the physical and emotional ambit of the family while boys are much more often left to fend for themselves, both physically and emotionally (Bagley and Young, 1980).

English boys and girls from middle class areas are relatively field independent, and significantly more so than working class English children, age controlled. Nevertheless, when age is taken into account, even middle class English children are significantly more field dependent than working class Japanese children.

Boys in Gujerat are more field dependent than any other male group we tested, and it is interesting to observe in this context that Sinha (1978) has complained that since CEFT is an abstract test using Western symbols, Indian children quickly lose motivation to complete the more difficult items. He devised instead an ingenious test in which children had to find hidden robbers and hidden treasure!

Forty-two Rajkot children were tested with the Group Embedded Figures Test, and the combined results of this with the CEFT scores for 30 Rajkot subjects supports Sinha's finding of difficulty in the formal skill of perceptual disembedding. In contrast to this finding we must however consider the Japanese results: despite the abstract nature and cultural strangeness of the test, most Japanese 9-year-olds examined did better on the CEFT than most American 14-year-olds in the normative samples (Witkin et al., 1971).

MIGRATION AND FIELD INDEPENDENCE

There is some evidence (see the review above) that migration, and the exposure to a variety of new cultural influences including different educational systems and pressures to socialise children in particular ways, may lead to a general 'modernisation' whose thrust is to influence the development of self-non-self differentiation. This possibility seems to emerge most clearly with the Jamaican children in England. In such children the large sex difference on the CEFT has narrowed considerably, and Jamaican boys have levels of field-dependence which are similar to those of their English peers of similar age and social class backgrounds (Table 1). Just as Ghuman (1975) had found that Punjabi boys in Birmingham, England possessed conceptual and cognitive styles similar to those of their English peers (and unlike those of non-migrant Punjabi boys in the Punjab), so children of Jamaican parents in Britain were orienting to their environment in conceptual terms quite similar to those of their English peers (Bagley and Young, 1980). It is salient however that some Jamaican families in England, mostly of lower class origin and unilingual in Jamaican creole, do seem to have considerable difficulty in orienting to their new environment; this is reflected to some degree in the scholastic underachievement of their children (Bagley, Bart and Wong, 1978).

Gujerati boys in London are more field independent than boys in Gujerat (our small American sample shows the same trend towards field independence). While this finding is in keeping with the modernisation hypotheses, it involves a paradox: in Gujerat higher caste children were more field-dependent. This result emerged with both the CEFT and the Group Embedded Figures Test which was used with an additional sample in Gujerat. Vyas (1982) interprets this in terms of the restrictive socialisation which upper caste children (as an elite group with truncated social interactions) are subject to. Lower caste children, in contrast are socialised in a less inclusive manner, which seems to foster self differentiation.

Children of Gujerati migrants in Britain and America came in the main, from upper caste groups. Inferentially, caste and its associated forms of socialisation become much less important in these migrant families, amongst whom considerable acculturation takes places: high status is still important, but this is sought through Western style achievement motivation, which implies greater cognitive flexibility for children in these families.

PARENTAL AUTHORITARIANISM AND FIELD DEPENDENCE

The hypothesis that restrictive, punitive and controlling parental socialisation will be associated with field dependence is a reasonable one in the light of earlier work by Witkin and his colleagues (Witkin, 1969). Miller's (1970) scale which we adapted was strongly predictive of scholastic underachievement in the original validation sample, and it was a reasonable hypothesis that the socialisation practices which the scale measured would predict other aspects of cognition in 10-year-olds.

The results of comparing scores on the Parental Authoritarism scale with those on the CEFT yielded, contrary to expectation, largley non-significant results without any clear trend. The only two significant results were in the opposite direction to that predicted. In Jamaican girls in Jamaica parental punitiveness and control of activities was associated with more field independence. Boys in Jamaica (who were subjected to very severe levels of parental punitiveness) tended to be less field dependent than girls, whose lack of self-non-self differentiation had its basis in a gentler, more inclusive socialisation into female roles. The more girls in Jamaica were socialised like boys, we concluded, the more likely were they to be more field independent. Such trends did not emerge in children of Jamaican parents in London (who had migrated from rural areas similar to the one studied in our Jamaican fieldwork).

In Gujerat only boys were studied because of the strictness of control of female children, who if they were educated at all, were not enrolled in the same school as boys. For the boys in our Indian sample, parental strictness and punitiveness was associated with field independence. This paradox was explained by the intervening variable of caste: higher caste boys were more field dependent (presumably a reflection of the retentitive socialisation associated with higher caste membership) but were socialised in a less punitive manner than lower caste children. What is implied in these results is that the aspect of socialisation which influences psychological differentiation is not directly measured by the scale we have used. In defence of its validity, however, our present results do strongly support Miller's (1970) original findings: parental authoritarianism is strongly related to underachievement in the British samples on a conventional test of verbal reasoning (Schonell, 1956). In addition, parental authoritarianism was clearly related to poor self-esteem, a finding elaborated below.

SELF-ESTEEM AND FIELD INDEPENDENT COGNITIVE STYLE

In his earlier work, Witkin et al. (1962) had implied that lack of self-differentiation might be associated with restricted self-concept and poorer self-esteem. Such an association is clearly asserted in Ziller's (1972) work on self-esteem. Detailed work with a sub-sample of our British subjects could not however establish any direct or significant relationship between Coopersmith's self-esteem inventory (Coopersmith, 1967) and scores on the CEFT. These two dimensions of personality were on the face of things completely orthogonal, independent aspects of personal function. Principal components analysis of the individual items in the Coopersmith and Miller items together with the CEFT clarified this (Bagley and Wong, 1982). The highly field independent child was found to be one who was likely to be an only child of busy, working parents, socialised for independence, self-recreation, self-care and personal choice and motivation.

Further work using the Piers-Harris scale and the CEFT with an ethnically mixed group of British 10-year-olds drew two main conclusions:

1. Field independence and high self-esteem are connected only in children who have been socialised to operate independently of group situations, and whose present family and school contexts, provide positive reinforcements for their group independent personality style.

2. Field dependence and poor self-esteem are connected only in children whose need for group support and affiliation, and group situations in the school context, are not being met.

These results applied both to English and West Indian children in the London schools we studied, and the picture that emerged was of heterogeneity of cognitive style within the ethnic groups studied. Although some West Indian children displayed both group dependence and lack of psychological differentiation others displayed quite opposite characteristics, whilst the majority had an average position on both dimensions. With regard to self-esteem West Indian and Asian children did not show any differential levels in comparison with English children (Bagley, Verma and Mallick, 1981).

FIELD INDEPENDENCE AND VERBAL REASONING

In the groups in England consistent, significant correlations of between 0.3 and 0.4 were found between CEFT scores and the test of Verbal Reasoning used (Schonell, 1956). This finding is in keeping with recent studies which have implied that disembedding skills are quite closely influenced by modern forms of schooling to a degree which can confound the socialisation influences identified in earlier studies (Serpell, 1976).

In Jamaica and in Gujerat this finding was, paradoxically, reversed. Girls in rural Jamaica showed considerable scholastic superiority in comparison with boys: in part this was due to the rigid streaming process which condemned boys to an inferior education; but in addition because of traditional social structure and wider trends in the educational system, girls in Jamaica are intellectually superior at all levels (Bagley, 1979). But, it will be observed from Table 1, rural Jamaican girls have very poor disembedding skills, and in this sample of rural Jamaican children scholastic achievement and CEFT scores are inversely related, a correlation which disappears when sex is controlled. This trend did not emerge in our London sample of Jamaican children, in whom sex difference in scholastic achievement were minimal (Bagley, 1981).

In the boys in Gujerat those from higher castes had the highest levels of scholastic achievement; but these high caste boys also had somewhat lower CEFT scores. The small positive correlation between disembedding skills and achievement <u>increased</u> significantly when the intervening variable of caste was controlled for.

DISCUSSION AND CONCLUSION

Our programme of comparative research has had a number of aims. First, in the tradition of research in crosscultural psychology we have attempted to look at the same psychological processes in different cultures, attempting to see if variations follow the same pattern, in terms of social and structural antecedents. The picture which has emerged is much more complex than that we had anticipated before the research began. Socialisation is a subtle influence on cognitive style, and is difficult to infer or measure accurately. But the influence of socialisation styles upon cognitive styles does not seem to be as direct as Witkin and his colleagues had implied. Our Japanese results are important for they represent a significant discontinuity in the schema proposed by Witkin. Apparently an extreme group dependence and apparent lack of self-non-self differentiation is paralleled in Japanese children by remarkable skills in perceptual disembedding. Results from Jamaica and Gujerat also imply that socialisation, sex, social status interact in complex ways to produce different levels of disembedding skills. The patterns which we have identified in different cultural groups imply description of emic rather than etic processes (cf Berry, 1979).

A second aim of this research has been to examine the effects of migration and living in a new culture on cognitive style. Cross-cultural analysis to elucidate this process has to face the fact that those migrating may be a quite different group from those not migrating. Vyas (1982) argues however that, given the long tradition of emigration from Gujerat this is unlikely to be true except for the lowest SES groups. Similarly, our view of Jamaica as a migrant culture in which all classes have migrated to some degree is supported by Thomas-Hope (1981). Only in the case of Japanese children in London have we been dealing with a group of rather different social antecedents from those of the group within Japan.

The evidence suggests that following migration children rapidly orient, in cognitive terms, to their new environment, and acquire the conceptual modes of thinking and perceiving which new culture demands. Nevertheless, traditional cognitive styles, especially as they relate to family organisation, are frequently retained (Bagley, 1981 b). The child of immigrant parents retains a certain duality of thinking, perceiving and feeling. This is illustrated in our comparative work on self-esteem in Indian children, in India and in Britain (Bagley, Verma and Mallick, 1981). The structure and levels of self-esteem (inferred from principal components analysis of the Coopersmith scale) in Indian children in Britain more closely resemble those of English children; but certain components of self-esteem in the Indian children in Britain bear a distinct resemblance to components in children in urban India (Verma, Bagley and Mallick, 1980). Children of migrant Indian parents are orienting to different aspects of culture simultaneously, and thus have a particularly complex set of affective and cognitive styles. Work on personality variables confirms this complex picture (Bagley, Verma and Mallick, 1982).

What implications do our findings have for the practice of multicultural education? The implications are largely negative. Although group oriented educational styles have important implications, especially in the sphere of interethnic interaction (Hansell and Slavin, 1981), more formal approaches which emphasise individual aspects of learning can also be valuable (Wheldall et al., 1981). Indeed in Britain, an overemphasis on group processes to the exclusion of individual educational needs seems to have had distinctively harmful effects on the educational progress of some young children (Donaldson, 1978).

Although local, community schools may concentrate on producing a 'social individual' - a child who is both socially oriented and has his or her individual needs and aspirations met (Skrimshire, 1981), policies which have aimed to accommodate the special needs of children of immigrants have been a distinct failure, in Britain at least (Stone, 1981). Part of the problem is that minority children, even from a single ethnic group, are not homogeneous with regard to their affective and cognitive styles. Although patterns of regularities can sometimes be detected these rarely explain enough variance to justify any particular educational strategies. In multicultural education as indeed in education generally, the focus on the needs of individuals in a positive and non-stereotyped way are crucial (Jeffcoate, 1979).

We must acknowledge the criticisms of multiculturalism and multicultural education from radical scholars in minority communities, who argue that a naive stress on 'differences', whether cognitive, cultural or otherwise, detracts from the real issue in inter-ethnic relations, namely discrimination and inequalities of power and denial of access to high status employment, training and resources. Moodley (1981) has argued this case powerfully in the Canadian context, suggesting the official multicultural policy disguises, ignores or falsifies profound differences in power between ethnic groups.

In Britain, Mullard (1980 and 1981) has argued that multicultural education is a masking ideology which, in its stress on 'ethnicism' is little better than the racism which it purports to counter. Naive concepts of multicultural education, he argues, ignore the realities of economic exploitation of certain ethnic groups, and the historical and structural interconnections of class and racial exploitation.

A non-Marxist but equally pungent critique has been advanced by Stone (1981) who argues that although practitioners of multicultural education do not usually ally themselves with the still prevalent ideologies of 'scientific racism' (which argue that black underachievement has a biological or genetic basis), nevertheless they subscribe to ideologies of 'cultural deprivation' reflected in 'poor self-esteem' which many teachers interpret (in self-fulfilling ways) as an indicator of the lack of potential of black children.

In our recent writings on education and ethnic relations we have argued that bias in teacher perceptions of minority children are a major problem for educational practice, and imply the need for important changes in teacher training. The thrust of our argument has been for the individualisation of teaching, and a methodological individualism which recognises and enhances the intrinsic aspirations (cultural, social and personal) of each pupil (Verma and Bagley, 1975, 1979 and 1981; Bagley and Verma, 1979 and 1982; Bagley, Verma, Mallick and Young, 1979).

Teachers, then, should be aware of their personal cognitive styles and frames of emotional and value reference, alter these if necessary, and use this cultural and cognitive understanding constructively in relating to the individual needs of each pupil. Culture is connected with, but never determines these individual needs.

In one of his last writings, the late Herman Witkin (1978) argued, in a lecture on cognitive styles in personal and cultural adaptation that:

> Cognitive styles stand apart from most of the earlier approaches in the scope of what they encompass of behavior in the person, in their conceptual underpinning, in their attention to person-situation interactions, and in the developmental context in which they have been placed. Because of these features, it seems appropriate to say that cognitive styles are really concerned with individuality and with diversity among people rather than with individual differences in the usual narrow sense.
> (Witkin, 1978, p. 63)

Individuality and diversity considered within an educational context which recognises the realities of power, exploitation and their reflection in biased educational systems, and the realities of cultural imperialism and cultural estrangement, is a cornerstone of a multicultural education which may lead to 'integration' in the sense defined by Pettigrew (1971) and Berry (1979).

Such integration is compatible with the development of community schools which serve particular ethnic and linguistic communities (cf Bhatnagar, 1981). Indeed, an important index of the social power of any ethnic community is the degree to which that community can mobilise resources to provide elementary schools serving the linguistic and cultural needs expressed by a significant proportion of the ethnic group. The survey by Pavin and Young (1980) shows that the most vigorous and powerful group in this respect (apart from the French and the English) are the Ukranians of Canada. Elementary schools serving the linguistic needs of Native children were not detected in that survey. In Alberta, we have not been able to discover an elementary school which teaches children in the Blackfoot language; though Blackfoot has survived the ethnocidal practices of an earlier administration, multicultural educational policies have singularly failed to provide any meaningful or realistic support for the linguistic and cultural heritage of Native peoples in Canada.

NOTES

1. Paper given to "Perspectives on Multiculturalism in Education: An Invitational Symposium," Queen's University, Kingston, Ontario, November 1981. A shortened version of this paper was published in the conference proceedings, Multicultural Education in Canada, Toronto: Allyn and Bacon, 1983.

The research reported in this paper is based on collaboration with Saburo Iwawaki, Kanka Mallick, Gajendra K. Verma, Harshad Vyas, Loretta Young and Joyce Siu-Ying Wong.

We are indebted to Herman Witkin for his patient correspondence with us about this research, and lament his untimely death in 1979.

REFERENCES

Bagley, C., Bart, M. and Wong, J. (1978). 'Cognition and Scholastic Success in West Indian 10-Year-Olds in London: A Comparative Study', Educational Studies, vol. 4, pp. 7-17.

Bagley, C. (1979), 'A Comparative Perspective on the Education of Black Children in Britain', Comparative Education, vol. 15, pp. 63-81.

Bagley, C. and Verma, G. (1979), Racial Prejudice, the Individual and Society, Saxon House, Farnborough, U.K.

Bagley, C., Verma, G., Mallick, K. and Young, L. (1979), Personality, Self-Esteem and Prejudice, Saxon House, Farnborough, U.K.

Bagley, C., Wong, J. and Young, L. (1980), 'Parental Behaviour and Cognitive Styles in 10-Year-Olds in England and Jamaica', New Community, vol. 8, pp. 37-50.

Bagley, C., Verma, G. and Mallick, K. (1982), 'The Comparative Structure of Self-Esteem in British and Indian Adolescents', in Verma, G. and Bagley, C. (eds.), Self Concept, Achievement and Multicultural Education, MacMillan, London.

Bagley, C. (1981), 'Asian Children in Britain: Education, Culture and Social Welfare', paper presented to the Annual Meeting of the Canadian Asian Studies Association, Halifax, May, 1981. (A revision of 'A Perspective on the Education of Asian Children in Britain', Indian Educational Review, 1980, July, pp. 1-21).

Bagley, C., Bart, M. and Wong, J. (1981), 'Achievement, Behaviour Disorder and Social Circumstances in West Indian Children and Other Ethnic Groups', in Verma, G. and Bagley, C. (eds.), Self-Concept, Achievement and Multicultural Education, MacMillan, London.

Bagley, C. (1982), 'Cognitive Styles, Ethnicity, Social Class and Socialisation on Cross-Cultural Perspective', in Bagley, C. and Verma, G. (eds.), Multicultural Childhood, Gower Press, Aldershot, U.K.

Bagley, C. and Verma, G. (1982), Multicultural Childhood: Cognitive Styles, Ethnicity and Education, Gower Press, Aldershot, U.K.

Bagley, C., Verma, G. and Mallick, K. (1982), 'Psychological Dimensions of Urban Education in India', in Bagley, C. and Verma, G. (eds.), Multicultural Childhood, Gower Press, Aldershot, U.K.

Bagley, C., Iwawaki, S. and Young, L. (1982), 'Japanese Children: Group Oriented But Not Field Dependent?' in Bagley C. and Verma, G. (eds.), Multicultural Childhood, Gower Press, Aldershot, U.K.

Bagley, C. and Wong, J. (1982), 'Self-Esteem, Cognitive Style and Group Independence in English 10-Year-Olds' in Bagley, C. and Verma, G. (eds.), Multicultural Childhood, Gower Press, Aldershot, U.K.

Berry, J. 1976), Human Ecology and Cognitive Style, Sage Publications, Beverly Hills, CA.

Berry, J. (1977), 'Nomadic Style and Cognitive Style', in McGurk, H. (ed.), Ecology and Culture, North Holland Publishing.

Berry, J. (1979), 'Research in Multicultural Societies: Implications of Cross-Cultural Methods', Journal of Cross-Cultural Psychology, vol. 10, pp. 415-434.

Bhatnagar, J. (1981), 'Language and Culture Maintenance Programmes in Canada', in Verma, G. and Bagley C. (eds.), Self-Concept, Achievement and Multicultural Education, MacMillan, London.

Campfens, H. (1980), The Integration of Ethno-Cultural Minorities: A Pluralist Approach - The Netherlands and Canada, Ministry of Cultural Affairs, The Hague.

Coopersmith, S. (1967), The Antecedents of Self-Esteem, Freeman, San Francisco.

Craig, D. (1971), 'The Use of Language by 7 Year Old Jamaican Children Living in Contrasting Socioeconomic Environments', PhD dissertation, University of London.

Donaldson, M. (1978), Children's Minds, Fontana/Collins, London.

Elkind, D. (1981), 'Forms and Traits in the Conception and Measurement of General Intelligence', Intelligence, vol. 5, pp. 101-120.

Ghuman, P. (1975), The Cultural Context of Thinking: A Comparative Study of Punjabi and English Boys, National Foundation for Educational Research, Windsor, U.K.

Ghuman, P. (1977), 'An Exploratory Study of Witkin's Dimension in Relation to Social Class, Personality Factors and Piagetian Tests', Social Behaviour and Personality, vol. 5, pp. 87-91.

Ghuman, P. (1978), 'A Comparative Study of Cognitive Styles in Three Ethnic Groups', paper given to the Annual Conference of the British Psychological Society, September, 1981.

Hansell, S. and Slavin, R. (1981), 'Co-Operative Learning and the Structure of Interracial Friendships', Sociology of Education, vol. 54, pp. 98-106.

Irwin, M., Engle, P., Klein, R. and Yarborough, C. (1976), 'Traditionalism and Field Dependence', Journal of Cross-Cultural Psychology, vol. 7, pp. 463-473.

Jeffcoate, R. (1979), Positive Image: Toward a Multi-racial Curriculum, Chameleon Books, London.

Kogan, N. (1977), Cognitive Styles in Infancy and Early Childhood, Erlbaum, New York.

Kirkness, V. (1981), 'The Education of Canadian Indian Children', Child Welfare, vol. 60, pp. 447-455.

Laosa, L. (1977), 'Multicultural Education: How Psychology Can Contribute', Journal of Teacher Education, vol. 28, pp. 26-30.

Lloyd, B. (1972), *Perception and Cognition: A Cross-Cultural Perspective*, Penguin Books, London.
Lynn, R. (1977), 'The Intelligence of the Japanese', *Bulletin of the British Psychological Society*, vol. 30, pp. 69-72.
Machtiger, H. (1974), 'An Exploration of the Relationship of Cognitive Style to Learning Disabilities in Primary School Children', PhD, dissertation, University of London.
Miller, G. (1970), *Educational Opportunity and the Home*, Longman, London.
Moodley, K. (1980), 'Canadian Ethnicity in Comparative Perspective', in Dahlie, J. and Fernando, T. (eds.), *Ethnicity, Power and Politics in Canada*, Methuen, Toronto,
Mullard, C. (1980), *Racism in Society and Schools: History, Policy and Practice*, Centre for Multicultural Education, Occasional Paper No. 1, University of London, London.
Mullard, C. (1981), 'Black Kids in White Schools: Multiracial Education', *Plural Societies*, in press.
Pannu, R. and Young, L. (1980), 'Ethnic Schools in Three Canadian Cities: A Study of Multiculturalism', *Alberta Journal of Educational Research*, vol. 26, pp. 242-261.
Pettigrew, T. (1971), *Racially Separate or Together?*, McGraw-Hill, New York.
Ramirez, M., Castaneda, A. and Herold, P. (1974), 'The Relationship of Acculturation to Cognitive Style Among Mexican Americans', *Journal of Cross-Cultural Psychology*, vol. 5, pp. 212-219.
Schonell, F. (1956), *Diagnostic and Attainment Testing*, Oliver and Boyd, Edinburgh.
Serpell, R. (1976), *Culture's Influence on Behaviour*, Methuen, London.
Sinha, D. (1978), 'Story-Pictorial EFT: A Culturally Appropriate Test for Perceptual Disembedding', *Indian Journal of Psychology*, vol. 53, pp. 1-18.
Stone, M. (1981), *The Education of the Black Child in Britain: The Myth of Multiracial Education*. Fontana, London.
Skrimshire, A. (1981), 'Community Schools and the Education of the 'Social Individual', *Oxford Review of Education*, vol. 7, pp. 53-65.
Thomas-Hope, E. (1981), 'Identity and Adaptation of Migrants from the English-Speaking Caribbean in Britain and North America', in Verma, G. and Bagley, C. (eds.), *Self-Concept, Achievement*

and Multicultural Education, MacMillan, London.
Verma, G. and Bagley, C. (eds.) (1975), Race and Education Across Cultures, Heinemann, London.
Verma, G. and Bagley, C. (eds.) (1979), Race, Education and Identity, MacMillan, London.
Verma, G. and Bagley, C. (eds.) (1981), Self-Concept, Achievement and Multicultural Education, MacMillan, London.
Verma, G., Bagley, C. and Mallick, K. (1980), Illusion and Reality in Indian Secondary Education, Gower Press, Aldershot, U.K.
Vernon, P. (1975), 'Intelligence Across Cultures', in Verma, G. and Bagley, C. (eds.), Race and Education Across Cultures, Heinemann, London.
Vyas, H. (1982), 'Education and Cognitive Styles: A Case Study of Gujerati Children in Britain, Eastern United States and India', in Bagley, C. and Verma, G. (eds.), Multicultural Childhood, Gower Press, Aldershot, U.K.
Wagner, D. (1978), 'The Effects of Formal Schooling on Cognitive Style', Journal of Social Psychology, vol. 106, pp. 145-151.
Witkin, H., Dyk, R., Faterson, H., Goodenough, D. and Karp, S. (1962), Psychological Differentiation, Wiley, New York.
Witkin, H. (1967), 'Cognitive Styles Across Cultures', International Journal of Psychology, vol. 2, pp. 233250.
Witkin, H. (1969), 'Social Influences in the Development of Cognitive Style', in Goslin, D. (ed.), Handbook of Socialisation Theory and Research, Rand McNally, New York.
Witkin, H., Oltman, P., Raskin, E., and Karp, S. (1971), A Manual for the Embedded Figures Test, Consulting Psychologists Press, Palo Alto, CA.
Witkin, H., Price-Williams, D., Bertin, D., Christiansen, B., Oltman, P., Ramirez, P. and Van Meel, M. and J. (1974), 'Social Conformity and Psychological Differentiation', International Journal of Psychology, vol. 9, pp. 11-29.
Witkin, H. and Berry, J. (1975), 'Psychological Differentiation in Cross-Cultural Perspective', Journal of Cross-Cultural Psychology, vol. 6, pp. 4-87.
Witkin, H. and Goodenough, D. (1977a), 'Psychological Differentiation in Cross-Cultural Perspective', Journal of Cross-Cultural Psychology, vol. 6, pp. 4-87.

Witkin, H., Moore, C., Goodenough, D. and Cox, P. (1977d), Field-Dependent and Field-Independent Cognitive Styles and Their Educational Implications', <u>Review of Educational Research</u>, vol. 47, pp. 1-64.

Witkin, H. (1978), <u>Cognitive Styles in Personal and Cultural Adaptation</u>, Clark University Press, Worcester, Mass.

Wheldall, K., Morris, M., Vaughan, P. and Ng, Y. (1981), 'Rows Versus Tables: An Example of the Use of Behavioural Ecology in Two Classes of 11-Year-Old Children', <u>Educational Psychology</u>, vol. 1, p. 2.

Ziller, R. (1972), <u>Manual for the Self-Other Orientation Inventories</u>, University of Delaware Press.

Table 1.1: Mean Scores on the Children's Embedded Figures Test

Group	Mean	Standard Deviation
Japanese boys in Nagoya, Japan (N = 32; mean age 9.09 years)	24.12	1.66
Japanese girls in Nagoya, Japan (N = 31; mean age 9.48 years)	23.90	1.64
Japanese boys in Hamamatsu, Japan (N = 85; mean age 9.17 years)	20.76	2.70
Japanese girls in Hamamatsu, Japan (N = 87; mean age 9.24 years)	20.40	3.11
Japanese boys in London (N = 23; mean age 9.7 years)	23.37	1.86
Japanese girls in London (N = 19; mean age 9.5 years)	22.95	2.50
American boys (Witkin et al., 1971) (N = 20; age range 9-10)	16.6	5.4
American girls (Witkin et al., 1971) (N = 20; age range 9-10)	16.3	5.7
American boys (Witkin et al., 1971) (N = 20; age range 11-12)	18.9	5.5
American girls (Witkin et al., 1971) (N = 20; age range 11-12)	17.2	4.8
English boys in middle class areas (N = 50; mean age 10.3 years)	20.86	3.73
English girls in middle class areas (N = 50; mean age 10.3 years)	20.84	3.68

Table 1.1   (continued)

Group	Mean	Standard Deviation
English boys in working class areas (N = 21; mean age 10.8 years)	19.38	3.63
English girls in working class areas (N = 24; mean age 10.4 years)	18.92	3.81
Jamaican boys in working class areas of London (N = 45; mean age 10.4 years)	18.09	3.80
Jamaican girls in working class areas of London (N = 42; mean age 10.6 years)	17.52	3.61
Jamaican boys in rural Jamaica (N = 48; mean age 10.2 years)	15.82	3.76
Jamaican girls in rural Jamaica (N = 80; mean age 10.1 years)	12.29	4.04
Gujerati boys in Rajkot, Gujerat, India (N = 30; mean age 10.8 years)	14.8	7.17
Gujerati boys in London (N = 27; mean age 10.5 years)	18.15	5.04

Note: The higher the score, the more the perceptual field independence. Maximum possible score on the CEFT is 25.0.

Table 1.2: Mean Scores on the Measure of Parental Authoritarianism

Group	N	Mean	Standard Deviation
Japanese boys in Japan (Nagoya)	32	10.93	4.31
Japanese girls in Japan (Nagoya)	31	9.49	3.76
Japanese boys in Japan (Hamamatsu)	85	11.29	3.61
Japanese girls in Japan (Hamamatsu)	87	10.53	4.10
Japanese boys in London	23	11.36	4.12
Japanese girls in London	19	9.70	4.25
English boys, middle class areas of England	53	9.86	4.08
English girls, middle class areas of England	50	8.87	3.98
English boys, working class areas of England	21	12.96	4.63
English girls, working class areas of England	24	12.01	4.29

Table 1.2 (continued)

Group	N	Mean	Standard Deviation
Jamaican boys, working class areas of England	46	15.40	5.27
Jamaican girls, working class areas of England	42	14.55	4.91
Jamaican boys, rural Jamaica	48	17.92	3.76
Jamaican girls, rural Jamaica	80	15.58	3.88
Gujerati boys, in Gujerat, India	72	16.54	5.40

Note: The higher the score, the more the parental authoritarian described by the child.

APPENDIX

The Measure of Parental Authoritarianism
for Completion by Children

Instructions: Look at the following sentences. If the sentence applies to you, put a circle around YES. If it does not apply to you, put a circle around NO.

---

1. My parents are very ready to answer all my questions.   YES   NO

2. My parents make all the rules and decisions without consulting me.   YES   NO

3. I can talk to my parents about anything, even things they don't like.   YES   NO

4. My parents are cross with me every time I argue.   YES   NO

5. At home I am allowed to make a lot of my own decisions.   YES   NO

6. If I am naughty at home I usually get a beating.   YES   NO

7. If I break a rule at home I can usually get out of being punished.   YES   NO

8. My parents never praise me when I do something well.   YES   NO

9. My parents think children are the most important people at home.   YES   NO

10. I quite often get a good hiding at home.   YES   NO

11. If I am naughty my parents always try to understand.   YES   NO

APPENDIX cont'd

12. At home I sometimes get into
    trouble when I ask questions.   YES   NO

13. There are things my parents
    won't let me talk about.   YES   NO

14. At home I can make very few
    decisions of my own.   YES   NO

15. My parents are strict.   YES   NO

Scoring:

    NO   (items 1, 2, 5, 7, 9, 11) score 2.

    YES (items 2, 4, 5, 8, 10, 12, 13, 14, 15)
         score 2.
      Any item not completed score 1.

Any Item not completed score 1.

Discard if more than five items not completed.

Chapter Twelve

THE WELFARE, ADAPTATION AND IDENTITY OF CHILDREN FROM INTERCULTURAL MARRIAGE (1)

Christopher Bagley
and Loretta Young

Marriage between partners of different racial or ethnic groups has in the past been an act of extreme deviance in the racist societies of Colonial Europe and North America (Washington, 1970). While concubinage and sexual exploitation has been common - and always involved white men exploiting black women, with offspring disowned by fathers and relegated to 'half-caste' status (Henriques, 1974; Day, 1974) - transracial marriage itself was extremely rare in the nineteenth and early twentieth centuries. Of the European colonial powers, Britain was the most racist in this respect, and the Netherlands probably the least. The treatment by the Dutch of their Indonesian 'Eurasian' offspring stands in marked contrast to the treatment the British afforded to Anglo-Indians (Bagley, 1973).

In Britain, migration from the former colonies in Africa, the Caribbean and Asia has taken place since 1945, but has now been diminished by restrictive immigration laws which mean that only dependents of migrants already in Britain may, after much delay and difficulty, enter the country. The number of black and Asian people now in Britain is difficult to ascertain, but they probably account for less than five percent of the total adult population. However, in parts of major urban centres such as London, Birmingham, Leeds-Bradford and Manchester, black and Asian children form at least a quarter of all children. This is because the migrants have settled predominantly in areas of available housing and employment; and since they are on average much younger than the indigenous population and have rather higher fertility, in a number of urban areas children of black and Asian origin form up to half of the child population.

These ethnic and demographic changes have had many influences in British urban life. Many schools are arenas not only for inter-ethnic mixing, but inter-ethnic conflict as well (Verma and Bagley, 1975). The frustrations of urban living and lack of employment experienced by many young whites in Britain is often expressed in terms of racial hostility (Bagley et al., 1979). However among sectors of the White, Black and Asian populations genuine cross-ethnic friendships do frequently occur, and this is reflected in high rates of inter-ethnic marriage. About 20 percent of individuals whose origin is in Africa, the Caribbean or India are in an inter-ethnic or transracial marriage (Bagley, 1972). This estimate has attempted to take into account the numbers of white people who were born overseas (usually as part of the colonial apparatus), and the increasing number of black and Asian people born in Britain. Over a decade, from the late 1960s to the late 1970s this number has grown significantly. The one exception are those from Pakistan, and here a continuing Moslem identity has meant a high degree of endogamy (Bagley, 1979).

The growth of transracial marriage in Britain, with an increasing number of children who are 'mixed race' has led to the development of an important organisation in Britain called Harmony, which represents intercultural living as a positive asset for Britain, and presses the interests and identity of mixed-race children (Bentley, 1977). This group urges that mixed-race children are special, in their own right. They are neither white nor black but have a cultural identity which incorporates a diversity of cultural and ethnic backgrounds.

SOCIAL AND PSYCHOLOGICAL ASPECTS OF
INTER-ETHNIC MARRIAGE

Earlier American literature suggested that inter-ethnic marriages were more at risk for break-up or divorce than were monoethnic marriages: presumably this reflected both their atypical frequency and the social isolation and other stresses which such couples faced. More optimistic findings for recent years have been offered by Monohan (1970), who indicates that as the number of such marriages has increased in frequency, so their stability has increased to the point where they are more stable than monoethnic marriages. The maturity and reflection on potential difficulties involved, and the mutual support which such couples give, implies a greater rather than a lesser strength in marriage.

CHILDREN OF INTER-ETHNIC MARRIAGE

In parallel to these trends, earlier researchers pointed to identity problems in children of mixed marriages. However, Chang (1974) has found that mixed race children in America have rather better self-concept than their monoracial peers. The reason for this seems to be that both parents and others (such as teachers) see children of black-white marriages as both special and interesting.

ETHNIC AND SELF-EVALUATION IN MINORITY CHILDREN

Research in America on self-perception in black and white children has produced consistent but gloomy findings. Although black children are becoming more positive in their perception of black people (as measured by various projective tests), nevertheless, a considerable residue of ambiguity and self-doubt in this area remains (Verma and Bagley, 1979 and 1982).

The most sophisticated instruments for measuring how young children perceive others of similar and dissimilar ethnic status (and by inference, themselves) are those devised by John Williams and his colleagues (Williams and Morland, 1976; Williams et al., 1975). The two instruments devised are the Colour Meaning Test (CMT) and the Pre-School Racial Attitudes Measure (PRAM). The tests are suited for children aged 4 to 7, and the format of each is similar. In the CMT, subjects are asked to examine and evaluate pairs of identical animals, white or black; in the PRAM, subjects are required to evaluate pairs of adults or children who are identical in every respect, except that one figure is white and the other is black. Each pair of figures is accompanied by a short story about how good or bad, strong or weak, kind or unkind the person is, and the child is required to make a choice in these terms of one of the two figures white or black. Because of the forced choice element of the test, it is possible to classify responses on the basis of probability theory into responses which imply a white bias, lack of bias, or black bias. Ideally perhaps, black and white children should have no bias, or at least black children should have a black bias, and white children should have a white bias. Such bias would be perfectly natural, and would effectively mean that the children were reflecting a positive evaluation of themselves and their families.

The American results presented by Williams and Morland suggest that this is true only for white children. Some 53 percent of black American children had a white bias on the PRAM, and only 12 percent had a positive, black bias. Conversely, 61 percent of white children had a positive, white bias in their perceptions and evaluations of children and adults.

Replication of this work using the CMT and PRAM in Jamaica and England by Young (1978 and 1982) provided similar results. Fifty-three percent of a sample of black Jamaican children had a white bias, compared with 45 percent of a sample of black children of Jamaican parents who had migrated to Britain (sub-population of a larger group of U.K. West Indian children for whom data are presented in Table 1). Only 13 percent of the Jamaican children in the London group had a positive, black bias. But in the white children in London in the same school classes, 74 percent had a positive, white bias.

The CMT and the PRAM in these samples were strongly related to one another, indicating that negative evaluation of one's own ethnic group was based on the negative evaluation of that group's colour. Both tests, moreover, had good internal reliability indicating that the evaluations of any particular set of stimulus items (adults or children) could predict responses to any other set of stimulus items in the test with a fair degree of accuracy.

In order to establish whether evaluations of colour had implications for personal evaluation (self-esteem) we adapted Ziller's technique (Ziller, 1972) for use with young children. This involves the spatial positioning of three cardboard figures, the 'good boy' (or girl, as appropriate), the 'bad boy' and 'me'. The distance and relationship of the figure representing the subject from the 'good' and 'bad' figures was taken to be a measure of self-image (Young, 1978).

As predicted, black children with negative evaluation of black figures had somewhat poorer self-esteem, and white children with positive evaluation of white children had better self-esteem. Black children (mostly of West African rather than Jamaican parents) who evaluated black figures positively also tended to have higher levels of self-esteem. These results imply that evaluating one's ethnic group positively ('black bias' for black children, 'white bias' for white children) is associated with higher self-esteem.

A crucial question remains. How will the growing number of mixed-race children in Britain who are neither black nor white, and who have one black and one white parent, evaluate black and white people in tests such as the PRAM? We might expect, given some American findings, that such children would have relatively high levels of self-esteem and that in the age group four to seven children of transracial marriage will evaluate positively the male who looks like their father (whether white or black); and likewise will evaluate positively the female who looks like their mother (white or black).

ETHNIC AND SELF-EVALUATION IN YOUNG
MIXED-RACE CHILDREN

In order to test these hypotheses we obtained data on the PRAM and on the Ziller self-esteem test for 64 children aged between 4 and 7 (average age 5.8 years) from intact families in which one parent was black (originally from Africa or the Caribbean), and negro in appearance, and in which the other parent was a white European. Forty-two fathers and 22 mothers in this sample were black, a ratio which reflects fairly accurately the sex ratio implied by the published statistics on transracial marriage. Subjects were obtained through Harmony, the organisation representing multicultural families, and through personal contact. Only one child in each family was tested. Twenty-seven of the 64 subjects were girls. The test was administered on all occasions by L.Y., a black Jamaican. The evidence on 'race of tester' effect in the administration of the PRAM is unclear, but the use of a black tester might have biased responses of some children in a problack direction.

Table 1 shows the proportions of responses of the different groups which fall into 'white bias', 'no bias' and 'black bias' groups. The mixed-race display the most balanced responses, and are the only group who have a majority of responses in the neutral or no bias category. This could be because of random choosing of black or white figure as good or bad. Another possibility, investigated in Table 2, is that children of inter-ethnic marriage are evaluating people like their mother and father (black or white) positively. This would give the appearance of a balanced response in the overall scores.

Eight of the stimulus pairs in the PRAM are of older people or adults, (four males and four female pairs). We therefore analysed our U.K. data according to the overall proportions evaluating the white male and and the white female positively in these eight forced-choice evaluations. The hypothesis of evaluation based on the parental models of the mixed-race group is strongly supported by the data in Table 2. Seventy-four percent of children with a white mother evaluate the white females positively; and 71 percent of these same children who have a black father evaluated black males positively. By contrast, black and white children whose parents were both the same colour had equivalent evaluations of the white female and male figures, which were also consistent with the proportions falling into the different 'bias' groups in Table 1. Significance testing of the results in Table 2 indicated a generally significant trend in the results in a direction indicating positive evaluation of people like their parents in the mixed-race group. Checks on the influence of sex of child (identification with the same-sexed parent might complicate the pattern); and the presence of other siblings of differing sexes and colours, revealed no consistent or significant effect.

Self-esteem levels have been compared across various ethnic groups. The variations are highly significant, and indicate that the mixed-race children have the most favourable levels of self-esteem. It should be stressed in interpreting this result that the mixed-race children are a specially selected group, having parents in the network of our acquaintances who take a special pride and interest in the positive evaluation of both black and white culture, and their essential compatabilities. Children of such couples are given a very positive sense of identity by their parents, and selected peer groups. These children come too from a largely middle class background. In contrast, the young children in the London and Jamaican schools we have tested come from largely working class backgrounds, and many come from disadvantaged backgrounds in which positive identity development is incidental rather than central.

CONCLUSIONS

This study of how mixed-race children with one black and one white parent has produced optimistic conclusions. Such children do not have the negative colour biases which many black children display, and their evaluations of colour seem to be based on positive evaluations of their black and white parents. This positive identification is reflected in high levels of self-esteem.

Other minority group parents can produce adequate conceptions of self and of personal ethnicity and colour. The West African parents in our sample seem to have been successful in this, despite the many negative messages and symbols which black people and their children receive about their ethnicity from the wider environment (Bagley and Verma, 1979). White adoptive parents of black children can often be successful in this respect too (Bagley and Young, 1979).

A particularly disadvantaged group are mixed-race children of single, white parents who often suffer both social disadvantage and lack of support for the development of positive ethnic identity in their children. A high degree of behavioural disturbance often develops in such children (Lambert, 1970; Batta et al., 1975). These children need special support particularly from groups like Harmony which is struggling, with limited resources to offer help, both practical and ideological, to disadvantaged families with mixed-race children. The basic message of this valuable group is that mixed-race children are neither black nor white, but combine the essence and quality of differing cultures and colours. The culture and ethnicity of these children is essentially a new phenomenon, precious for the individuals involved, and precious for society as a whole.

NOTES

1. Based on a paper presented to the Third Annual Intercultural Conference of the Society for International Education, Training and Research, University of Bradford, England.

REFERENCES

Bagley, C., 'Pattterns of Inter-Ethnic Marriage in Britain', Phylon, vol. 33, 1972, pp. 373-379.

Bagler, C., The Dutch Plural Society: A Comparative Study in Race Relations, Oxford University Press, London, 1973.

Bagley, C., 'Introduction, to Inter-Ethnic Marriage in Britain and the United States from 1970-1977', Sage Race Relations Abstracts, vol. 4, 1979, pp. 1-22.

Bagley, C. and Young, L., 'The Identity, Adjustment and Achievement of Transracially Adopted Children: A Review and Empirical Report', in Verma, G. and Bagley, C. (eds.), Race, Education and Identity, MacMillan, London, 1979.

Bagley, C. and Verma, G., Racial Prejudice, The Individual and Society, Saxon House, Farnborough, U.K. 1979.

Bagley, C., Verma, G., Mallick, K. and Young, L., Personality, Self-Esteem and Prejudice, Saxon House, Farnborough, U.K., 1979.

Batta, J., McCulloch, M. and Smith, N., 'A Study of Juvenile Delinquency Amongst Asians and Half-Asians', British Journal of Criminology, vol. 15, 1975, pp. 32-42.

Bentley, S., 'Harmony: Multi-Racial Families in Britain', New Community, vol. 5, 1977, pp. 495-497.

Chang, T., 'The Self-Concept of Children in Ethnically Different Marriages', California Journal of Educational Research, vol. 25, 1974, pp. 242-252.

Day, B., Sexual Life Between Blacks and Whites, Collins, London, 1974.

Henriques, F., Children of Caliban: Miscegenation, Secker and Warburg, London, 1974.

Lambert, J., Crime, Police and Race Relations, Oxford University Press, London, 1970.

Monohan, T., 'Are Interracial Marriages Really Less Stable?', Social Forces, vol. 48, 1970, pp. 461-473.

Verma, G. and Bagley, C. (eds.), Race and Education Across Cultures, Heinemann, London, 1975.

Verma, G. and Bagley, C. (eds.), Race, Education and Identity, MacMillan, London, 1979.

Verma G. and Bagley, C. (eds.), Self-Esteem, Achievement and Multicultural Education, MacMillan, London, 1982.

Washington, J., Marriage in Black and White, Beacon Press, Boston, 1970.

Williams, J. and Morland, K., *Race, Color and the Young Child*, University of North Carolina Press, Chapel Hill, N.C., 1976.

Williams, J. et al., 'Pre-School Racial Attitudes Measure II', *Educational and Psychological Measurement*, vol. 35, 1975, pp. 3-18.

Young, L., 'A Comparative Study of the Evaluative Meaning of Colour: Implications for Identity and the Development of Self-Esteem in Young Black Children', M.Phil. thesis, University of Surrey, 1978.

Young, L. and Bagley, C., 'Identity, Self-Esteem and Evaluation of Colour and Ethnicity in Young Children in Jamaica and London', in Verma, G. and Bagley, C. (eds.), *Self-Esteem, Achievement and Multicultural Education*, MacMillan, London, 1982.

Ziller, R., *The Social Self*, Pergamon Press, Oxford, 1972.

Table 1.1: Proportions of Different Ethnic Groups with Three Types of Response to the Pre-School Racial Attitude Questionnaire

Score on PRAM	'Black bias' 0-9	'No bias' 10-14	'White bias' 15-24
Mixed Race children N = 64	25.0	54.7	20.3
White English N = 100	5.0	21.0	74.0
UK West Indian N = 113	16.8	43.4	39.8
UK African N = 23	43.5	43.5	13.0
Rural Jamaican N = 117	3.4	42.7	53.0
White American N = 159	10.1	28.9	61.0
Black American N = 176	12.5	34.1	53.4

Note: Data on American children taken from Williams and Morland. Data on U.K. children, apart from the mixed-race group, from Young and Bagley.

Table 1.2: Aggregated Proportions of Children from Different Ethnic Groups in U.K. Evaluating White and Black Adult Male and Female Figures Positively in the PRAM Test

Group	Aggregate percent choosing:			
	White female positively	Black female positively	White male positively	Black male positively
Mother white, father black N = 42	74.0	26.0	29.0	71.0
Mother black, father white N = 22	36.0	64.0	64.0	36.0
Father & mother black (UK West Indians) N = 113	41.6	58.4	38.0	62.0
Father and mother white N = 100	72.0	28.0	80.0	20.0

Significance (Chi-Squared)		Evaluation of white female	Evaluation of white male
(a) Mother white, father black	cf Father & Mother black	.001	N.S.
(b) Mother white, father black	cf Father & Mother white	N.S.	.001
(c) Mother black, father white	cf Father & Mother black	N.S.	.001
(d) Mother black, father white	cf Father & Mother white	.05	N.S.

Table 1.3: Ziller Self-Esteem Scores in Black, Mixed Race and White Children

Group	Ziller Self-Esteem Scores Mean
Mixed-Race N = 64	2.98
White English N = 100	2.78
African N = 23	2.52
UK West Indian N = 113	2.40
Rural Jamaican N = 117	1.75

Analysis of variance of self-esteem scores across ethnic categories F (d.f. 4, 416), 7.66, p less than .001).

The higher the score, the more positive the self-esteem.

Chapter Thirteen

NATIVE INDIAN AND METIS CHILDREN IN CANADA:
VICTIMS OF THE CHILD WELFARE SYSTEM

Bradford Morse

INTRODUCTION

Although it has been clearly and decisively documented in a number of research studies, few professionals within the Canadian child welfare system and certainly not in any international dimension have appreciated the immensity of the tragedy that is naively being perpetrated upon the Native Indian and Metis peoples of Canada by child welfare policies, practices, and statutes. (1)
   Despite the presence of thousands of Native children in the care of child welfare agencies in numbers far higher than their population warrants, our child welfare system has comfortably ignored the fact that something has definitely gone wrong in the last 20 years. One might presume simply from seeing the articles and photographs of Indian and Metis children available for adoption that regularly appear in our daily newspapers, if not as a result of available data demonstrating caseload rates of fourty percent and higher west of Thunder Bay, Ontario, that our governments were readily aware of the magnitude of this disaster and were actively working on solutions to rectify it. Although some positive signs have risen on the horizon in the last few years, unfortunately, the general evidence does not support such a presumption.
   This article will begin to attempt to discuss this topic in detail by briefly sketching the position of Indian and Metis people within Canadian society so as to prepare a foundation upon which one can explore the present situation regarding the delivery of child welfare services to Native people in terms of the quantity and quality of these services. This will then be followed by an examination of the various possible explanations for why

the relationship between the child welfare system and indigenous peoples has led to disaster for the latter. Finally, several of the options available for remedying this situation will be canvassed.

WHO ARE THE INDIAN AND METIS PEOPLES?

Although it is not possible to answer this question fully in this article,(2) it is important to possess some appreciation of who the Indian and Metis peoples are and what their present position is within Canadian society, both legally and socially, before one can understand the child welfare situation. The Indian people are the original residents of what is now southern Canada (below the treeline) who have occupied and enjoyed this land for tens of thousands of years as have the Inuit (also originally known as 'Eskimos' or 'Eskimaux' based upon their name in the Cree language) in the far North. Although there are some philosophical, economic and racial similarities among the Indian people, they are not a homogeneous group - just as all Europeans are not culturally, linguistically or even physically the same. They speak hundreds of different dialects derived from some eleven distinct linguistic groupings. Native people belong to dozens of different nations, many of which have developed very different cultures, life-styles, governmental structures, and family patterns. As Indian society has evolved in recent decades, the degree of these differences has declined, although they have by no means disappeared.

Therefore, one should not assume that, for example, the child-rearing practices of one Indian nation will be the same as another. This obviously has an impact upon a number of aspects of the child welfare system, such as evaluating parent-child interaction or developing child welfare programmes.

The Metis people also are not all the same. There are economic differences, as some Metis have adopted a traditional Indian lifestyle of hunting, fishing and trapping, whereas others are still the traders and small businessmen that they were in the last century, while others are part of the wage economy. They also differ as a result of their cultural background in that some Metis are francophone and Catholic whereas others are anglophone and Protestant. Furthermore, the Metis have different Indian backgrounds which may dramatically affect their attitudes towards the world.

Another important factor to be kept in mind is that the Aboriginal Peoples of Canada have been legally subdivided into categories which fall within the spheres of influence of either the federal or provincial government.

The federal government has the authority under s.91(24) of the <u>British North America Act</u> (3), to legislate in relation to "Indians, and Lands reserved for the Indians". This power has been exercised in the passage of special legislation called the <u>Indian Act</u> (4). This latter statute possesses a complex system for registering Indians, administering their lands, and regulating their lives. The idea of defining who the Indian people are has existed since colonial times with the passage of early legislation concerning Indians in 1850, and it has been maintained in all subsequent statutes (5).

The courts have held that this constitutional authority in s. 91(24) also clearly extends federal jurisdiction to include the Inuit (6). Although the national organization which represents the Metis and non-status Indians has consistently argued for the last decade that they too are a federal responsibility as being 'Indians' within the meaning of s. 91(24) of the <u>B.N.A. Act</u>, the Government of Canada has continually resisted this position. Since the issue has never been submitted to the courts, one can only guess at what the legal position really is. It does appear, however, that there is considerable merit to the opinion of the Native Council of Canada and that it would likely be adopted by the courts.

As far as the new <u>Constitution Act</u> (7) of 1981 is concerned, the Metis do now have some constitutional recognition, although not within s. 91(24) of the <u>B.N.A. Act</u>, as s. 35(2) specifically defines the 'aboriginal peoples of Canada' as including the Metis along with the Indian and Inuit peoples for the purpose of the <u>Constitution Act, 1981</u>. This may cause the federal government to change its position and accept a special responsibility for the Metis and non-status Indians. Such an acceptance would not necessarily lead to separate federal legislation as the Parliament has not acted on its authority regarding the Inuit in the 43 years since the courts have declared that they are 'Indians' within our constitutional framework.

The foregoing is relevant to a discussion of Indian and Metis child welfare for two reasons, namely: (1) it explains why it is impossible to precisely determine the size of the aboriginal population within Canada's borders as only two of the three aboriginal groups have been considered by the federal government to fall within its constitutional jurisdiction; and (2) it begins to indicate one of the underlying reasons for the jurisdictional nightmare that exists in the child welfare field.

The federal government's narrow view of its authority has led to the passage of Indian legislation which has had the effect of dividing the Indian people into those who are legal or 'status' Indians, and are thereby subject to the advantages and disadvantages that go with the Indian Act, and those who are legally non-Indian despite their Indian ancestry. The so-called non-status Indians have none of the unique rights of those who are legally Indians and they are, therefore, regarded by the provincial and federal government as being ordinary citizens. Their position in law is, then, similar to the one held by the Metis.

One example of this policy in action has been in regard to data collection. The federal government can be very precise in stating exactly how many registered Indians there are in Canada, of which there are just over 300,000 belonging to some 573 bands. The Department of Indian Affairs and Northern Development (hereinafter referred to as DIAND) is not quite as precise in reference to the Inuit, who are approximately 23,000 in total. DIAND has no idea, however, when it comes to ascertaining the numbers of Metis and non-status Indians in Canada. In fact, DIAND has no relationship with these people or their organizations as it leaves such contact to the Secretary of State Department.

Statistics Canada had never included Indian ancestry among its categories until the 1981 census. Prior to that time, these people were forced into the 'other' slot. Since the 1981 census data will not be tabulated and released until late 1983 at the earliest, and since the provinces have also not gathered this information, one must rely upon the estimates for Metis and non-status Indians which range from 260,000 to one million people. The best one can really state is that there are approximately one to one and a half million Aboriginal People residing in what is now called Canada, or roughly 5 percent of our total population.

THE EXTENT OF THE PRESENT TRAGEDY

Indian, Metis and Inuit families across Canada are in a state of crisis. The situation is so serious, and the statistics are so alarming, that one might be tempted to say that Aboriginal families are under a state of siege. Although there is always cause for hope, and there have been a few positive developments in recent years, the stability of Aboriginal families is crumbling as the social conditions are deteriorating, both within their communities and in urban centers. This is particularly evident in the child welfare area for people of Indian ancestry (status Indians, non-status Indians and the Metis) due to their far greater contact than the Inuit with urban centers and the social service system.

Since many non-status Indian and Metis children are often not recognized as such, the available statistics must definitely be viewed as being on the conservative side. Nevertheless, one recent study (Hepworth, 1980) indicated that 20 percent of all children in the care of the child welfare system in Canada in 1977, totalling 15,500 children, were of Indian ancestry. Hepworth's data demonstrated that this figure represented three times the national average, whereas a recent government study (DIAND, 1980) suggested that the rate of status Indian children in care was five times higher than the non-Indian average.

Hepworth analyzed the statistics in reference to each province and discovered some frightening results. Children of Indian ancestry represent 30 percent of the total number of children in care in B.C., 44 percent in Alberta, 51.5 percent in Saskatchewan, and an astounding 60 percent in Manitoba. Even in Ontario, where the provincial rate is just under 9 percent, the reality in the northern region overall is 19 percent. Johnston (1981b) indicates that in the Kenora district the Indian child welfare rate is an incredible 85 percent. The latest data (Johnston, 1982) demonstrates that the overrepresentation of children of Indian ancestry in the child welfare system is continuing and, in some cases, is getting worse.

These figures are even more startling when one realizes that the divorce rates of status Indians are only one half the national average and the proportion of children released for adoption at birth, or thereafter, by unmarried Indian and Metis women is dramatically less than the general pattern.

Despite the fivefold increase in child care expenditures by DIAND over the last two decades, family conditions on reserves are worsening. The increase in the federal financial commitment to child care expenses for status Indians has neither minimized this tragedy nor has it provided any direct tangible benefits to Indian communities.

These disheartening statistics do, however, need to be placed in an overall context that reflects the life situation of Indian and Metis peoples in Canada. One must also consider the social, economic, educational and health conditions of these people as a whole in order to gain some perspective on the child welfare area.

According to the Department of Indian Affairs and Northern Development (1980), despite a 64 percent increase in Indian reserve housing since 1958, at least one-third of all Indian families live in crowded conditions with almost one-fifth of reserve homes having two or more families as occupants. In 1977, approximately 11,000 new houses were needed and 24 percent of existing homes required major repairs. Less than 40 percent of rural and remote reserve housing had running water, sewage and indoor plumbing. Lack of running water and poor quality housing results in an extraordinarily high number of fires and a fire death rate six times the national average. It also means that much of reserve housing is unlikely to meet the standards of acceptability of child welfare agencies.

Inadequate and inferior housing also affects the health situation of registered Indians. Indian children can expect an average life span of ten years less than that of the national population, with violent deaths and suicides occurring three times more than the non-Indian public. There have, however, been some significant improvements in health care in recent years, such as a reduction in infant mortality from six times the national rate to twice the average in 1977. Nevertheless, there is also some suggestion that recent improvements in health care face a reversal due to industrial pollution as a minimum of 20 Indian communities, involving some 10,000 Indians, are confronted by severe environmental hazards at the present time.

Indians also suffer heavily from the 'last hired, first fired' syndrome within our economy. The most optimistic figures place on-reserve Indian participation in the labour force at only two-thirds of the national rate, whereas other estimates of Indian unemployment runs as high as 75 percent. On many reserves, unemployment is the reality for almost 100 percent of the residents with those who are fortunate enough to find work often being limited to seasonal employment. Simultaneously, traditional economic activities are becoming increasingly more marginal as fish and game populations decline due to encroaching industrialization and the competition of sportsmen.

The position of Indian and Metis within the criminal justice system is also shocking. They are three times more likely to spend time in federal penitentiaries than non-Natives and represent over 40 percent of the provincial prison population in some provinces and the territories. Several of the womens prisons on the Prairies contain an inmate population that is almost 100 percent Indian and Metis. This is further compounded by an Indian juvenile delinquency rate that is also three times higher than their numbers warrant. The result is that Indians face an incredibly large likelihood of having family members, or themselves, spend time incarcerated.

The only cause for some optimism is in the area of education. Even here, however, the high school "drop-out" rate is still extremely high as only one in five registered Indians completes grade 12. Although the presence of poverty, allegedly poor quality education, racism, the irrelevance of a school system that fosters middle class goals, and the conflict between the values and beliefs of Indian culture and those held by the dominant society tend to explain these unsatisfactory statistics, one must be impressed with the determination and drive of those Indians who represent a jump in university enrollment from almost zero in 1957 to over 2,500 students in 1979.

THE PROBABLE EXPLANATIONS

This writer would suggest that there are at least five plausible rationales for the presence of a major crisis within the child welfare system in relation to Indian and Metis people. Each one represents, however, only a partial explanation for the present situation so that they must be examined both individually and collectively.

The first factor, actually, has already been addressed, that is, the disadvantaged position of Aboriginal People within Canadian society. The destruction of the traditional Indian and Metis economies without an adequate replacement has played a role in generating a disproportionate rate of criminality. This means an increased use of incarceration leading to single parent or no parent families for extended periods of time with obvious impact upon child-rearing. The relationship between crime and the use of alcohol by Aboriginal People is well-known (Brody, 1971; Dosman, 1972). This cycle of despair also clearly impinges heavily upon family stability.

The previously documented absence of adequate housing has two negative effects regarding child welfare. Overcrowding naturally causes tension within the home that engenders family violence and instability. Furthermore, it makes it extremely difficult for the traditional response to children in need of care (namely, for members of the extended family to absorb any extra children on a temporary or permanent basis) to function properly and effectively.

A weak socio-economic situation in Indian, Metis and Inuit communities creates the appearance of material, if not also physical, deprivation on the part of their children. Social workers tend to conclude that these children are in an unacceptable family situation requiring apprehension. Such a conclusion leads to the next two explanations for the current tragedy.

A second major cause of abnormal child apprehension rates in southern Canada is a function of the application of ethnocentric values to all families by the social service system. Our society relies upon one set of standards to govern the welfare of our children which are founded upon white, middle class values derived from a northwestern European experience. Different cultural attitudes concerning child-rearing or, for that matter, life objectives are disregarded. Such an approach not only can harm minority ethnic or racial groups, but it also fails to reflect the reality of Canadian society.

Regarding Native people, this has meant that the courts, the statutes, and the policies all tend to reflect a common perception, that is, that these people are unable to adequately meet their own family needs through their own policies, programs, and laws. An attitude, based on notions of guardianship and superiority, has been adopted by our society in recent decades that has justified, if not necessitated, the intervention of the state and its agents into the Indian and Metis family structure.

This action has been well intentioned but it has been misguided and has had disastrous consequences. The interventionistic approach of the social service agencies has been aided by the general lack of regard on the part of the legal system towards the rights of Aboriginal people and the validity of their traditional family laws.

Different cultural values also lead to different perceptions of the problem and how to resolve it. The legislation in this field, and the guidelines developed for children's aid staff in implementing it, are very broad and flexible. This can give the professional staff considerable latitude in interpreting specific provisions relating to child neglect in light of their own cultural values and biases. Unfortunately, this can result in culturally insensitive interventions in Native families. Roman Komar, advisor to the Government of Ontario, has warned child care workers that:

> ...they can, consciously or unconsciously become the vehicle for the imposition of North American middle-class standards of child care upon people whose social and cultural standards happen to be different. Thus, the poor, immigrants and native peoples seem to be singled out for special attention and it is here that Courts must be vigilant to prevent misuse of the law by agencies.

There is also a tendency for poorer communication with clients and a lower quality of services to result as a further repercussion of cultural misunderstanding. Neil Stuart, in a recent report (Stuart, 1978) on the quality of child welfare services delivered to the Indian population of the Sudbury and Manitoulin districts, stated that:

Indians in care are less likely to get specialized services than other children, were more likely to stay in care longer than non-Indian children, and were less likely to be discharged home. Workers on Indian cases were more likely to be less experienced than workers in non-Indian cases.

Failure to recognize and to react properly to cultural misunderstanding results in the overzealous use of apprehension to resolve a 'problem'. Social workers are unable to do their real job, that is, to assist Native families to remain viable and retain control over their own children. Prevention is in reality largely unpracticed regarding Indian and Metis families and supportive services, such as homemakers, are generally not offered. If a social worker cannot speak to and truly understand an Indian parent, how then can the worker provide positive aid?

The entrenchment of cultural values that only reflect those of the dominant society also generates a third partial rationale. It has caused some people to internalize these values to such a degree that they are prepared to give up their children to white, middle-class homes so that their kids may have a better chance to 'make it' in our society. For others, the acceptance of these external values has not been complete. They, then, undergo an internal struggle as they have lost some respect for their own approaches to their traditional mode of life and caring for their children. This process can cause confusion and, in some cases, a rejection of both societies (Hudson and McKenzie, 1981).

Other parents reject the validity of white values but accept the reality that those values are enforced upon them. Thus, they become passive when pressured by social workers or after the apprehension of their children. Several writers (Sanders, 1975; Jackson and Morse, 1974; Girard, 1979) one federally commissioned study (Canadian Corrections Association, 1967), and the Royal Commission on Family and Children's Law of British Columbia (1975) have all commented upon the powerlessness and subsequent apathy that this generates. What compounds this tragedy is that the apathy is frequently misinterpreted as abandonment or lack of concern such that the negative perceptions of the social worker are reinforced before the family court judge by the absence of the parents at the hearing. Thus, the likelihood of a child of Indian ancestry being returned to his/her natural parents is extremely low, which only tends to further the view that opposition is pointless.

A fourth factor is the impact of the ongoing jurisdictional struggle between the federal and provincial governments regarding who has financial and administrative responsibility for status Indian children. Although the Government of Canada has constitutional authority over Indians, it has failed to enact any legislation for Indian children except regarding their education. Provincial legislation is relied upon to fill this vacuum for all aspects of family law, other than the federal Divorce Act, by virtue of s.88 of the Indian Act. This means that no special legislation designed to meet the particular needs and values of Indian people is in place anywhere in Canada.

This abdication of federal responsibility has caused several provinces to be unwilling to extend child welfare and other social services to status Indians except in 'life-or-death' situations (Hepworth) without a guarantee of full reimbursement by the federal government. Even where formal or informal cost-sharing or 'bill-back' agreements are in place, status Indians are still not eligible for the full range of services and benefits.

This has also meant that Indian families must accept the existing services or none at all. They have no input or control over the quality or quantity of these services and, therefore, they must accept whatever is available or is imposed upon them. A frequent defect in the philosophy underlying social services that prevails is the concentration upon individual or family problems. The connection between the individual, the family, and the community is generally ignored resulting in the exclusion of band councils or Metis and non-status Indian organizations and their staff from any involvement in the social services that are provided.

The fifth and final suggestion that accounts for at least a portion of the current conditions is the continuing manifestations of colonialism. Hudson and McKenzie argue forcefully that the child welfare system is an agent in the colonization of Aboriginal people along with the education and health care systems. All three are involved in the separation of children from their families, communities, and culture as part of the colonialist drive towards assimilation. Although this writer has never plotted such a relationship, there does appear to be a connection between the decline of residential schools for status Indians and the rise of Indian child apprehensions.

This is not intended to imply that social workers are consciously motivated by colonialist imperatives. It does mean, however, that the relationship between the child welfare system and the Aboriginal people is colonialist in nature and is perceived of as such by many. The general characteristics of a colonial relationship - the decisionmaking power concerning critical issues affecting the colonized lies in the hands of the colonizers; the dominant group gives little weight to the values, lifestyle and laws of the dominated; the colonialists interact with the indigenous people in a manner that reflects the lower status and power of the latter; the colonizers import their standards, cultural values, laws and systems and impose them upon the colonized so as to eliminate the latter's traditional structures; the economic benefits primarily go to the immigrants - are all present in the child welfare system of today.

It is for this reason that many Indian and Metis communities are beginning to define the child welfare system as a mechanism for cultural genocide. The B.C. Royal Commission observed this reaction and commented:

> The Adoption Act is sometimes viewed as one more weapon employed by white society to destroy the Indian culture. It is seen as a means of taking away the right of Indian bands to take care of their own children and as means of placing Indian children in white homes where they would lose contact with their own race.

The repercussions of this phenomenon can be devastating. Many of the parents fall into total despair and alcoholism while the children become lost between two cultures while belonging to neither. Far too many of these children run the cycle of foster and group homes until they end up in jail or as a suicide victim.

THE STATE OF THE LAW

Although Indian and Inuit customary law regarding marriage and adoption, among other areas, has been consistently recognized by Canadian courts since the pre-Confederation area (Morse, 1982), the reality is that general provincial legislation is applied to all Indina, Metis and Inuit people in the social service field. The constitutionality of this has never been questioned regarding the latter two groups, although it appears to be valid bsed upon a similar underlying theory as regarding status Indians by virtue of s.88 of the Indian Act.

The only limitations on provincial legislative authority to date, in the absence of a federal statute on the matter, is that a province cannot expressly exclude Indians from what would otherwise be general legislation, (8) nor can it affect their 'Indianness' in any way (9). It is also arguable that a band-by-law, as the Spallumcheen Indian Band of British Columbia has done, would oust the application of provincial legislation regarding on-reserve behaviour (MacDonald, 1981).

As this writer has written elsewhere (Morse, 1981) it does appear possible, given these limitations, for a province to carefully draft its legislation in such a way as to make positive reforms that would expressly refer to the Indian and Metis population within its borders. The B.C. Royal Commission made concrete recommendations some years ago for provincial legislative action, which unfortunately were never implemented, while the Province of Ontario is currently considering a number of initiatives in this area. The new child welfare statute enacted in British Columbia in 1981 at least imposed a requirement for notice to be given to the Chief regarding any judicial hearings to be held affecting band children.

RECOMMENDATIONS FOR CHANGE

What is not needed is more social workers to do more diagnostic and home assessments, follow-up services, crisis intervention, etc. Rather, a wholistic approach is needed to confront the child welfare issue within the total context of the conditions of Aboriginal people in Canadian society.

Economic advancement and self-sufficiency for Aboriginal people and their communities on their terms must become a prime objective. For many communities this will require the emphasis to be placed upon developing the traditional economy and renewable resources. For others it will mean developing a wage economy that coincides with traditional values. It will also entail a just resolution of land claims so as to promote economic and social self-determination.

It will further necessitate a re-evaluation of the child welfare system's culturally biased standards and delivery mechanisms so as to reflect the value and richness of our cultural differences. In doing so, it becomes essential to respect the critical importance of maintaining a child's culture, language and identity through culturally suitable placements whenever removal from the home is unavoidable.

All three of these thrusts - economic revival, respect for cultural differences, and cultural bonding - would be beneficial to many other segments of our society and should, therefore, be generally considered as valuable objectives. In the context of Aboriginal people they are even more essential as they will assist in the resurrection of the spirit and the decolonization of the original inhabitants of the land.

There must also be a change in the orientation of the social services system and its professionals away from an individual or family problem focus towards the philosophy of the indigenous population. That is, full respect must be given to the perception of children as the hope and future of the people as a whole rather than as the private property of the parents. This translates into the necessity for community involvement in the setting of policy for service delivery and in the actual decision-making process regarding specific cases. For example, the Spallumcheen By-law gives initial authority for resolving cases to the Band Council with a right of appeal to the Band as a whole. Some other Indian communities have established local child care committees to reach any necessary decisions with the possibility for review by the Band Council.

The only method of effectively obtaining these objectives is to transfer the actual delivery of the service and the control over it to Aboriginal people themselves. This would ensure that these people would be both the service deliverers AND the decision-makers. That requires a transfer of the program and its standards and its legislative base and its judicial function. Only this approach will generate a proactive strategy as opposed to crisis intervention and reactive responses.

CONCLUSIONS

Interest in the field of child welfare as it relates to Indian and Metis peoples has been mushrooming in recent years. There have been several national conferences sponsored by the Canadian Indian Lawyers Association in the last two years as well as regional conferences and a national policy workshop conducted by the National Indian Brotherhood. The Canadian Council on Social Development is presently carrying out a major two year research project following upon the heals of its general study on foster care and adoption. Several other articles not already mentioned have appeared recently in Canada (Johnston, 1981a; Chartier and Mercredi, 1982; Johnston, 1982). In addition, DIAND is about to embark upon two significant, external research projects regarding the possibility of a federal Indian Child Welfare Act, to build upon their ongoing internal province-by-province evaluation (Girard, note 3).

There are also a number of very positive developments in the way of actual changes to the system being made or actively considered besides these research efforts. There are now a number of Indian child care workers and certified social workers, in part as a result of the Indian Social Work Education Program of the University of Regina, delivering social services to Indian and Metis people in many parts of Canada. Many bands are involved, to varying degrees, in delivering child welfare programmes on reserves in Ontario and Quebec. In the latter province, these programmes are delivered by the regional social service centres using Indian staff through consultation with local bands. In Ontario, the projects differ quite radically from the minimum, with Children's Aid Societies simply hiring a few Indian employees, to joint projects between bands and child welfare agencies, to exclusively band controlled services.

The most noticed development in the last year has been the signing of the Canada-Manitoba-Indian Child Welfare Agreement on February 22, 1982 by the three parties. This Agreement builds upon the foundation laid by the most extensive Indian controlled project in the country, the Dakota Ojibway Child and Family Services, which has a staff of 23 and a budget of over one million dollars annually to handle all child welfare services, other than adoption, on eight reserves in Manitoba. The Agreement establishes a framework within which individual subsidiary agreements can be signed covering child welfare and juvenile probation programmes under provincial legislation for each reserve in Manitoba paid for by the federal government. Although it contains a set of guiding principles for service delivery, the Agreement does not alter the substantive law nor does it apply to off-reserve Indians or the Metis. It simply authorizes the development of individual projects to be administered and created by a willing band.

The Ontario government released a public discussion paper in the Summer of 1982 concerning all aspects of legislation that affects children, other than education. It contained a number of recommendations and suggestions oriented towards making provincial legislation more culturally sensitive and in keeping with Indian and Metis needs. It raised the possibility of transferring control over service delivery, project design, and judicial decision-making authority to Indian and Metis entities anywhere within the Province. Depending upon public reaction (there will be a special consultation process with Indian and Metis people in Ontario) these proposals could be implemented in a new omnibus bill scheduled for presentation to the Legislature in the Fall of 1983.

The final development of note is the aforementioned Spallumcheen By-law. This piece of legislation has been recognized by the federal and B.C. governments as warranting a transfer of funds from Canada and band children from the wardship of the Superintendent of Child Welfare to the control of the Band Council. These events, in and of themselves, are not unique as they are mirrored in several of the jurisdictions already mentioned. The special element in the Spallumcheen situation is that any placement or guardianship decisions are made by the Band Council, as opposed to a family court judge, under band law rather than under the provincial statute.

It is this writer's view, which he has outlined in greater detail elsewhere (Morse, 1981) that the best hope for the elimination of the child welfare 'problem' among Aboriginal people lies in a return to the past. That is, a return to a position where Indian, Metis and Inuit communities perceived of their children as the community's future, their most valuable resource and of concern to them all. This is not a romanticized view reflecting the restoration of pre-colonial times, for that era will not return. We are part of the 20th century and facing the 21st. It does, however, suggest the revival of certain traditional values, but within a modern context. It means that the guiding principles become control over services, standards and laws so as to ensure that they respond to the values and needs of Aboriginal People.

This is not farfetched as just south of our imaginary border, in the United States, one finds a situation where Indian laws govern all child welfare matters before Indian tribal courts. This is supported by federal legislation, the <u>Indian Child Welfare Act</u> of 1978, which directs local or state agencies and state courts to transfer all child welfare cases to tribal courts if the parents consent. These tribal courts are created under tribal law to administer customary and modern tribal law with full faith and credit given to their decisions by federal and state courts. This, then, means that Indian judges are applying appropriate Indian enacted or traditional child welfare law to Indian families. Although there is a severe shortage of funds to make this initiative fully effective it is interesting to note that this legislation has apparently resulted in a drastic reduction in the number of Indian children being in the care of child welfare agencies or being adopted by non-Indian parents. In fact, it has led to an increasing demand for Canadian children of Indian ancestry to be adopted south of the border by these agencies.

Therefore, there is little question concerning the ability of our society and our governments to transform our child welfare system regarding Aboriginal People. There can also be no doubt concerning the desire of Indian and Metis people to participate in this total transformation. Nor is there any question, at least in this writer's opinion, concerning the wisdom of such a change. The sole obstacle appears to be a lack of will on the part of most governments and the self-interest of the child welfare agencies in favour of the status quo. One can only hope that this will disappear in the near future so that the present tragedy can be eradicated from the future. It won't be easy, but it can and must be done as we have little to lose beyond the repetition of our mistakes.

NOTES

1. Strictly speaking an 'Indian' in the Canadian context denotes a person registered under the Indian Act, and entitled to 'reservation' status. People so registered may be wholly or partly descended from the original ("aboriginal") people of North America. A number of people who are fully aboriginaly are "nonstatus Indians". A larger number of Metis (literally "mixed" in the French term) people have partial descent from the aboriginal people, and part from early settlers. Metis people are particularly likely to be descended from unions between early French settlers and native people. Alberta is the only Canadian Province where there are legally sanctioned Metis settlements.

2. For further information, see, B. Morse, "The Original Peoples of Canada" (1982) 5 Canadian Legal Aid Bulletin, No. 1, 1-16 and sources cited therein.
3. R.S.C. 1970, App. II, No. 5.
4. R.S.C. 1970, c. I-6.
5. An Act for the Better Protection of the Lands and Property of the Indians in Lower Canada, S.C. 1850, C. 42, 13 & 14 Vict., s. 5.
6. For the complete text of all Indian legislation, both pre- and post-confederation, see, Gail Hinge, ed., Consolidation of Indian Legislation - Vol. I: United Kingdom and Canada (unpublished, available from the Department of Indian and Northern Affairs).
7. Reference re Eskimos, (1939) S.C.R. 104; 2 D.L.R. 417.
8. S.C. 1981.
9. Nelson v. Children's Aid Society of Eastern Manitoba, (1975) 5 W.W.R. 45 (Man. C.A.).
10. Director of Child Welfare of Manitoba v. B., (1979) 6 W.W.R. 229 (Man. Prov. Ct.).
11. See, e.g., National Parents et al. v. Superintendent of Child Welfare et al., 60 D.L.R. (3d) 148 (S.C.C. 1975); Kruger and Manuel v. The Queen, (1977) 4 W.W.R. 294 (S.C.C.); and The Queen v. Sutherland et al., (1980) 5 W.W.R. 456 (S.C.C.).

REFERENCES

Brody, H. Indians on Skid Row. Ottawa: Information Canada, 1972.
Canadian Corrections Association. Indians and the Law. Ottawa: Canadian Corrections Association, 1967.
Chartier, C. and Mercredi, O. "The Status of Child Welfare Services for the Indigenous People of Canada: The Problem, the Law and the Solution". Canadian Legal Aid Bulletin, 5, No. 2, 1982.
Department of Indian Affairs and Northern Development. Indian Conditions: A Survey. Ottawa: 1980.
Dosman, E.J. Indians: The Urban Dilemma. Toronto: McClelland and Stewart Ltd., 1972.
Girard, J. Background Paper for the Evaluation of Child Welfare Services. Ottawa: Department of Indian Affairs and Northern Development, March 1979.

Hepworth, H.P. *Foster Care and Adoption in Canada*. Ottawa: Canadian Council on Social Development, 1980.

Hudson, P. and McKenzie, B. "Child Welfare and Native People: The Extension of Colonialism". *The Social Worker/Le Travailleur Social*, 49, No. 2, 1981, pp. 63-66 and 87-88.

Jackson, M. and Morse, B. *Summary of Prince George Native People's Conference*. Unpublished manuscript, May 1974. (Available from Attorney General's Department of British Columbia).

Johnston, P. "Indian Control of Child Welfare: A Historic Step". *Perception*, 5, No. 1, 1981, pp. 7-9.

Johnston, P. "Planting the Roots for Indian Social Services". *Perception*, 5, No. 2, 1981, pp. 18-19 and 32-33.

Johnston, P. "The Crisis of Native Child Welfare". *Canadian Legal Aid Bulletin*, 5, No. 2, 1982.

Komar, R.N. *Manual for Clerks and Staff of the Ontario Provincial Courts (Family Division) on the Child Welfare Act, 1978; Part II: Protection and Care of Children*. Toronto: Ministry of Community and Social Services.

MacDonald, J.A. *The Spallumcheen Indian Band By-law and Its Potential Impact on Native Indian Child Welfare Policy in British Columbia*. Vancouver: School of Social Work, University of British Columbia, 1981.

Morse, B. *Indian Child Welfare: Options for Change*. Toronto: Ministry of Community and Social Services, May 1981.

Morse, B. "Indian and Inuit Family Law and the Canadian Legal System". *American Indian Law Review*, 8, No. 2, 1982 (in press).

Morse, B. "The Original Peoples of Canada". *Canadian Legal Aid Bulletin*, 5, No. 1, 1982, pp. 1-16.

Royal Commission on Family and Children's Law of British Columbia, Tenth Report. *Native Families and the Law*. Victoria: Queen's Printer, 1975.

Sanders, D. *Family Law and Native People*. Ottawa: Law Reform Commission of Canada, 1975.

Stuart, N. *Study of Child Welfare Services Provided to Indian People in the Sudbury and Manitoulin Districts*. Unpublished manuscript, 1978. (Available from Ministry of Community and Social Services).

Chapter Fourteen

A MATCHED-GUISE METHODOLOGY FOR MEASURING
MINORITY ATTITUDES TOWARD AMERICAN-SIGN-LANGUAGE
SPEAKERS (1)

    R. Bruce Anderson and
    Robert Benford

According to Charrow and Wilbur (1975) nearly 500,000 deaf people use a system of communication called American Sign Language (ASL), which makes it the third most widely used non-English language in the United States. Anyone who doubts that this system of communication is appropriately called <u>a language</u> should take the time to peruse the second edition of Stokoe's <u>Sign Language Structure</u> (1978) and Klima and Bellugi's <u>The Signs of Language</u> (1979). Either of these volumes alone should be adequate to convince the reader that ASL is indeed a language with a range of expressive potential comparable to vocal-auditory languages. Further, ASL has in common with oral languages the fact that many of its 'speakers' learned it as the mother tongue or native language. In this paper we use the term speaker to refer to a person communicating in either an oral language such as English or a manual language such as ASL. While an English speaker 'speaks to the ears', an ASL speaker 'speaks to the eyes', and for a native speaker of either language the mode of communication is as comfortably natural as the alternative mode is for a native speaker of the other. A native speaker of ASL, or Native Signer, may either be a deaf person, or the hearing child of deaf parents. Of course other people, both deaf and hearing, also use ASL as a usual or frequent means of communication. Among the half-million deaf users of ASL, many but not all would be classified as native speakers. For these people any oral use of English (or any other oral language) is generally precluded due to the prelingual occurrence of their deafness. For them acquisition of second language skills in English (or other non gestural languages) will be limited to reading and writing and possibly speech or 'lip' reading.

The fact that prelingually deaf people are generally unable to respond orally to utterances in the oral language of the society in which they live -- even if they can (partially) understand them through speech reading -- marks them as different as surely as an immigrant's accented speech or the skin color of a racial minority member. Many people who became deaf after the acquisition of an oral language eventually come to speak that language in a distorted manner that also sets them apart. Even if such post-lingually deaf persons can produce near normal spoken English, the fact that they are restricted in their ability to understand it sets them apart and makes them minority group members as well. Being different, of course, is not a sufficient condition for minority group membership. Gliedman and Roth (1980) discuss the handicapped in broad terms and argue that being handicapped results in stigmatisation that is similar to that occurring with other groups which we more commonly agree to call minorities. Schlesinger and Meadow (1972) and Meadow (1978) present evidence that deafness is a stigmatising handicap. Furth (1966) asserts that both scholars and members of society in general have historically considered the deaf to be 'sub-human' -- incapable of education and culture.

The literature describing the experiences of deaf children growing up in a hearing society shows many parallels to the experiences of racial and other minorities. Of particular interest to us was the evidence that deaf people often internalise many of the negative images that their handicap arouses in others. If, for example, a parent is ashamed or embarrassed that his child is deaf - a relatively common situation - this attitude will be communicated to the child. Eventually such communication of negative feelings influence the child's self-identity (Meadow, 1978). As the deaf child grows up he will receive non-verbal cues regarding the attitudes of those around him -- cues that include indicators of pity, sympathy, overprotectiveness, and the like. As these cues influence the child's self-concept he may increasingly fulfill the expectations through adopting a 'sick role' and exhibiting dependent and socially immature behavior (Koetitz, 1976). At least one study reports that young deaf people perceive the attitudes of the hearing to be <u>more</u> negative than is actually the case (Schroedel and Schiff, 1972).

We thus have a picture of deaf people constituting a linguistic minority and having experiences similar to those of other minorities. We also see them as internalising some of the negative images that are held by the dominant group members -- and possibly even exaggerating the stereotypic perceptions. These ideas, sketched briefly in the previous paragraphs, reminded us of the attitude studies published by Lambert and his associates during the 1960's. These studies (Lambert, et al., 1960; Anisfeld and Lambert, 1964; Lambert, Anisfeld and Yeni-Komshian, 1965; and Lambert, Frankel and Tucker, 1966) employed a 'matched-guise' procedure which they found better suited to eliciting the private reactions of subjects than traditional direct attitude questionnaires. In brief, what Lambert and his associates did was as follows.

First they developed stimulus materials which consisted of audio tapes of a number of voices reading the same passage. Though there were a number of variations in their design over the several studies, typically the stimulus tape included about 8 or 10 voices, half of which spoke one language and half spoke the other. If there were eight voices on a given tape, there were only 4 speakers. Thus, for example, the first voice might have Jacques speaking in French, the second Marie speaking in English, and so forth. If this was the case, then the fifth voice would be Jacques speaking in English, the sixth Marie speaking in French, and on through the original speaker sequence. Thus each of the speakers was heard twice, speaking French once and English the other time. These speakers were carefully selected bilinguals who could pass as native speakers of both languages under study.

These stimulus tapes were played for naive subjects who were unaware that they were listening to bilingual speakers. After each voice was heard the subjects were asked to judge the speaker on a series of attitude items. For analysis purposes, it was then possible to match the voices and compare the attitudes elicited by the two language guises. Thus attitudes elicited by Marie speaking French would be compared with attitudes elicited from the same subject by Marie speaking English. Since the subjects and the speakers were identical, this comparison of reactions to the matched-guises produced differences that were clearly attributable to the language and the attitudes it evoked. Results were generally systematic, and typically showed that the dominant-language-guise produced more favorable reactions than the minority language-guise. Further, when the subjects were chosen from a bilingual population, the differential between reactions to the two guises was generally minimal. When monolingual speakers of the dominant language were compared with monolingual speakers of the minority language, a common finding was that the former group of subjects actually had a less unfavorable reaction to the minority-language-guise than did minority language speaking subject.

The matched-guise methodology has, in our judgement, great merit. The problem is, can it be adapted for use where one language is oral and the other manual. If this can be done successfully, then one can investigate attitudes toward the deaf ASL speaker in a similar way to the Lambert group's studies of attitudes toward speakers of several oral languages and dialects. Since we believe that such investigations would provide valuable additions to our knowledge, we have worked to develop a matched-guise methodology that would fit the problem. In the process we have turned up a number of complications and side-issues which will be touched upon in the remainder of this paper describing our matched-guise methodology for use with a manual language.

A MANUAL-ORAL MATCHED-GUISE METHODOLOGY

Since one of the languages in which we were interested is manual (ASL) we immediately had to abandon the audio tape in favor of video recording. This, of course, made it impossible for us to have the same subject rate both guises on a single tape since the subject could not help but recognise the person as being one and the same who had performed under the other guise previously. Our design then must employ comparison groups of subjects randomly assigned to experimental conditions as has been traditionally done by behavioral scientists. This, in turn, meant that we required larger subject pools than Lambert and associates in order to achieve equally trustworthy results.

At least in his early studies in Montreal, it is reasonable to assume that all of Lambert's naive subjects had had some prior exposure to monolingual speakers of both languages employed in the study. Canadian broadcast media routinely transmit in both languages, and though there is generally separation into 'English' and 'French' channels, most listener can be expected to have heard at least some broadcasts employing the other (2) language. In contrast, monolingual ASL speakers in the United States have, undoubtedly had frequent experience with persons speaking English, whereas monolingual English speakers may be expected to have had little exposure to ASL. Thus for a Canadian we expected it rather natural to hear people speaking French and English -- even though the listener understands only one language. For our monolingual speakers of ASL and English, in contrast, we anticipated that the former would find it quite natural to see a video presentation in English while the latter would find a presentation in ASL a new experience. As far as we were aware, ASL is used on Television in the United States primarily for interpretation of English presentations for the deaf, and only occasionally as the language of original presentation. When it is the original language, interpretation into English is almost universally provided.

Our dilemma, then was whether or not to provide interpretation along with our video-taped stimulus presentation. If we did not, our design would parallel Lambert's more closely -- but our subjects were less likely than his to be comfortable with the experiment. On the other hand, if we provided interpretation our subjects were more likely to find the stimulus tapes 'natural'. If interpretation was provided, however, there would be two people appearing on the screen, and the attitude ratings might be confounded -- even with careful instructions to the subjects that they were to judge the original speaker, not the interpreter. We were unable to solve this dilemma <u>a priori</u>, and had therefore decided to seek an empirical solution through an expanded design that included both interpreted and uninterpreted video tapes that were otherwise identical.

Since our subjects eventually included members of three populations having differing language skills, our research instrument and instructions had to be understood by all. English monolingual subjects and subjects who were ASLEnglish bilinguals presented no problem. For these two populations our attitude questionnaire and all instructions might be in standard English. Subjects drawn from the population of ASL monolinguals, however presented a different situation. Of course living in an English speaking society provides considerable incentive for deaf people to learn English as a second language, and many learn to read and write it rather well. On the other hand, the educational level of deaf people in the United States averages only fifth grade. Our consultants who work with the deaf on a regular basis advised us, repeatedly, to keep all written instructions as simple as possible, and to minimise or eliminate the need for deaf respondents to write English. They suggested that we communicate instructions to our deaf respondents in ASL.

This suggestion, while reasonable, raised serious issues of stimulus condition comparability that were different only in detail from issues first addressed by Anderson in 1967. In solving the problem of communication with our deaf, ASL monolingual respondents and maintaining comparability of experimental conditions across subject language-skill groups, we again opted for leaving the issue open for empirical solution. We prepared two sets of video tapes. On one set an announcer provided instructions simultaneously in both ASL and English and also went through the questionnaire one item at a time. The pace through the questionnaire was such that respondents were able to answer each item as it was explained. Explanations were, of course, simultaneously in English and ASL. On the other set of tapes only the announcer's general introduction at the beginning of the tape was retained. No explanation of the individual questions was provided beyond that on the printed page before the subject. By comparison of results generated by these two sets of tapes we had the possibility of sorting out the effects of the ASL-English video-taped explanation, if any. Using either set of tapes provided empirically constant stimuli across subject language-skill groups.

Summarising to this point, we had a design that began with bilingual ASL-English speakers, who could pass as natives in either language, presenting themselves as monolingual. Two video tapes were made -- such that each speaker was presented as an English monolingual on one and as an ASL monolingual on the other. In order to deal with the expected differential exposure of our subject populations to the two languages, a second set of tapes had also been made. The second set was identical to the first except that interpretation had been added so that when the main speaker, who dominated the screen was speaking English an interpretation into ASL was superimposed in the upper right-hand corner of the screen. When the main speaker was speaking ASL, the superimposed interpreter interpreted into English. The structure of these four basic stimulus tapes is summarised in Table 1. In addition to the two language conditions (English and ASL) and two interpretation conditions (interpreted and uninterpreted) we have also discussed two testing conditions (explained on the tape and unexplained) in previous paragraphs. Since our experimental design was essentially an Analysis-of-Variance design, the introduction of testing conditions increased our required number of tapes to eight. The four additional tapes were identical to those summarized in Table 1, except that they also included the interspersed explanation of the questionnaire.

In addition to the three independent variables discussed above, there were several other variables that we had wished to explore on a more modest scale. The first of these was the impact of visual versus auditory cues on the attitude ratings. We wondered whether or not the simple fact that we were using video tape where Lambert and his colleagues used audio tape might make a difference. We decided, therefore, to make an audio tape of our six speakers doing the English guise. This tape was presented to a randomly selected group of English monolingual subjects who were asked to make identical judgements on the basis of the auditory stimuli alone. Suitable comparisons have enabled us to assess the effects of the visual component of the stimulus materials on the attitudes elicited.

Another aspect of the visual stimulus that we will explore through a single tape comparison is color. All of the eight 'main tapes' discussed above are created in color from the masters filmed in the campus studio. We shall also make, from one of these, a tape that is in black and white, but otherwise identical. Comparison of the attitudes which it evokes with those evoked by the color version will allow us to draw inferences about the effects of color, if any obtain. Should such effects obtain it might be desirable to make additional black and white tapes to facilitate assessment of the interaction of these effects with the variables of primary interest.

Table 1.1: Structure of the Television Stimulus Tapes

		Stimulus Tape[3]			
		Uninterpreted		Interpreted	
Speaker[4]	Tape:	A	B	C	D
1		ASL[5]	English	ASL	English
3		English	ASL	English	ASL
6		ASL	English	ASL	English
4		ASL	English	ASL	English
2		English	ASL	English	ASL
5		English	ASL	English	ASL

Finally, we shall make at least one tape in which captioning, rather than interpretation is employed. We expect that deaf respondents will prefer interpretation to captioning, but would be interested in exploring the impact upon attitudes among all three language-skill populations. Whether or not we are able to do so ultimately will depend upon our ability to acquire adequate funding to expand the number of subjects to include additional groups of deaf and bilingual respondents with captions instead of interpretation superimposed on the basic tapes.

SUMMARY

Table 2 summarises the analysis of variance design showing that the full array of potential combinations of the variables we have discussed as having potential impact upon attitudinal responses would require 144 different experimental conditions. After elimination of those logically possible conditions that are either empirically empty or redundant there remain 80 conditions. We propose to begin our investigation by examining only the effects of language-skill population, guise,

Table 1.2: Potential Analysis-of-Variance Design, and Modified Design Proposed for Measuring Attitudes Toward American Sign Language Speakers#

	Subject Language-Skill Population Groups:					
	ASL Monolinguals		ASL-English Bilinguals		English Monolinguals	
Guise Presented	ASL	ENG	ASL	ENG	ASL	ENG
Interpreted Explained Color						
Audio Only	*	*	*		*	
Video						
Black & White						
Audio Only	*	*	*	**	*	**
Video						
Unexplained Color						
Audio Only	*	*	*		*	
Video						
Black & White						
Audio Only	*	*	*	**	*	**
Video						
Uninterpreted Explained Color						
Audio Only	Details of this portion identical to the above					
.						
.						
.						
Captioned Explained Color						
.	Details of this portion identical to the above					
.						
.						

\# The potential array of experimental conditions is shown in its entirety for interpreted video tapes. Identical sets of conditions would also be theoretically possible for uninterpreted and captioned video tapes.
* The cells would be empirically empty.
**These cells would be empirically redundant on cells shown above them in the table, and all "audio" cells would be redundant under the captioned condition.

presence or absence of interpretation, and presence or absence of explanation, and will probably not examine all 24 conditions that these variables generate at the outset. With respect to the other variables, color/black & white, audio/video, and captioning we anticipate limited exploratory studies using conditions that take these variables one-at-a-time and control for all other conditions. Only if they generate significant differences under these highly controlled conditions will we expand the design toward its potential complexity in order to examine interaction effects.

At present our first tapes are in hand, and the first groups of English Monolingual subjects have responded. Though very preliminary and therefore necessarily tentative, our evidence to date suggests that it will be possible to employ the matched-guise methodology described here to investigate factors influencing attitudes towards speakers of American Sign Language.

NOTES

1. We wish to thank Mrs. Smith for her contributions, many of which have influenced the development of our thinking and design. We would also like to acknowledge the contributions of consultants Duffer Childry, Stella Fitzgerald, and Reva Pleake of Eastfield College, and the North Central Texas Registry of Interpreters for the Deaf for locating the bilinguals who appear on our stimulus tapes. Lynette Waltisperger who has made and edited our tapes, together with the bilinguals who are their starts also deserve our gratitude. The materials included in this paper reflect contributions of all these people.

2. Our focus here is on monolingual speakers. Thus for a monolingual speaker of English, French is the "other" language, and vice versa.

3. Column headings identify the four experimental conditions. Entries in the cells of this table indicate the language of the presentation made by each speaker. The two tapes which included interpretation (C and D) were identical to the uninterpreted tapes (A and B), except that an interpreter interpreted the presentation into the other language. Where interpretation was included the interpreter was presented in a reduced image in the upper right-hand corner of the screen. The physical position of the main speaker on the screen

was identical in both interpreted and uninterpreted versions.

4. Numbers assigned to speakers refer to the sequence in which the original tapes were made. Sequencing for stimulus tapes, as well as which language is to be used on Tape A were randomly determined. Sequencing remains constant over all four tapes, and languages alternate from the first to the second tape under each interpretation condition.

5. ASL refers to American Sign Language. All speakers were native signers except one who learned ASL at an early age and could pass as native. All speakers could also pass as native speakers of American English.

REFERENCES

Anderson, R. Bruce W., 'On the Comparability of Meaningful Stimuli in Cross-Cultural Research', Sociometry, vol. 30, 1967, pp. 124-136.

Anisfeld, E. and Lambert, W.E., 'Evaluational Reactions of Bilingual and Monolingual Children to Spoken Languages', Journal of Abnormal and Social Psychology, vol. 69, 1964, pp. 89-97.

Charrow, V.R. and Wilbur, R.B., 'The Deaf Child as a Linguistic Minority', Theory Into Practice, vol. 14, 1975, pp. 353-359.

Furth, H.G., Thinking Without Language: Psychological Implications of Deafness, The Free Press, New York, 1966.

Gliedman, J. and Roth, W., The Unexpected Minority: Handicapped Children in America, Harcourt Brace Janovich, New York, 1980.

Klima, E.S. and Bellugi, U., The Signs of Language, Harvard University Press, Cambridge, Mass., 1979.

Koetitz, L.E., 'Cognitive and Psycho-Social Develpment in Deaf Children: A Review of the Literature', Education and Training of the Mentally Retarded, vol. 11, 1976, pp. 66-72.

Lambert, W.E. et al., 'Evaluational Reactions to Spoken Languages', Journal of Abnormal and Social Psychology, vol. 60, 1960, pp. 44-51.

Lambert, W.E., Anisfeld, M. and Yeni-Komshian, G., 'Evaluational Reactions to Jewish and Arab Adolescents to Dialect and Language Variations', Journal of Personality and Social Psychology, vol. 2, 1965, p. 84-90.

Lambert, W.E., Frankel, H. and Tucker, G.R., 'Judging Personality Through Speech: A French-Canadian Example', *Journal of Communication*, vol. 16, 1966, pp. 305-321.

Meadow, K.P., 'Personality and Social Development of Deaf Persons', *Focus on Deafness: Selected Readings for Paraprofessionals*, Lawrence, E.D. (ed.), University Press of America, Washington, D.C., pp. 61-73.

Schlesinger, H.S. and Meadow, K.P., *Sound and Sign: Childhood Deafness and Mental Health*, University of California Press, Berkeley, 1972.

Schroedel, J. and Schiff, W., 'Attitudes Towards Deafness Among Several Deaf and Hearing Populations', *Rehabilitation Psychology*, vol. 19, 1972, pp. 59-70.

Stokoe, W.C., *Sign Language Structure*, Linstok Press, Silver Spring, Md., 1978.

AUTHOR INDEX

Adorno, T.W., 31, 35
Almeida, Z., 117
Ardener, S., 18

Bagley, C., 4, 7, 17, 20, 23, 33, 62-3, 100, 106, 110-1, 116, 123, 170, 217, 222-3, 226, 228-31 247-52
Ballard, G., 106
Banks, J., 161
Banton, M., 17
Baptiste, H., 59
Barker, G., 117
Balta, J., 254
Bauer, E., 100
Baumgartner-Karabak, A., 119
Bell, R., 118
Bender, E., 101
Bentley, S., 248
Berger, P., 34
Bereiter, C., 89
Berry, J., 220, 232
Bernstein, B., 158
Bhatnagar, J.K., 115
Bodenbender, W., 115
Bowhay, C., 7
Blumer, H., 19
Bohning, W.R., 100-2
Bolton, E., 61-2
Brittan, E., 20, 165
Brody, H., 8, 265
Buchignani, N., 59
Bullivant, M., 72, 158
Burgess, E.W., 29

Burnet, J., 59
Butterworth, E., 119

Caditz, J., 35
Campfens, H., 217
Carlyle, T., 21
Castles, S., 100, 113, 120
Chang, E.C., 32
Chang, T., 249
Charlot, M., 108
Charrow, V.R., 278
Cherrington, D., 72, 157
Chipman, L., 59
Claydon, L., 80
Clout, H., 100
Coopersmith, S., 28

Day, B., 247
Derrick, J., 116
Deutsch, M., 89
Dixon, R., 170
Donaldson, M., 229
Dosman, E.J., 265
Drake, G., 93

Edwards, J., 95-6
Ekstrand, L.H., 118, 120
Elkind, D., 218
Engelmann, S., 89
Fishman, J., 93-4
Figueroa, P., 17-19
Fitzpatrick, B., 79, 82

Furth, H.G., 279

Gartner-Harnach, V., 118
Ghuman, P., 66, 221
Gibson, M., 59
Giles, R., 157
Glass, R., 20
Glazer, N., 59
Gliedman, J., 279
Gleitman, H., 90
Gold, M., 161
Goldman, R., 116
Gould, J., 158
Granier, R., 102
Green, A., 22
Green, P., 16

Haavio-Mannila, E., 119
Habermas, J., 159
Hamilton-Guerson, D.J., 29
Hammar, T., 114
Hansell, S., 230
Harrant, S., 118
Hayakawa, S., 95
Henriques, F., 247
Hepworth, H.P., 62
Hess, R., 89
Higham, J., 93
Hodges, M., 164
Holborn, L.W., 101
Holden, G., 106
Holland, D., 18
Hudson, P., 267-8
Husband, C., 19, 21

Iwawaki, S., 222

Jackson, M., 267
Jeffcoate, R., 69, 159
Jenkins, R., 62
Jensen, A., 88, 87
Johannesson, I., 115
Johnston, P., 63

Kelley, H.H., 25, 33
Kim, Y.Y., 34
Kindelberger, C.P., 101
Kirkness, V., 218
Kitano, H.L., 34-5
Koetitz, L.E., 279
Kogan, N., 218

Kolb, W., 158
Kosack, G., 120
Kubat, D., 108
Kuhn, M.H., 33, 36

Lambert, J., 254
Lambert, W.E., 80, 279
Landis, D., 69
Lasonen, K., 81
Laosa, L., 218
Lawton, D., 158, 159
Lenneberg, E., 90
Lee, L.T., 102
Levine, D.W., 29-32, 36-7
Linton, R., 158
Lipkin, J., 115
Little, K., 21
Lloyd, B., 218
Lofland, L., 31
Luckman, T., 34
Lynch, J., 161, 162

MacDonald, J.A., 269
Machtiger, H., 221
Maggs, P.B., 102
Mallick, K., 4, 7, 120, 170
Marciano, J.P., 102
McDonald, J.R., 101
McKenzie, B., 267-8
McLemore, S.D., 29, 31
Mead, G.H., 33
Meadow, K.P., 279
Meredith, G., 61
Merton, R.K., 33
Miller, G., 224
Mitchell, R., 84
Monohan, T., 248
Moodley, K., 231
Morland, K., 249
Morris, L., 161
Morse, B., 267, 269
Mullard, C., 70, 231

Nandy, D., 65
Nasser, S., 78
Padilla, A.M., 34
Park, R.E., 29
Passow, A., 88
Pettigrew, T., 231

Porter, R.E., 29
Power, J., 101
Prentice, N.M., 32

Raoufi, S., 123
Raven, J., 95-6
Rees, O.A., 79, 82
Rex, J., 22
Rideau, R., 101
Rijk, J.T., 122
Rist, C.R., 100, 111, 125, 126
Ritter, E.H., 32
Rodriguez, R., 95
Rose, E., 16
Rossi, A.K., 33
Roth, W., 279
Rowley, G., 158
Rose, E., 21

Salt, J., 100
Samuda, J.R., 116
Sanders, D., 267
Savile, M.R., 81
Schiff, W., 279
Schonell, F., 227
Schuetz, A., 35
Scott, R., 170
Schroedel, J., 279
Segall, M.H., 35
Serpell, R., 219
Sharma, S., 78
Sharp, R., 22
Sherif, M., 33
Sikes, P., 158
Simmel, G., 29, 30
Skrimshire, A., 230
Slavin, R., 230
Smolicz, J., 69
Sowell, T., 93
Stenhouse, L., 162
Stone, M., 23, 71, 158, 231
Stonequist, E., 37
Street-Porter, R., 62
Stuart, N., 267
Sumner, W.C., 30

Taylor, F.M., 116
Thomas, D.R., 35
Tiryakian, E.A., 35

Tomlinson, S., 22
Toukomoa, P., 80
Townsend, H., 163
Triandis, H., 8
Troike, R.C., 81
Trudgill, P., 90
Tucker, G.R., 80

Urry, J., 34

Van den Berghe, P., 93
Verma, G.K., 4, 7, 20, 23, 33, 62, 75, 106, 116, 120, 170, 217, 228-30, 249, 253
Vernon, P., 218
Vyas, H., 230

Wagner, D., 219
Walvin, J., 21
Washington, J., 247
Widgren, J., 88
Wilbur, R.B., 279
Willey, R., 61-2
Williams, J., 249
Wilpert, C., 113
Wilson, G., 32
Witkin, H., 218-9, 226-7, 232
Wood, M.M., 30
Wong, J., 228

Young, 7, 18, 170, 222, 226, 232, 251, 253

Ziller, R., 28, 250
Zolf, L., 95

SUBJECT INDEX

Adoption,
  Native children, 269
African children,
  self-perception, 250
American Sign Language, 278
Asian studies, 144
Australia,
  Ethnic Schools, 206
  Greek Language pupils, 194
  Italian Language pupils, 200
  Language Teaching, 187-9, 190
  Lebanese, 184
  Multicultural Education, 59, 184-212
  Polish, 184
  Spanish Language pupils, 194
  Yugoslavians, 184

Bilingual Programmes,
  in Britain, 79, 81
Bilingualism, 66, 79, 81, 94
Black People,
  in Britain, 22
Books,
  Multicultural Education 163-182
Bradford,
  Multicultural Schools, 171-72

Britain,
  Cypriots, 20
  History of Race Relations, 15-16, 18
  Minority Children, 99-128
  Multicultural Education, 57-61, 60-75, 79
  Race Relations, 15-6, 18
British Empire, 22
Bullock Report, 66

Canada,
  Multicultural Policy, 23, 59
  Native Children, 259-76
Canadian Indians, 259-76
Colonialism,
  and Native Child Welfare, 268
Cognitive Styles,
  British Children, 217-33
  Education, 221, 230
  Indian Children, 217-33
  Jamaican Children, 217-33
  Japanese Children, 217-33

Mexican Children, 220
West Indian Children, 221
Compensatory Education, 71
Criminal Justice System,
  and Native People, 264
Culture,
  Defined, 146
  Language Education, 190-91
  Racial Differences, 22
Cultural identity,
  British Minorities, 32, 78
Cultural Values,
  Canada, 67
Curriculum Development, 74, 78-82
  Australian Schools, 149-50, 153-54
  British Schools, 143
  Multiculturalism, 173-76, 178

Deaf Children, 278-88
Department of Education
  and Science, 22
Discrimination,
  Britain, 20
Disadvantage,
  Achievement, 88-9
  Australian Schools, 187
  Defined, 96

Enculturation, 35
English Children,
  Cognitive Style, 222-23
English as a Second Language
  Australian Schools, 185
Ethnocentrism, 29-38
Ethnic Studies, 57, 59, 61
  Australian Schools, 144, 152-3, 190
  British Schools, 144
European Economic Community 66, 79

Field Independence-Dependence,
  Defined, 217
  Self-Esteem, 228
  Social Interaction, 219
  Socialization, 227

France,
  Minority Children, 99-128
  Public Schools, 109

Germany,
  Minority Children, 99-128

Host Community, 32-35

Identity,
  see Cultural Identity
Immigrant Children,
  Attitudes, 10, 35
  Education, 9-128
  Language Problems,
Indian Children,
  Cognitive Style, 224
Interculturalism, 73
Language, 90-91

Jamaican Children,
  Cognitive Style, 222-3
  Education, 229
  Self-Perception, 251, 256
Japanese Children,
  Cognitive Style, 223

Language Teaching,
  Australian Schools, 187-189
  Class Size, 23
  Parent Goals, 196, 203
  Teacher Goals, 196 203
  Teacher Training, 207-8

Mead's 'I' and 'me', 34
Metis of Canada, 259-270
Minority Groups,
  Achievement, 89
  Education, 94
  Policies, 87

Mixed Race Children, 247-52
Mother-Tongue Teaching, 79-83
Multicultural Education,
 Britain, 164
 General Policy, 87, 143-62
 Goals, 217
 Models, 57-75, 231
 School Books, 179, 186
Multilingualism,
 Advantages, 205
 Disadvantages, 205

Native People in Canada,
 Adoption, 269
 Child Welfare, 259-70
 Criminal Justice, 264
 Education, 264
National Union of Teachers, 64
Netherlands,
 Minority Children, 99-128

Pluralism, 93, 96
Plural Societies,
 Educational Issues, 57-75, 93-96
Prejudice,
 in Britain, 17
Publishers,
 Multicultural Education, 163-82
Punjabi Speakers,
 in Britain, 82

Race
 Cultural Differences, 22
 Defined, 18
Race Relations,
 Britain, 15-17
 Frames of Reference, 19-20
 Racism, 23
Racial Attitudes,
 Children, 249, 256-7
Rampton Committee, 16
Reference Groups, 32-34

Schools Council, 71
Second Language Teaching,
 Australia, 184-213

Self-Concept,
 see Self-Esteem
Self-Esteem, 16
 Field Dependence, 228
 Minority Children, 120-1
 Mixed-Race Children, 258
 West Indian Students, 20
 Young Children, 250
Self-Perception,
 see Self-Esteem
Social Control, 145
South Asians,
 in Britain, 85
South Asian Children,
 in Britain, 61-62, 85
Stranger,
 Attitudes to, 29-33
Sweden,
 Immigrant Children, 99-128

Teacher Education, 72
 Multicultural Education, 118-22

Unemployment,
 and Native People, 264
United Kingdom,
 see Britain
United States,
 Multicultural policy, 59, 60

Values,
 Education, 48
West Indians in Britain 16, 20, 221-3
West Germany,
 Minority Children, 99-128
Western Europe,
 Class and Race, 99-103
 Immigrant Workers, 100-102